W9-ADL-030

MERCENARY MARC SPECTOR DIED IN EGYPT UNDER A STATUE OF THE MOON GOD KHONSHU. IN THE SHADOW OF THE ANCIENT DEITY, MARC RETURNED TO LIFE AND TOOK ON KHONSHU'S ASPECT TO FIGHT CRIME FOR HIS OWN REDEMPTION. HE WENT COMPLETELY INSANE AND DISAPPEARED FOR A TIME, BUT RETURNED TO PROTECT THOSE WHO TRAVEL BY NIGHT. AT LEAST HE THINKS THAT'S WHAT HAPPENED...

MOON KNIGHT
LUNATIC

WRITER
JEFF LEMIRE

ARTIST
GREG SMALLWOOD

COLOR ARTIST
JORDIE BELLAIRE

ADDITIONAL ARTISTS, #5
**WILFREDO TORRES,
FRANCESCO FRANCAVILLA
& JAMES STOKOE**

ADDITIONAL COLOR ARTISTS, #5
**MICHAEL GARLAND,
FRANCESCO FRANCAVILLA
& JAMES STOKOE**

LETTERER
VC's CORY PETIT

COVER ART
GREG SMALLWOOD

ASSISTANT EDITOR
KATHLEEN WISNESKI

EDITOR
JAKE THOMAS

COLLECTION EDITOR: JENNIFER GRÜNWALD
ASSOCIATE MANAGING EDITOR: KATERI WOODY
ASSOCIATE EDITOR: SARAH BRUNSTAD
EDITOR, SPECIAL PROJECTS: MARK D. BEAZLEY
VP PRODUCTION & SPECIAL PROJECTS: JEFF YOUNGQUIST
SVP PRINT, SALES & MARKETING: DAVID GABRIEL
BOOK DESIGN: JAY BOWEN

EDITOR IN CHIEF: AXEL ALONSO
CHIEF CREATIVE OFFICER: JOE QUESADA
PUBLISHER: DAN BUCKLEY
EXECUTIVE PRODUCER: ALAN FINE

MOON KNIGHT VOL. 1: LUNATIC. Contains material originally published in magazine form as MOON KNIGHT #1-5. First printing 2016. ISBN# 978-0-7851-9953-3. Published by MARVEL WORLDWIDE, INC., a subsidiary of MARVEL ENTERTAINMENT, LLC. OFFICE OF PUBLICATION: 135 West 50th Street, New York, NY 10020. Copyright © 2016 MARVEL No similarity between any of the names, characters, persons, and/or institutions in this magazine with those of any living or dead person or institution is intended, and any such similarity which may exist is purely coincidental. **Printed in Canada.** ALAN FINE, President, Marvel Entertainment; DAN BUCKLEY, President, TV, Publishing & Brand Management; JOE QUESADA, Chief Creative Officer; TOM BREVOORT, SVP of Publishing; DAVID BOGART, SVP of Business Affairs & Operations, Publishing & Partnership; C.B. CEBULSKI, VP of Brand Management & Development, Asia; DAVID GABRIEL, SVP of Sales & Marketing, Publishing; JEFF YOUNGQUIST, VP of Production & Special Projects; DAN CARR, Executive Director of Publishing Technology; ALEX MORALES, Director of Publishing Operations; SUSAN CRESPI, Production Manager; STAN LEE, Chairman Emeritus. For information regarding advertising in Marvel Comics or on Marvel.com, please contact Vit DeBellis, Integrated Sales Manager, at vdebellis@marvel.com. For Marvel subscription inquiries, please call 888-511-5480. **Manufactured between 10/7/2016 and 11/14/2016 by SOLISCO PRINTERS, SCOTT, QC, CANADA.**

10 9 8 7 6 5 4 3 2 1

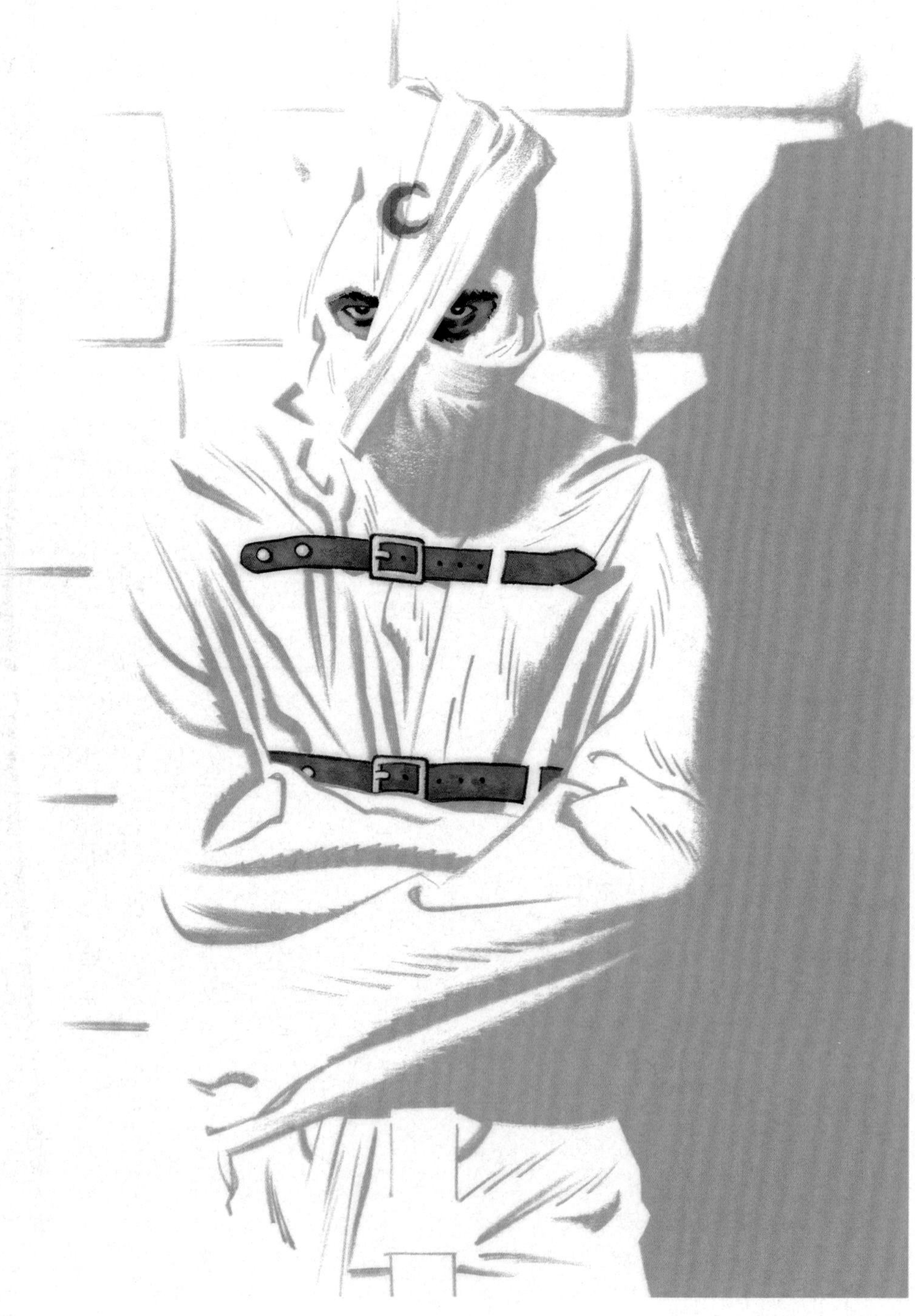

WELCOME TO NEW EGYPT
PART ONE

1

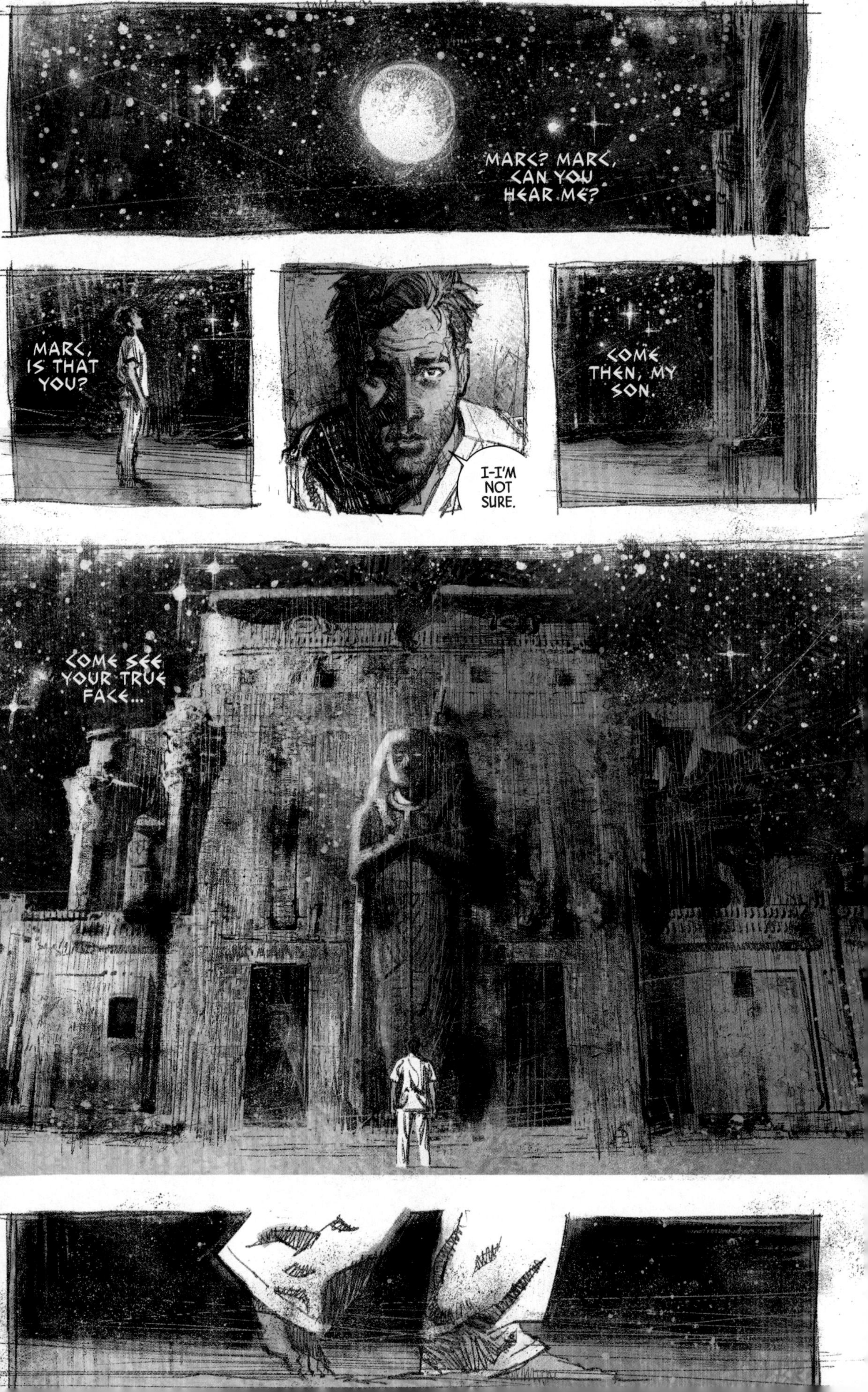
MARC? MARC, CAN YOU HEAR ME?
MARC, IS THAT YOU?
I-I'M NOT SURE.
COME THEN, MY SON.
COME SEE YOUR TRUE FACE...

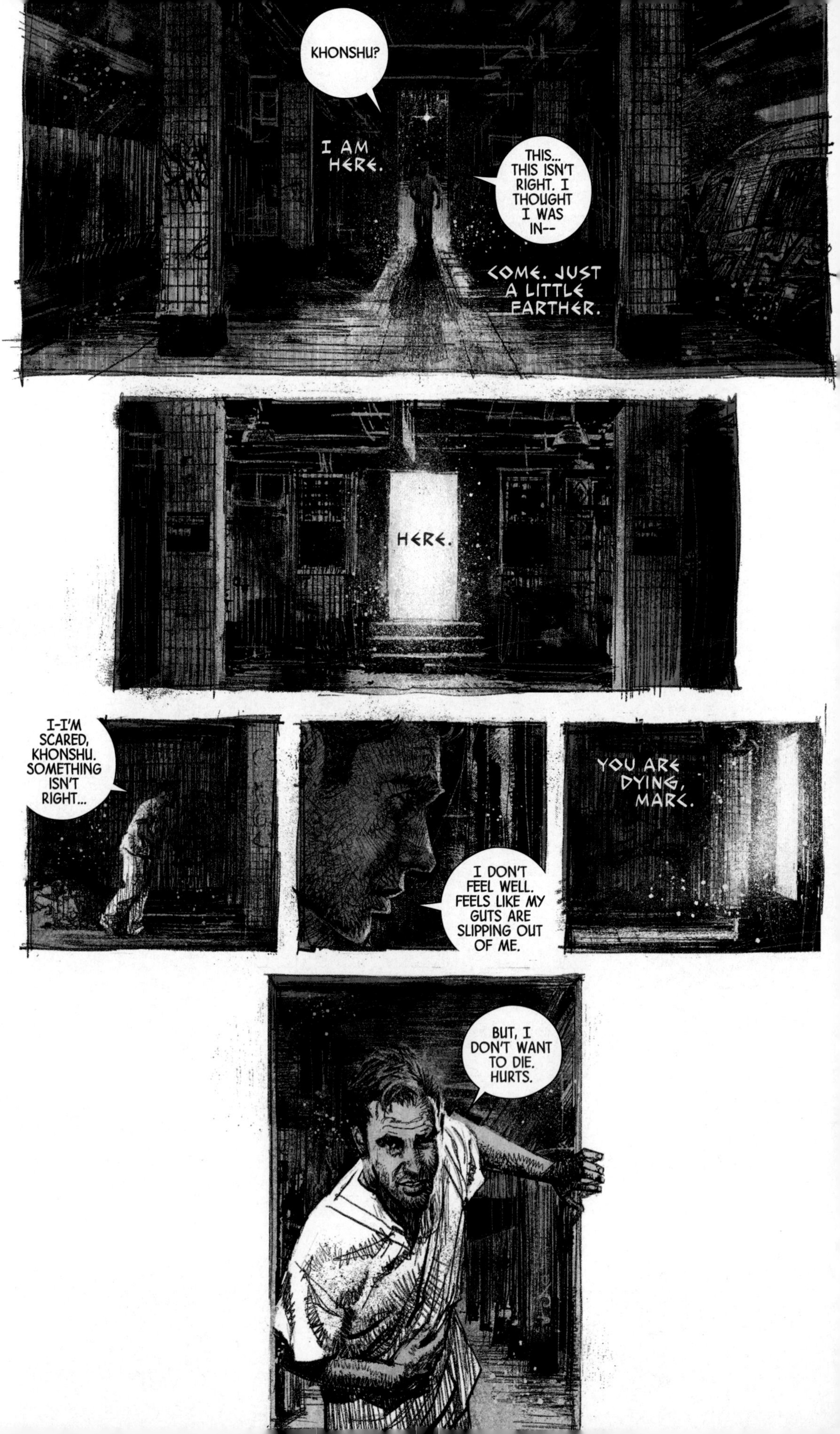
KHONSHU?
I AM HERE.
THIS... THIS ISN'T RIGHT. I THOUGHT I WAS IN--
COME. JUST A LITTLE FARTHER.
HERE.
I-I'M SCARED, KHONSHU. SOMETHING ISN'T RIGHT...
I DON'T FEEL WELL. FEELS LIKE MY GUTS ARE SLIPPING OUT OF ME.
YOU ARE DYING, MARC.
BUT, I DON'T WANT TO DIE. HURTS.

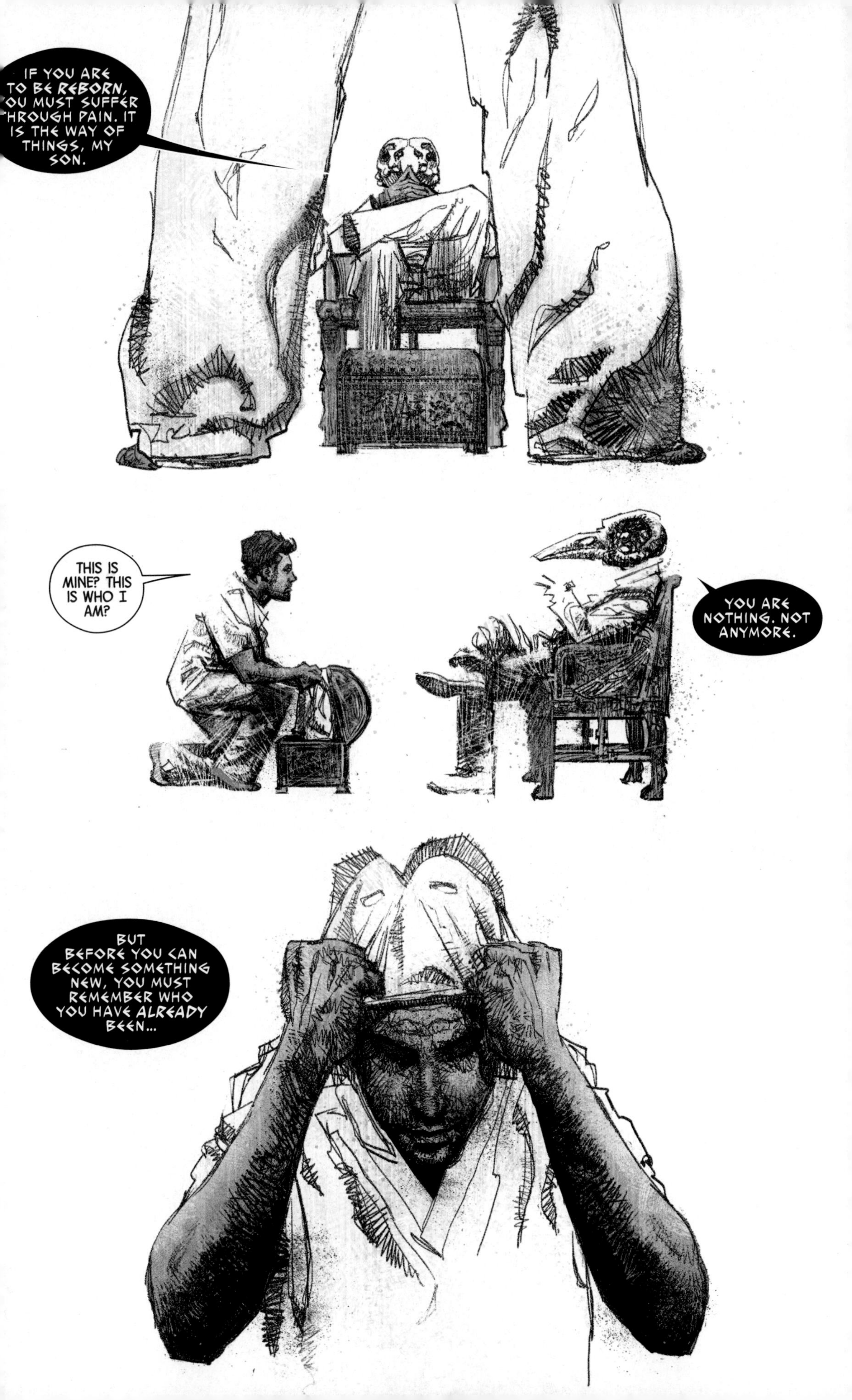
IF YOU ARE TO BE REBORN, OU MUST SUFFER HROUGH PAIN. IT IS THE WAY OF THINGS, MY SON.
THIS IS MINE? THIS IS WHO I AM?
YOU ARE NOTHING. NOT ANYMORE.
BUT BEFORE YOU CAN BECOME SOMETHING NEW, YOU MUST REMEMBER WHO YOU HAVE ALREADY BEEN...

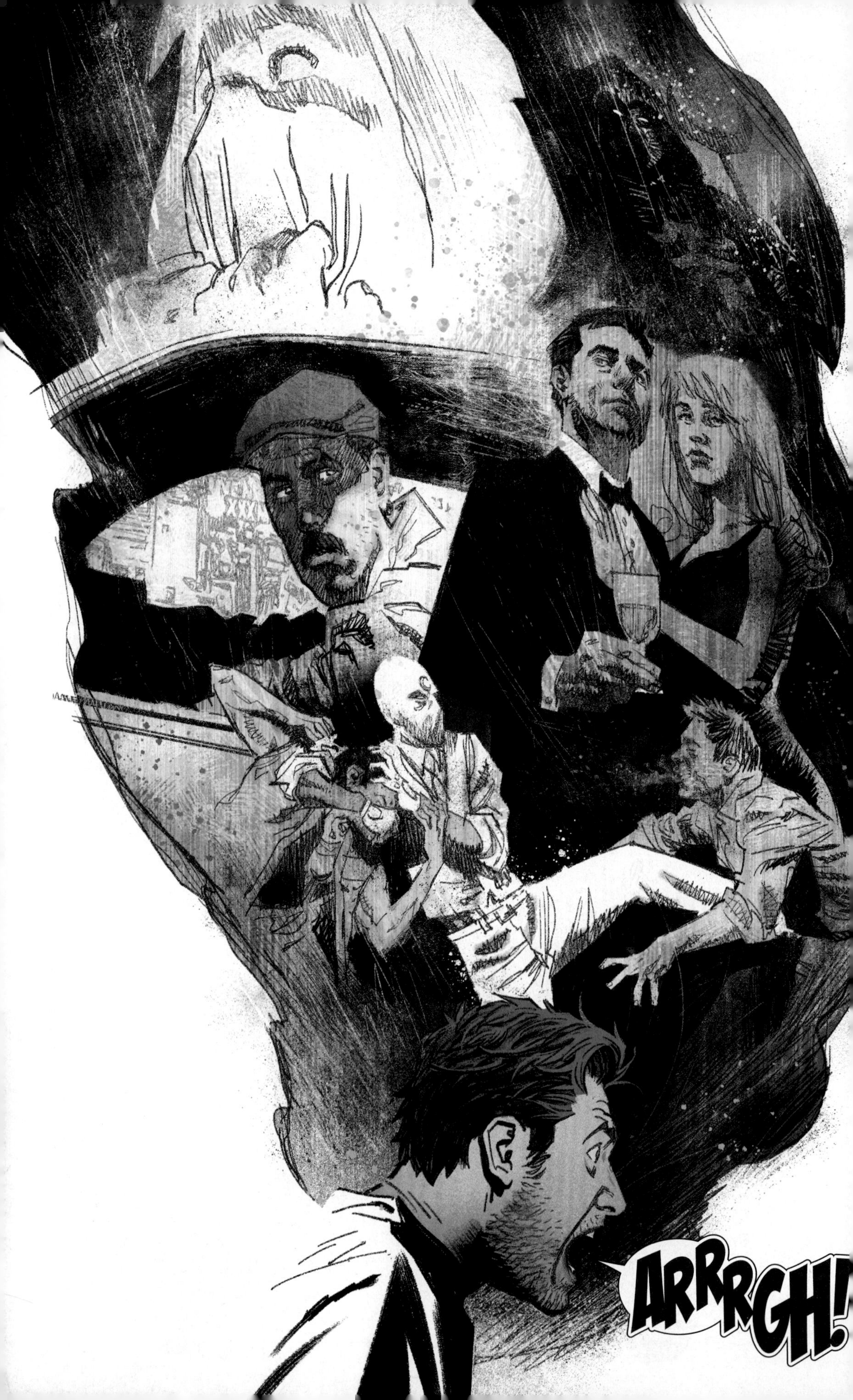
ARRRGH!

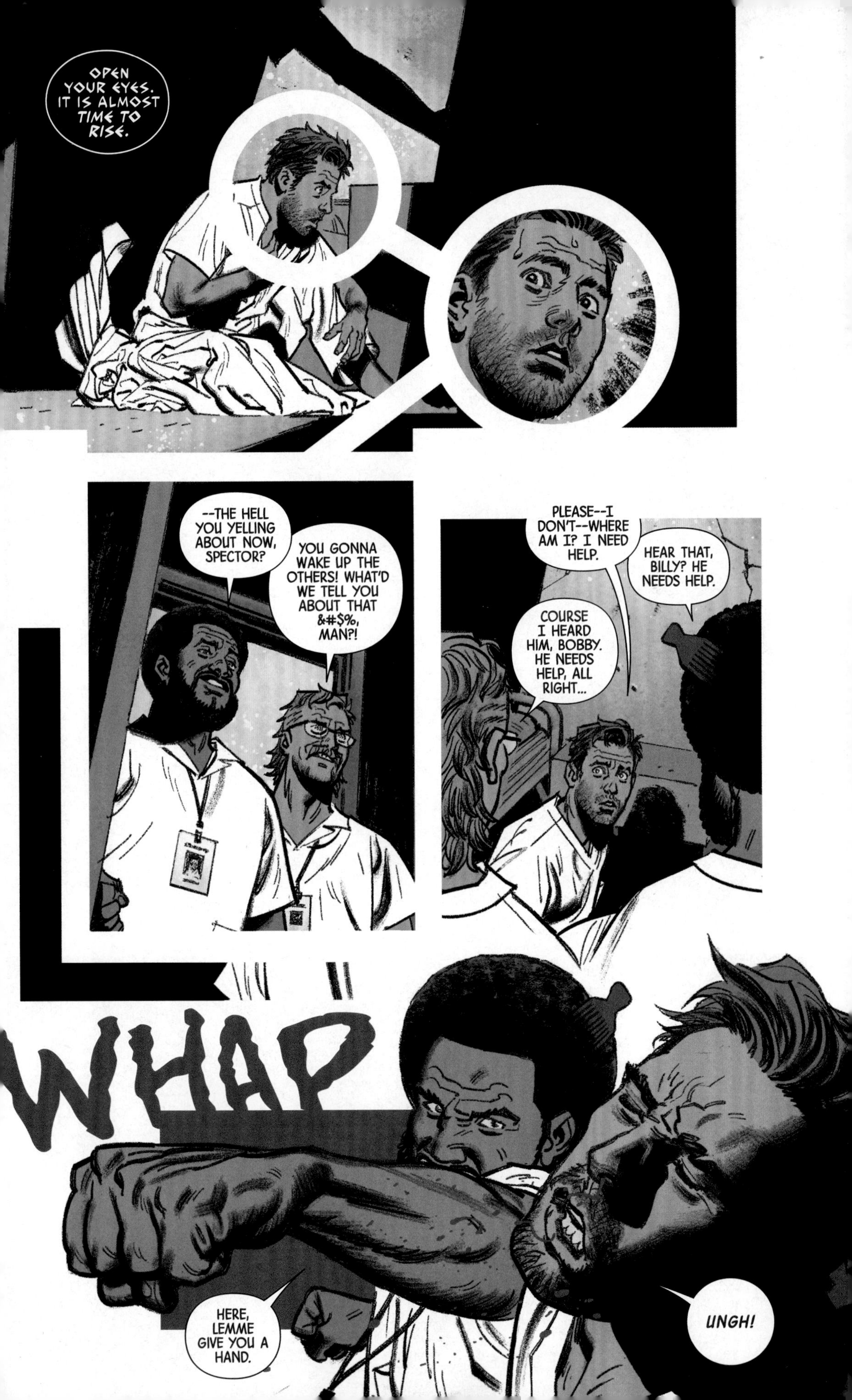
OPEN YOUR EYES. IT IS ALMOST TIME TO RISE.
--THE HELL YOU YELLING ABOUT NOW, SPECTOR?
YOU GONNA WAKE UP THE OTHERS! WHAT'D WE TELL YOU ABOUT THAT &#$%, MAN?!
PLEASE--I DON'T--WHERE AM I? I NEED HELP.
HEAR THAT, BILLY? HE NEEDS HELP.
COURSE I HEARD HIM, BOBBY. HE NEEDS HELP, ALL RIGHT...
WHAP
HERE, LEMME GIVE YOU A HAND.
UNGH!

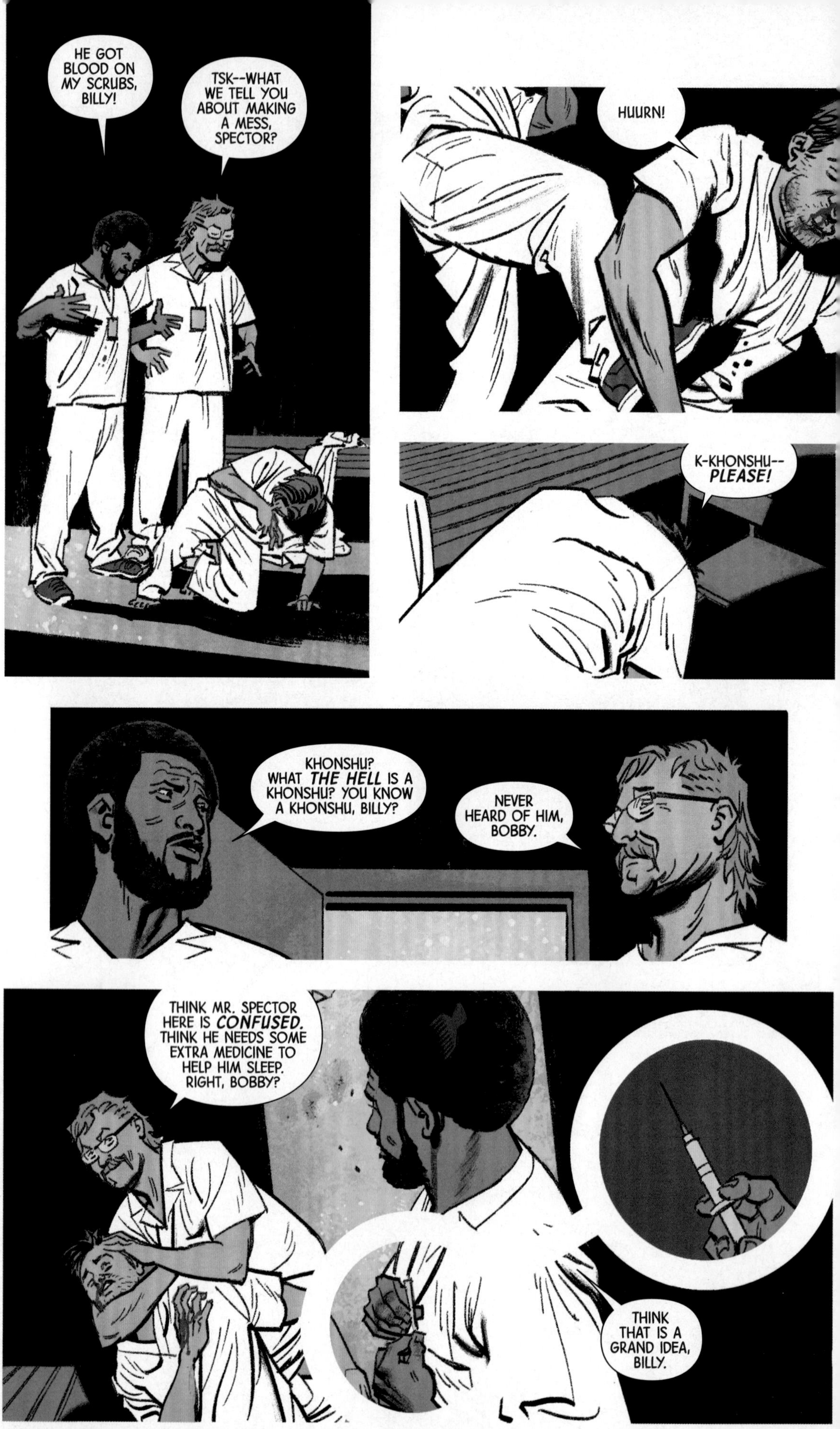
HE GOT BLOOD ON MY SCRUBS, BILLY!
TSK--WHAT WE TELL YOU ABOUT MAKING A MESS, SPECTOR?
HUURN!
K-KHONSHU-- PLEASE!
KHONSHU? WHAT THE HELL IS A KHONSHU? YOU KNOW A KHONSHU, BILLY?
NEVER HEARD OF HIM, BOBBY.
THINK MR. SPECTOR HERE IS CONFUSED. THINK HE NEEDS SOME EXTRA MEDICINE TO HELP HIM SLEEP. RIGHT, BOBBY?
THINK THAT IS A GRAND IDEA, BILLY.

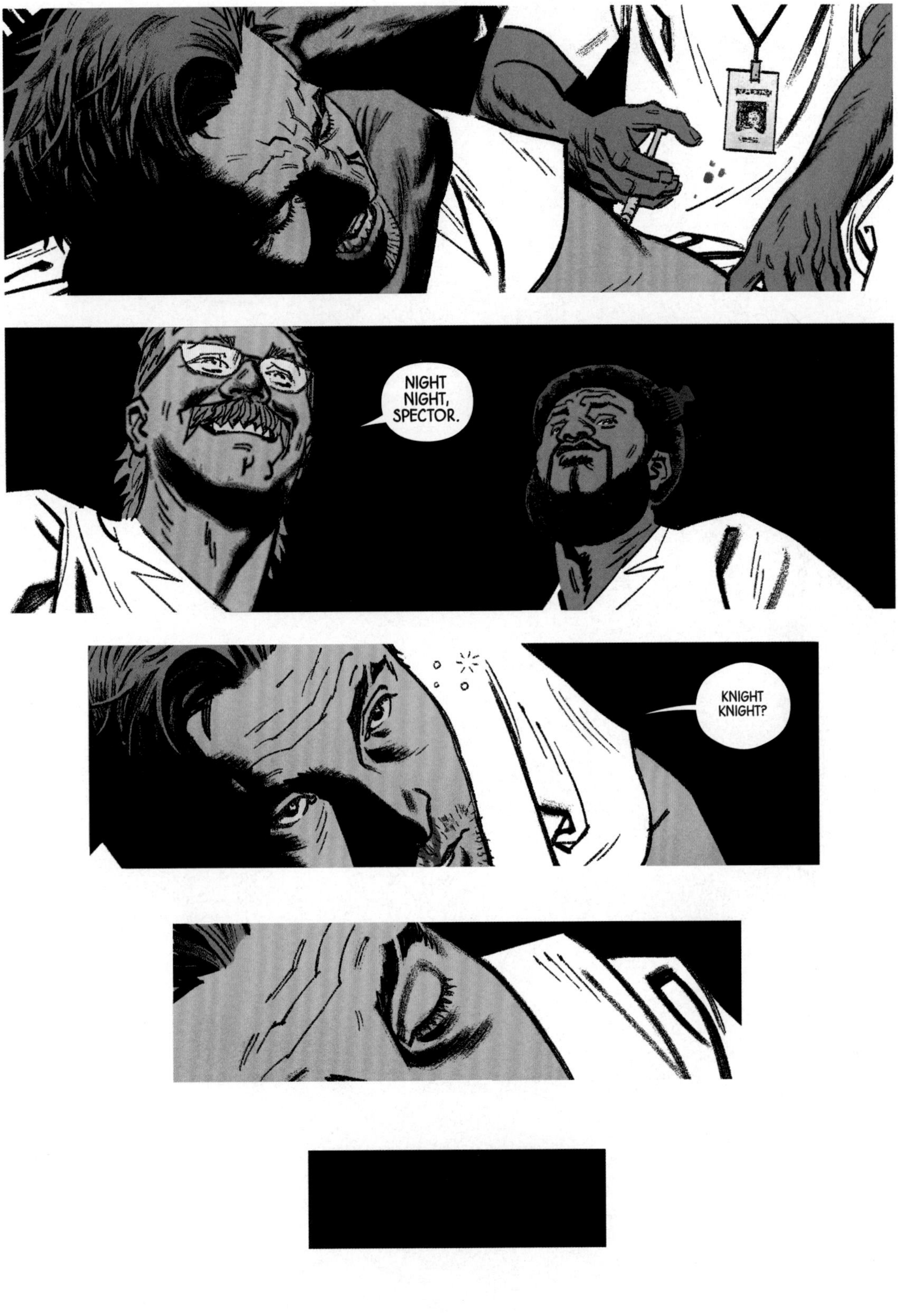
NIGHT NIGHT, SPECTOR.
KNIGHT KNIGHT?

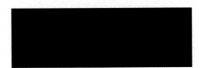

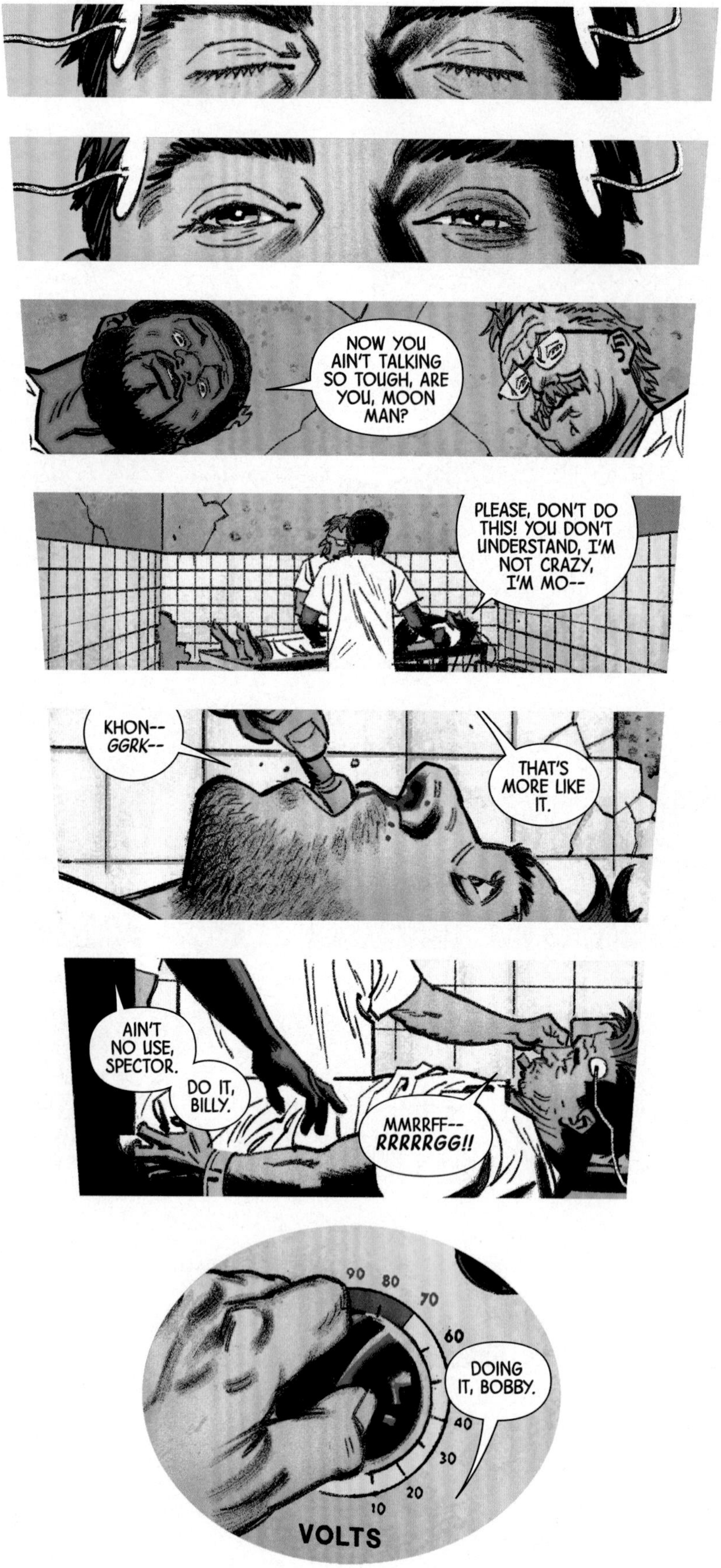
NOW YOU AIN'T TALKING SO TOUGH, ARE YOU, MOON MAN?
PLEASE, DON'T DO THIS! YOU DON'T UNDERSTAND, I'M NOT CRAZY, I'M MO--
KHON-- GGRK--
THAT'S MORE LIKE IT.
AIN'T NO USE, SPECTOR.
DO IT, BILLY.
MMRRFF-- RRRRRGG!!
90 80 70 60 40 30 20 10
VOLTS
DOING IT, BOBBY.

MMRGH!!!
60
50
40
30
20
10
200
190
180
MRRF...
HEH HEH...

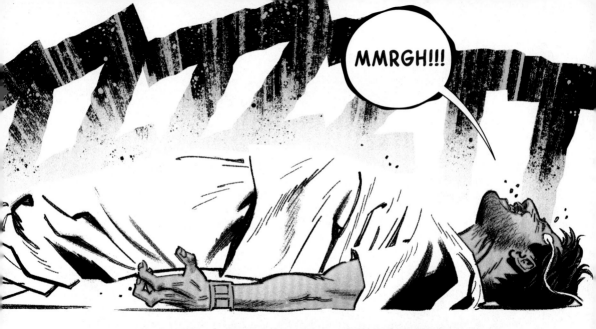

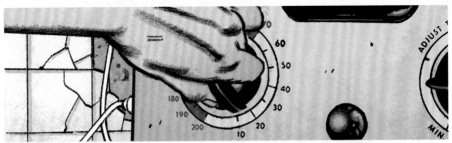

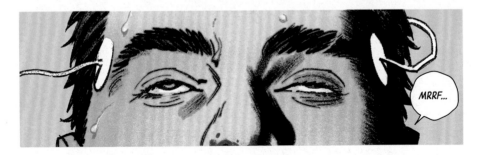

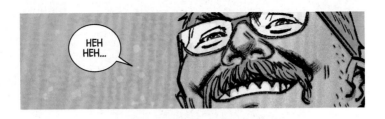

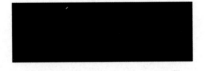

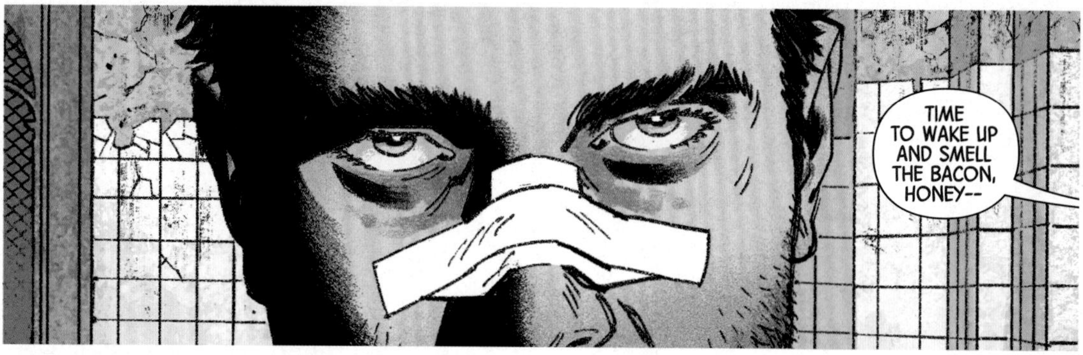
TIME TO WAKE UP AND SMELL THE BACON, HONEY--

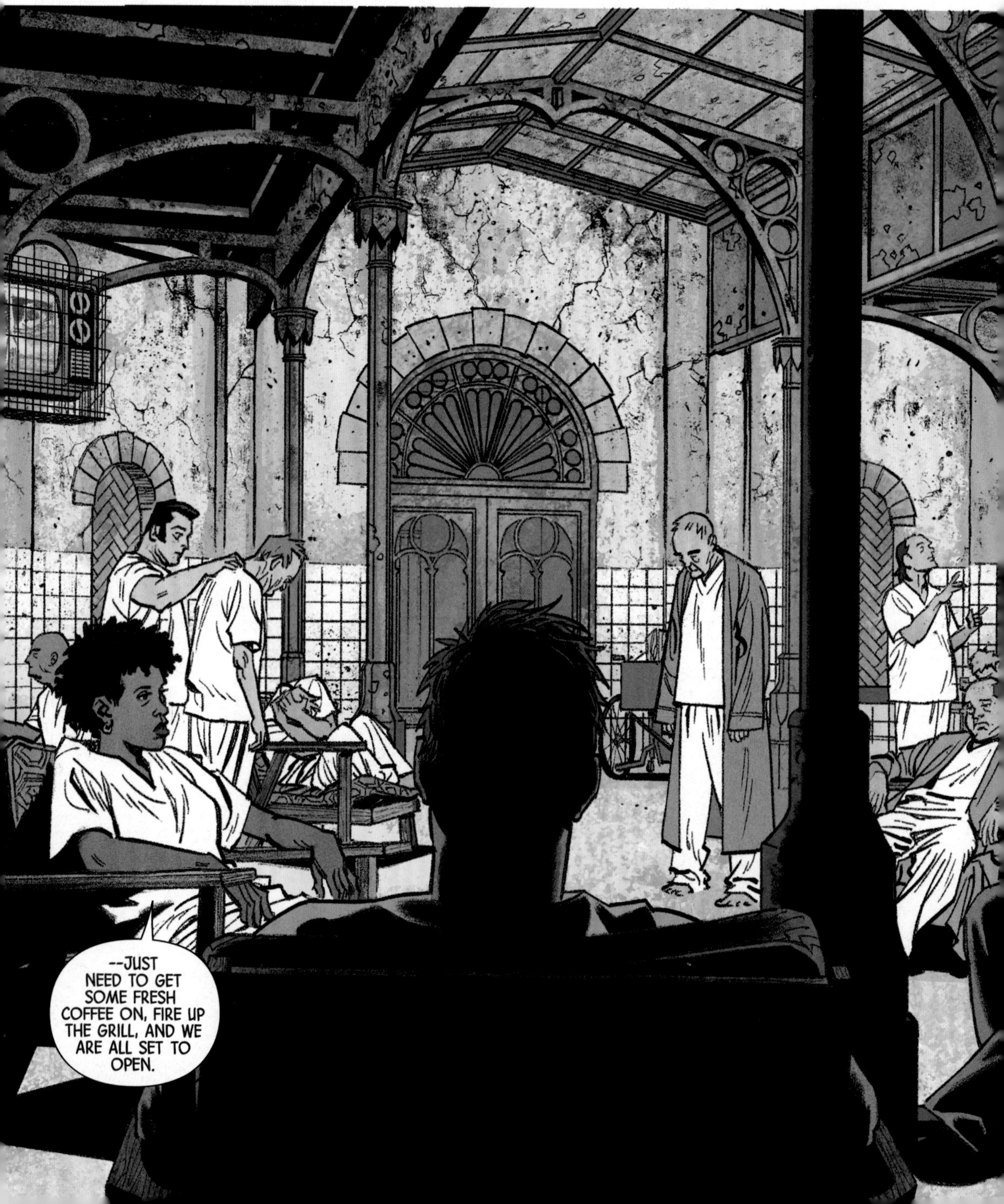
--JUST NEED TO GET SOME FRESH COFFEE ON, FIRE UP THE GRILL, AND WE ARE ALL SET TO OPEN.

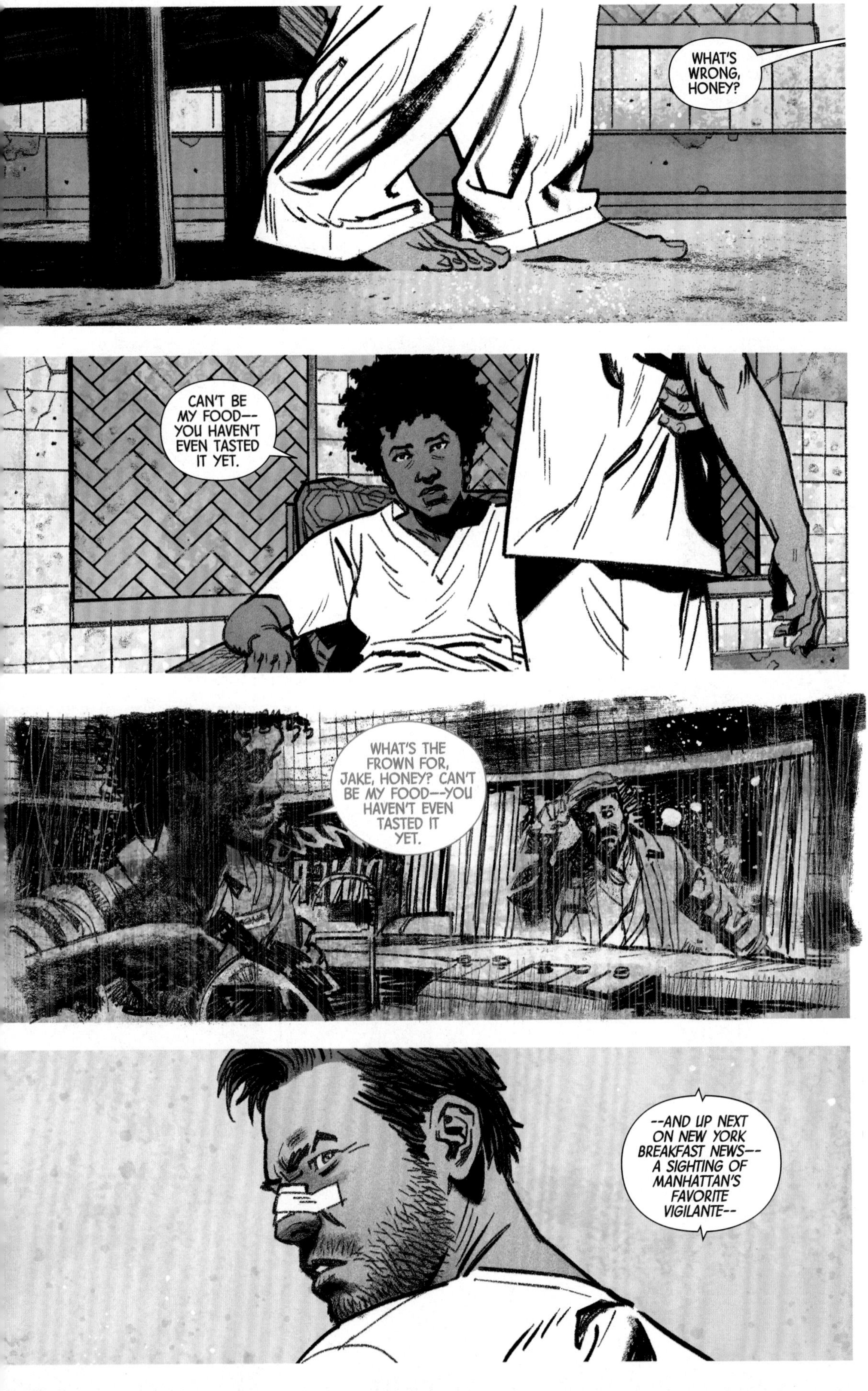
WHAT'S WRONG, HONEY?
CAN'T BE MY FOOD-- YOU HAVEN'T EVEN TASTED IT YET.
WHAT'S THE FROWN FOR, JAKE, HONEY? CAN'T BE MY FOOD--YOU HAVEN'T EVEN TASTED IT YET.
--AND UP NEXT ON NEW YORK BREAKFAST NEWS-- A SIGHTING OF MANHATTAN'S FAVORITE VIGILANTE--

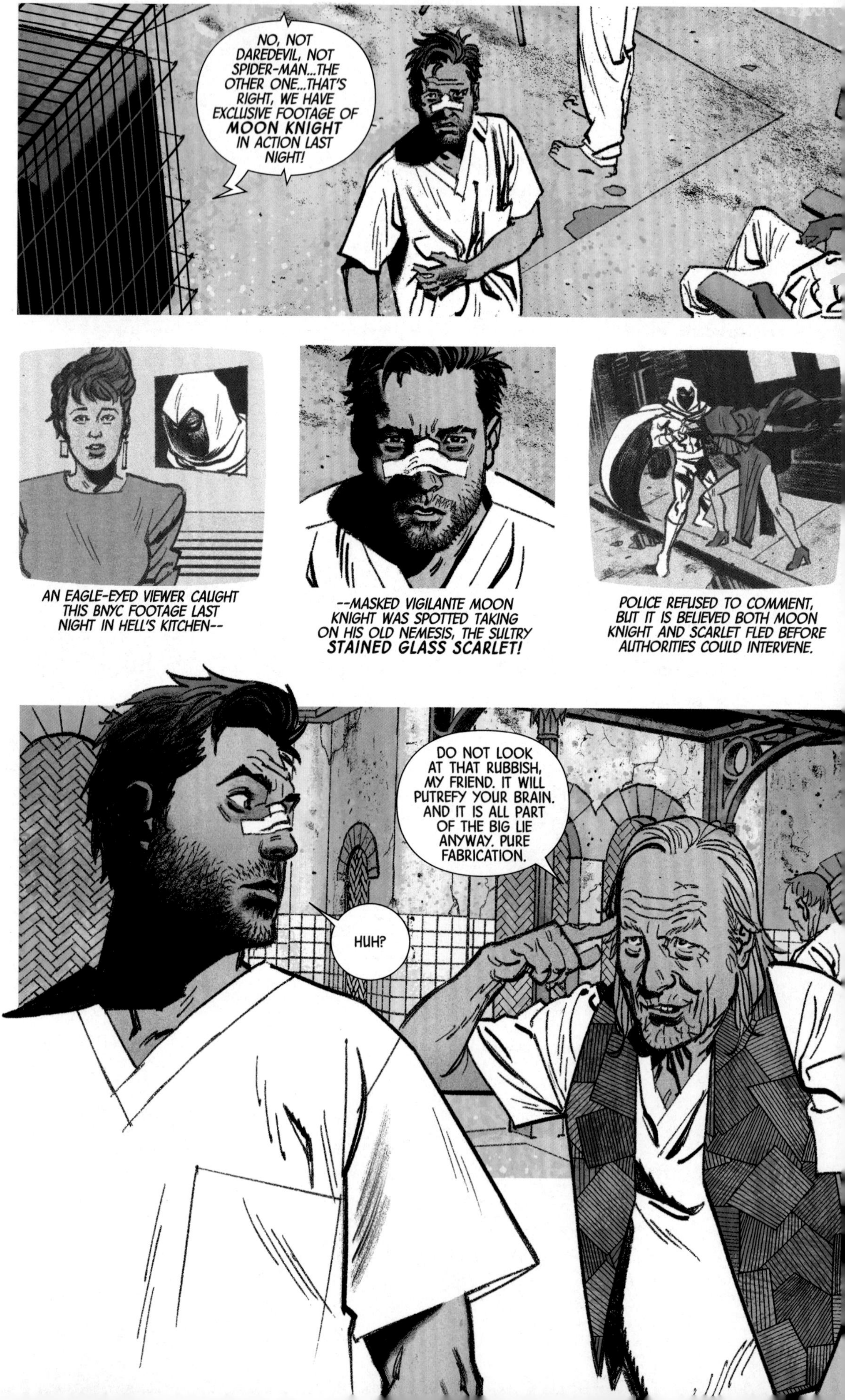
NO, NOT DAREDEVIL, NOT SPIDER-MAN...THE OTHER ONE...THAT'S RIGHT, WE HAVE EXCLUSIVE FOOTAGE OF MOON KNIGHT IN ACTION LAST NIGHT!
AN EAGLE-EYED VIEWER CAUGHT THIS BNYC FOOTAGE LAST NIGHT IN HELL'S KITCHEN--
--MASKED VIGILANTE MOON KNIGHT WAS SPOTTED TAKING ON HIS OLD NEMESIS, THE SULTRY STAINED GLASS SCARLET!
POLICE REFUSED TO COMMENT, BUT IT IS BELIEVED BOTH MOON KNIGHT AND SCARLET FLED BEFORE AUTHORITIES COULD INTERVENE.
DO NOT LOOK AT THAT RUBBISH, MY FRIEND. IT WILL PUTREFY YOUR BRAIN. AND IT IS ALL PART OF THE BIG LIE ANYWAY. PURE FABRICATION.
HUH?

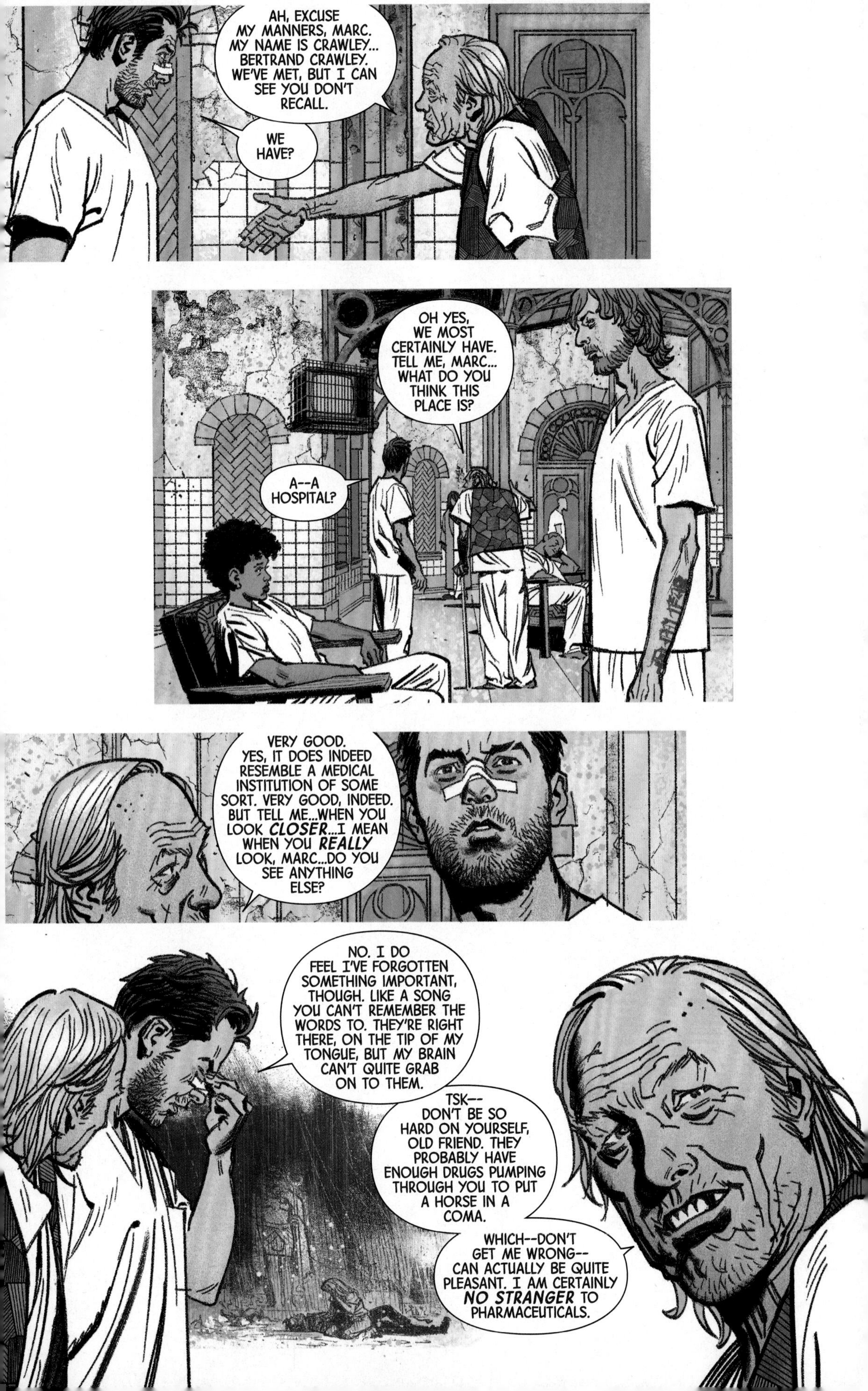
AH, EXCUSE MY MANNERS, MARC. MY NAME IS CRAWLEY... BERTRAND CRAWLEY. WE'VE MET, BUT I CAN SEE YOU DON'T RECALL.
WE HAVE?
OH YES, WE MOST CERTAINLY HAVE. TELL ME, MARC... WHAT DO YOU THINK THIS PLACE IS?
A--A HOSPITAL?
VERY GOOD. YES, IT DOES INDEED RESEMBLE A MEDICAL INSTITUTION OF SOME SORT. VERY GOOD, INDEED. BUT TELL ME...WHEN YOU LOOK CLOSER...I MEAN WHEN YOU REALLY LOOK, MARC...DO YOU SEE ANYTHING ELSE?
NO. I DO FEEL I'VE FORGOTTEN SOMETHING IMPORTANT, THOUGH. LIKE A SONG YOU CAN'T REMEMBER THE WORDS TO. THEY'RE RIGHT THERE, ON THE TIP OF MY TONGUE, BUT MY BRAIN CAN'T QUITE GRAB ON TO THEM.
TSK-- DON'T BE SO HARD ON YOURSELF, OLD FRIEND. THEY PROBABLY HAVE ENOUGH DRUGS PUMPING THROUGH YOU TO PUT A HORSE IN A COMA.
WHICH--DON'T GET ME WRONG-- CAN ACTUALLY BE QUITE PLEASANT. I AM CERTAINLY NO STRANGER TO PHARMACEUTICALS.

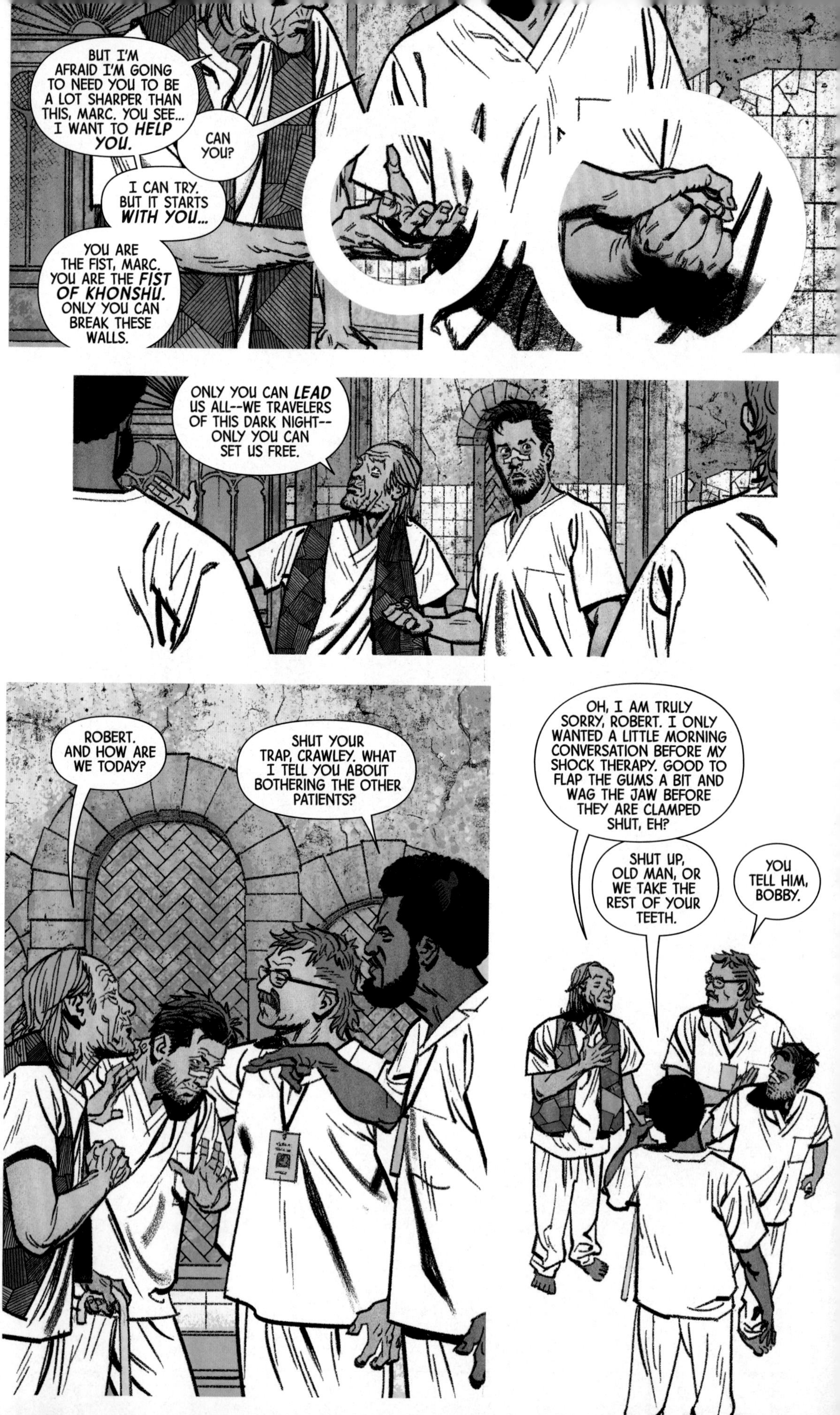
BUT I'M AFRAID I'M GOING TO NEED YOU TO BE A LOT SHARPER THAN THIS, MARC. YOU SEE... I WANT TO HELP YOU.
CAN YOU?
I CAN TRY. BUT IT STARTS WITH YOU...
YOU ARE THE FIST, MARC. YOU ARE THE FIST OF KHONSHU. ONLY YOU CAN BREAK THESE WALLS.
ONLY YOU CAN LEAD US ALL--WE TRAVELERS OF THIS DARK NIGHT--ONLY YOU CAN SET US FREE.
ROBERT. AND HOW ARE WE TODAY?
SHUT YOUR TRAP, CRAWLEY. WHAT I TELL YOU ABOUT BOTHERING THE OTHER PATIENTS?
OH, I AM TRULY SORRY, ROBERT. I ONLY WANTED A LITTLE MORNING CONVERSATION BEFORE MY SHOCK THERAPY. GOOD TO FLAP THE GUMS A BIT AND WAG THE JAW BEFORE THEY ARE CLAMPED SHUT, EH?
SHUT UP, OLD MAN, OR WE TAKE THE REST OF YOUR TEETH.
YOU TELL HIM, BOBBY.

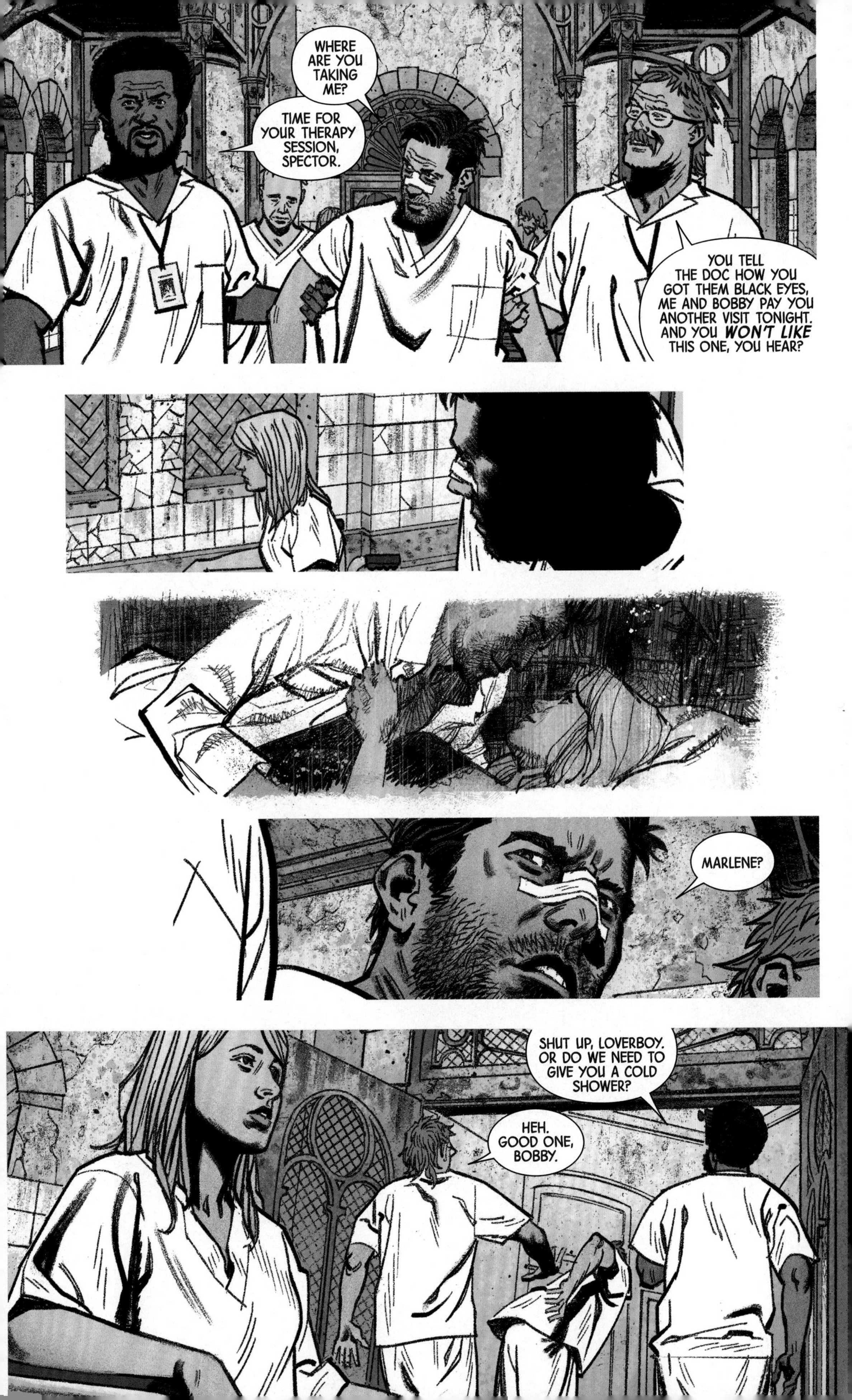
WHERE ARE YOU TAKING ME?
TIME FOR YOUR THERAPY SESSION, SPECTOR.
YOU TELL THE DOC HOW YOU GOT THEM BLACK EYES, ME AND BOBBY PAY YOU ANOTHER VISIT TONIGHT. AND YOU *WON'T LIKE* THIS ONE, YOU HEAR?
MARLENE?
SHUT UP, LOVERBOY. OR DO WE NEED TO GIVE YOU A COLD SHOWER?
HEH. GOOD ONE, BOBBY.

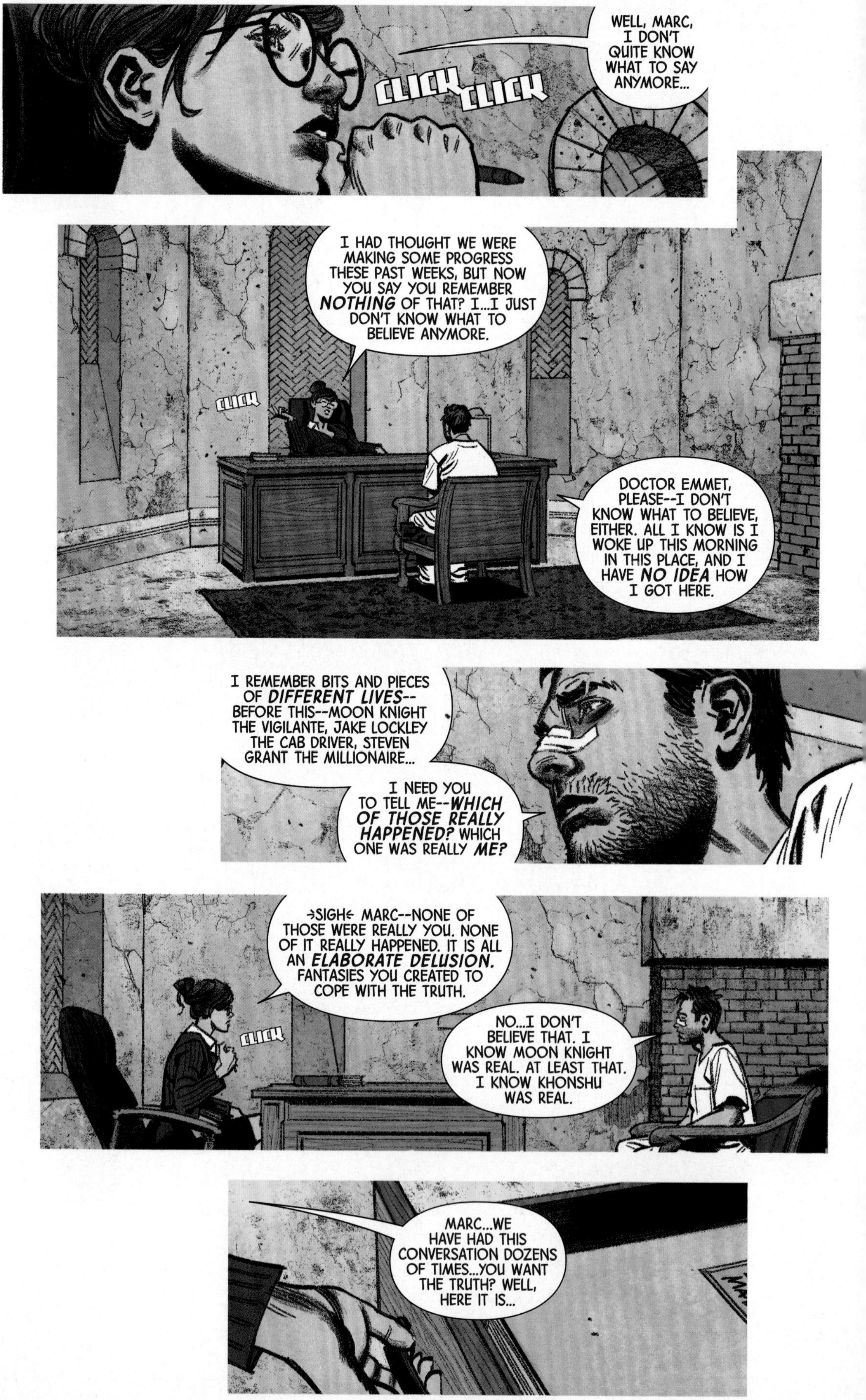

CLICK CLICK
WELL, MARC, I DON'T QUITE KNOW WHAT TO SAY ANYMORE...
I HAD THOUGHT WE WERE MAKING SOME PROGRESS THESE PAST WEEKS, BUT NOW YOU SAY YOU REMEMBER NOTHING OF THAT? I...I JUST DON'T KNOW WHAT TO BELIEVE ANYMORE.
CLICK
DOCTOR EMMET, PLEASE--I DON'T KNOW WHAT TO BELIEVE, EITHER. ALL I KNOW IS I WOKE UP THIS MORNING IN THIS PLACE, AND I HAVE NO IDEA HOW I GOT HERE.
I REMEMBER BITS AND PIECES OF DIFFERENT LIVES-- BEFORE THIS--MOON KNIGHT THE VIGILANTE, JAKE LOCKLEY THE CAB DRIVER, STEVEN GRANT THE MILLIONAIRE...
I NEED YOU TO TELL ME--WHICH OF THOSE REALLY HAPPENED? WHICH ONE WAS REALLY ME?
→SIGH← MARC--NONE OF THOSE WERE REALLY YOU. NONE OF IT REALLY HAPPENED. IT IS ALL AN ELABORATE DELUSION. FANTASIES YOU CREATED TO COPE WITH THE TRUTH.
CLICK
NO...I DON'T BELIEVE THAT. I KNOW MOON KNIGHT WAS REAL. AT LEAST THAT. I KNOW KHONSHU WAS REAL.
MARC...WE HAVE HAD THIS CONVERSATION DOZENS OF TIMES...YOU WANT THE TRUTH? WELL, HERE IT IS...

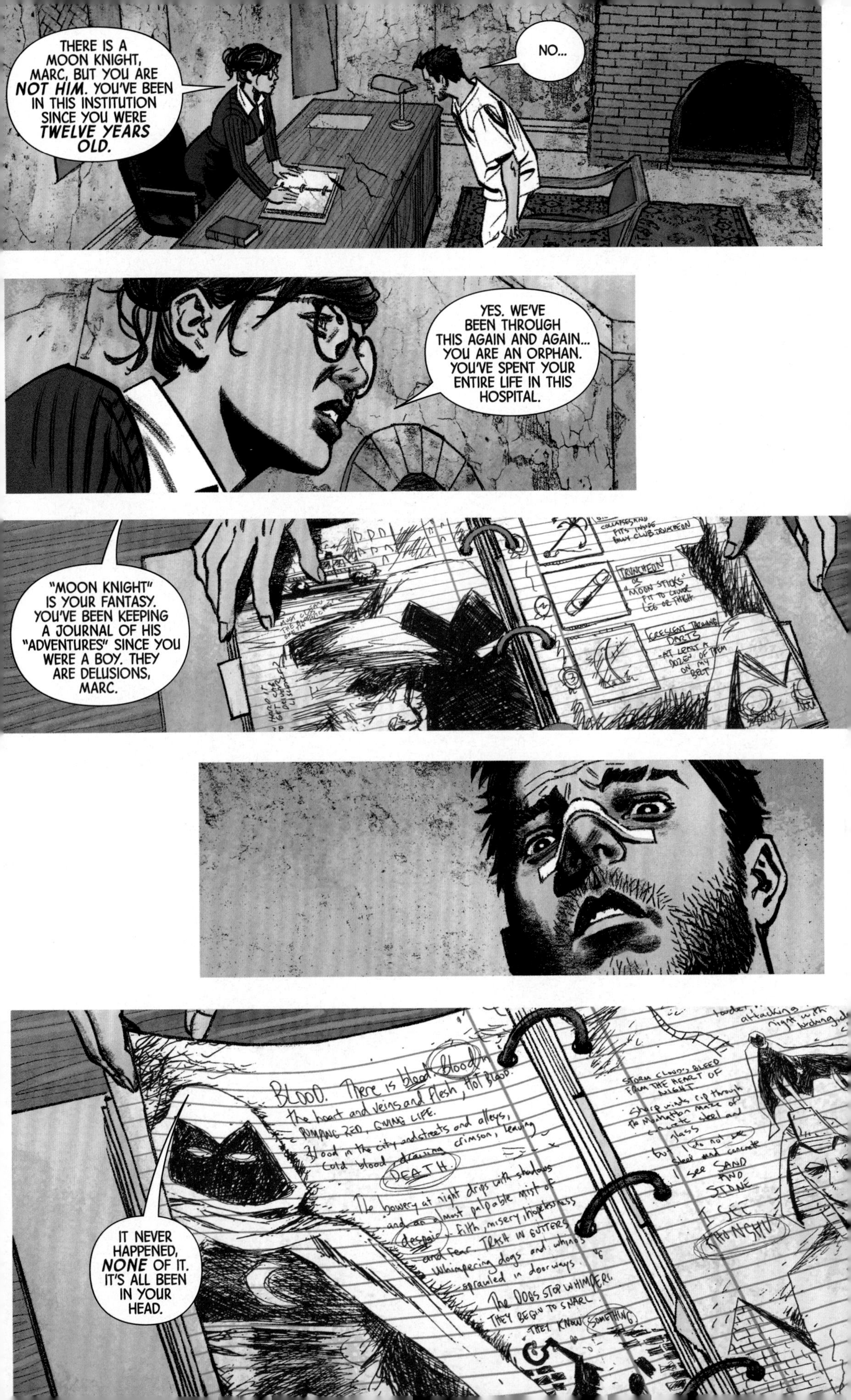
THERE IS A MOON KNIGHT, MARC, BUT YOU ARE *NOT HIM*. YOU'VE BEEN IN THIS INSTITUTION SINCE YOU WERE *TWELVE YEARS OLD.*
NO...
YES. WE'VE BEEN THROUGH THIS AGAIN AND AGAIN... YOU ARE AN ORPHAN. YOU'VE SPENT YOUR ENTIRE LIFE IN THIS HOSPITAL.
"MOON KNIGHT" IS YOUR FANTASY. YOU'VE BEEN KEEPING A JOURNAL OF HIS "ADVENTURES" SINCE YOU WERE A BOY. THEY ARE DELUSIONS, MARC.
IT NEVER HAPPENED, *NONE* OF IT. IT'S ALL BEEN IN YOUR HEAD.

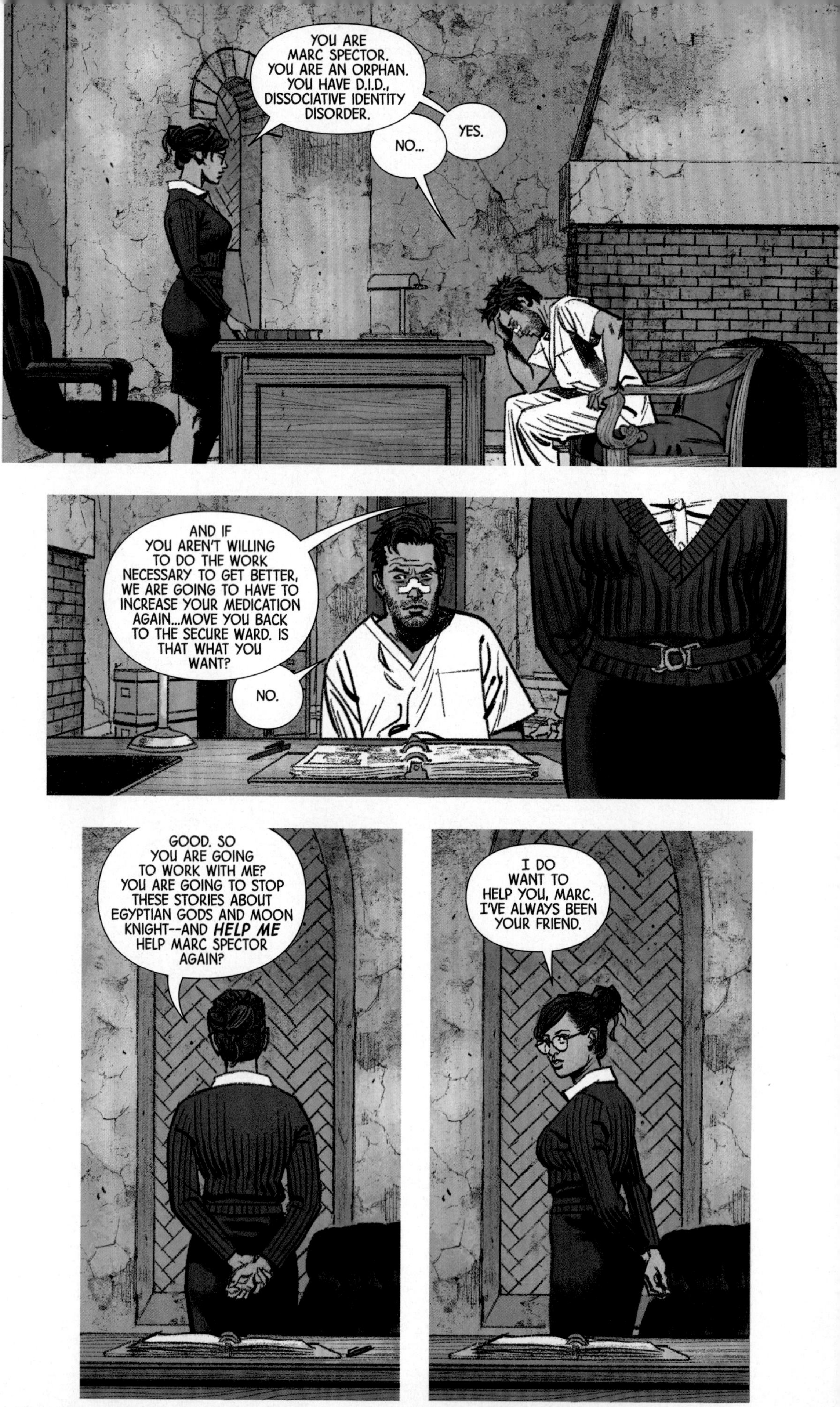
YOU ARE MARC SPECTOR. YOU ARE AN ORPHAN. YOU HAVE D.I.D., DISSOCIATIVE IDENTITY DISORDER.
NO...
YES.
AND IF YOU AREN'T WILLING TO DO THE WORK NECESSARY TO GET BETTER, WE ARE GOING TO HAVE TO INCREASE YOUR MEDICATION AGAIN...MOVE YOU BACK TO THE SECURE WARD. IS THAT WHAT YOU WANT?
NO.
GOOD. SO YOU ARE GOING TO WORK WITH ME? YOU ARE GOING TO STOP THESE STORIES ABOUT EGYPTIAN GODS AND MOON KNIGHT--AND *HELP ME* HELP MARC SPECTOR AGAIN?
I DO WANT TO HELP YOU, MARC. I'VE ALWAYS BEEN YOUR FRIEND.

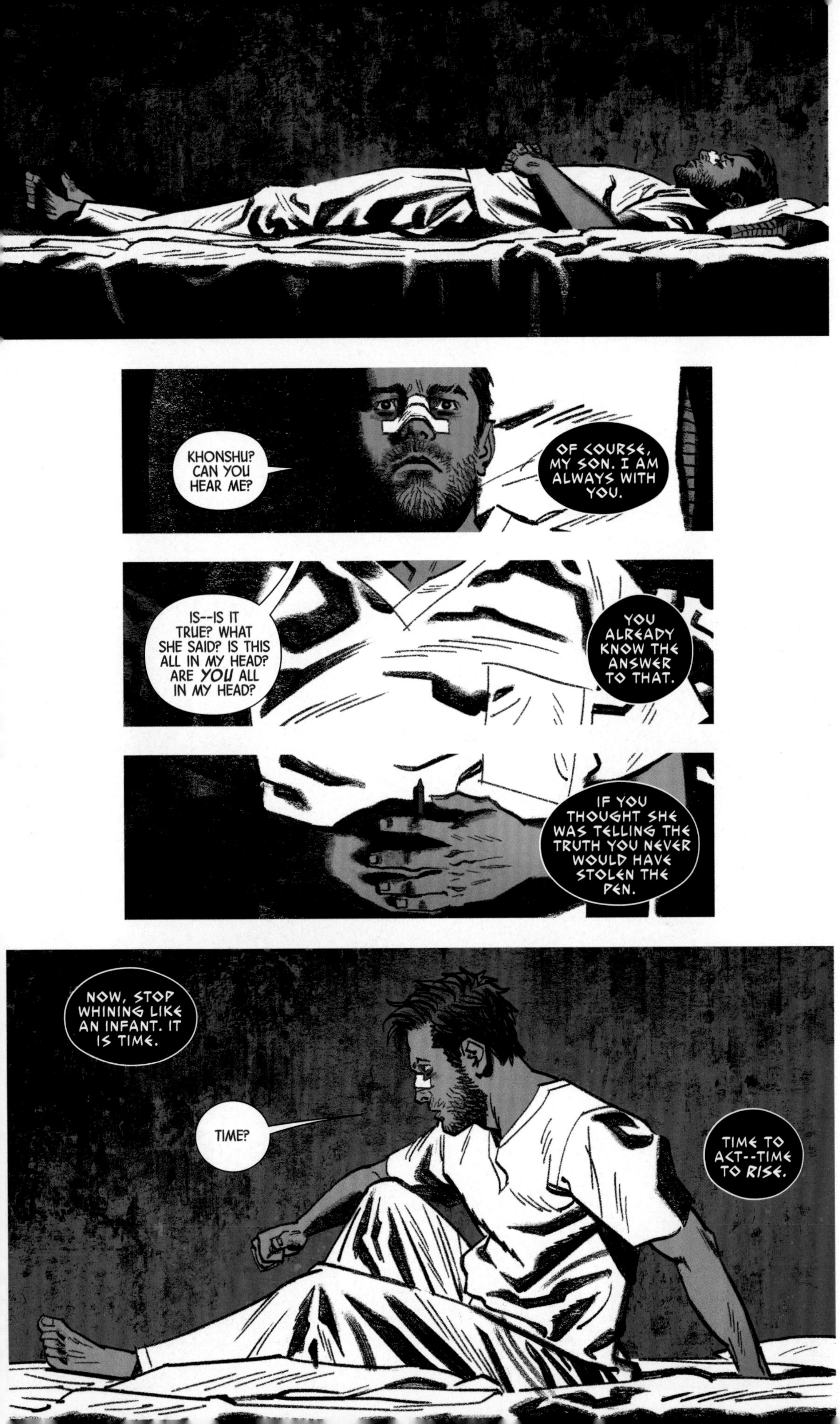
KHONSHU? CAN YOU HEAR ME?
OF COURSE, MY SON. I AM ALWAYS WITH YOU.
IS--IS IT TRUE? WHAT SHE SAID? IS THIS ALL IN MY HEAD? ARE YOU ALL IN MY HEAD?
YOU ALREADY KNOW THE ANSWER TO THAT.
IF YOU THOUGHT SHE WAS TELLING THE TRUTH YOU NEVER WOULD HAVE STOLEN THE PEN.
NOW, STOP WHINING LIKE AN INFANT. IT IS TIME.
TIME?
TIME TO ACT--TIME TO RISE.

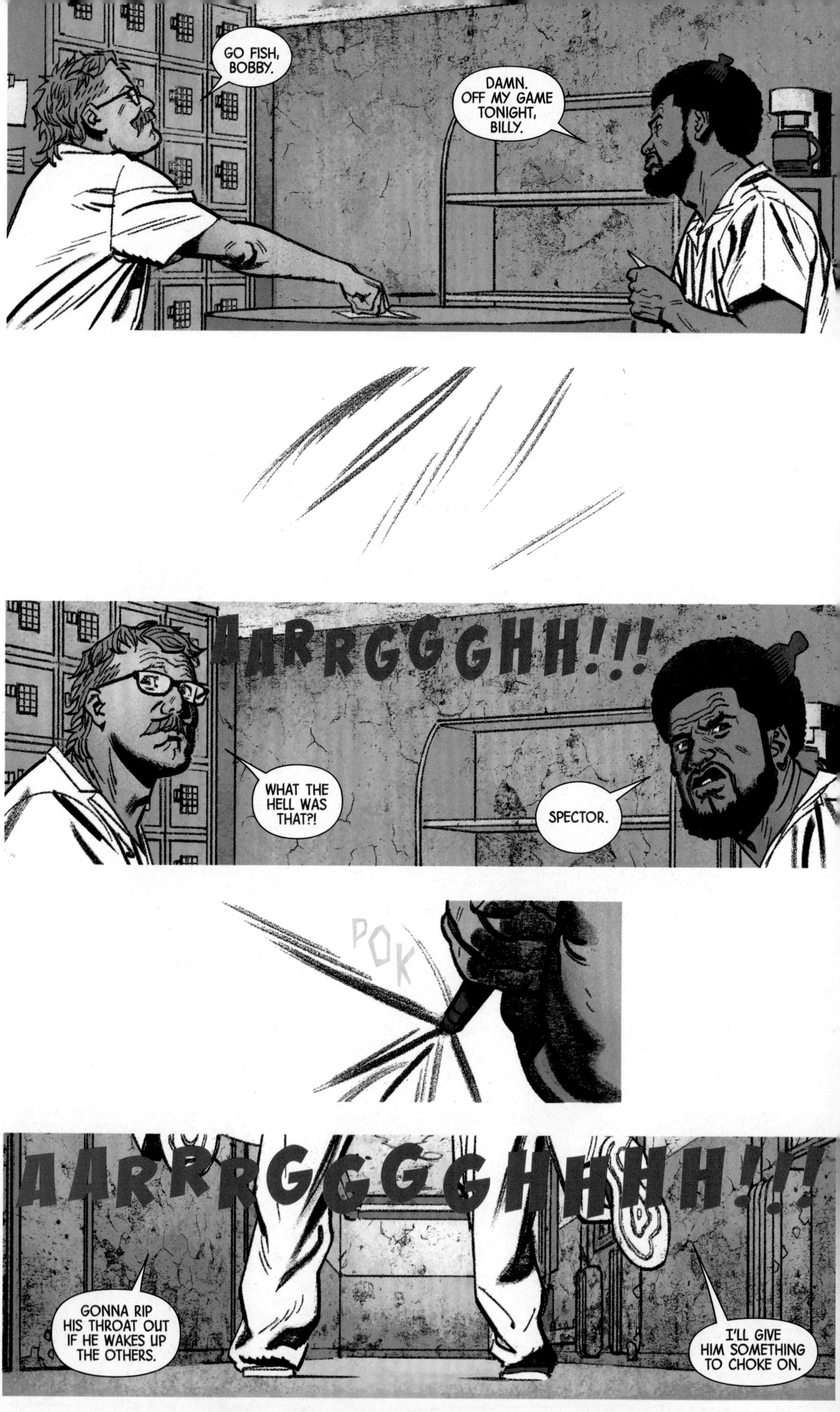
GO FISH, BOBBY.
DAMN. OFF MY GAME TONIGHT, BILLY.
AARRGGGHH!!!
WHAT THE HELL WAS THAT?!
SPECTOR.
POK
AARRRGGGGHHHH!!!
GONNA RIP HIS THROAT OUT IF HE WAKES UP THE OTHERS.
I'LL GIVE HIM SOMETHING TO CHOKE ON.

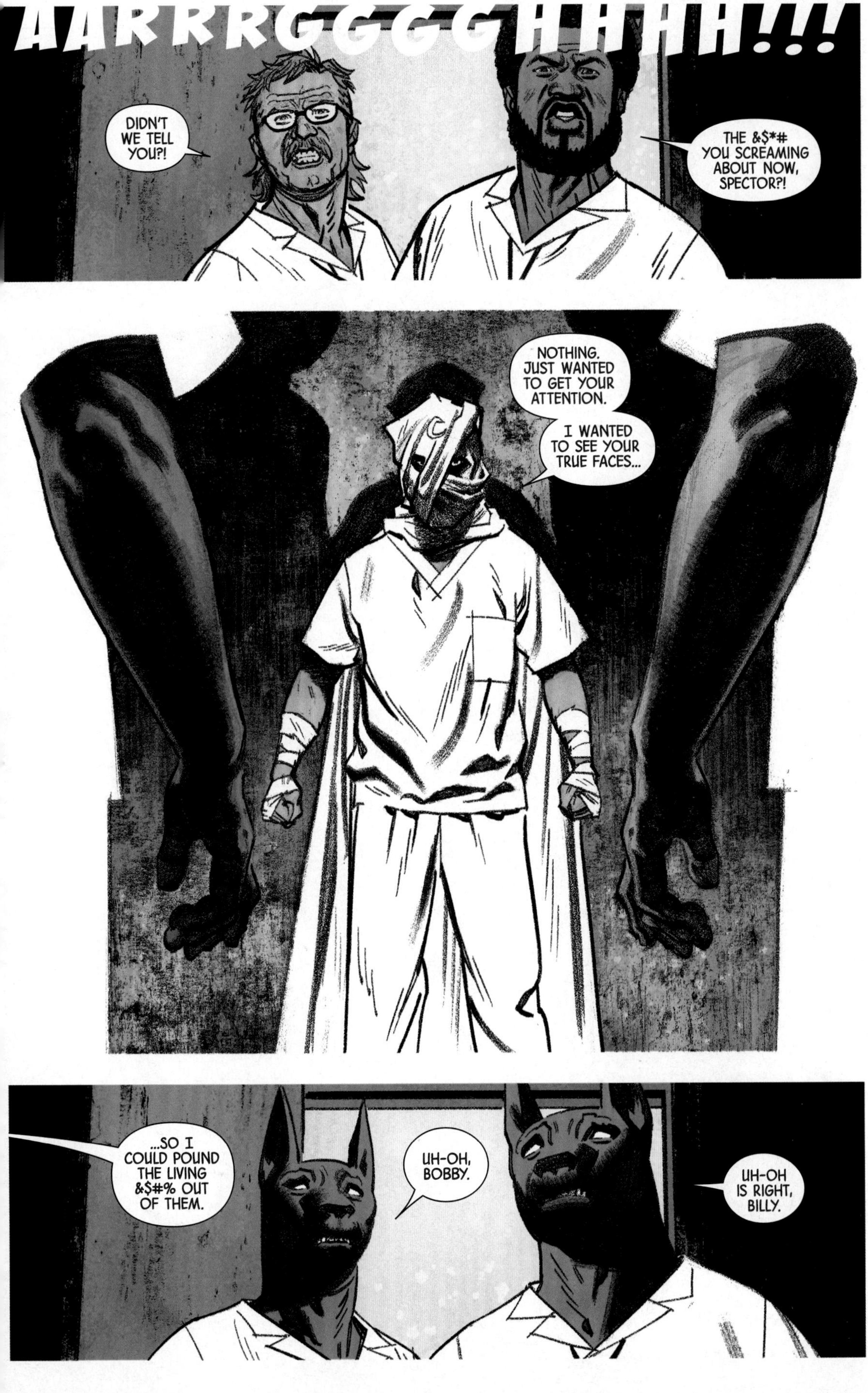
AARRRGGGGGHHHHH!!!
DIDN'T WE TELL YOU?!
THE &$*# YOU SCREAMING ABOUT NOW, SPECTOR?!
NOTHING. JUST WANTED TO GET YOUR ATTENTION.
I WANTED TO SEE YOUR TRUE FACES...
...SO I COULD POUND THE LIVING &$#% OUT OF THEM.
UH-OH, BOBBY.
UH-OH IS RIGHT, BILLY.

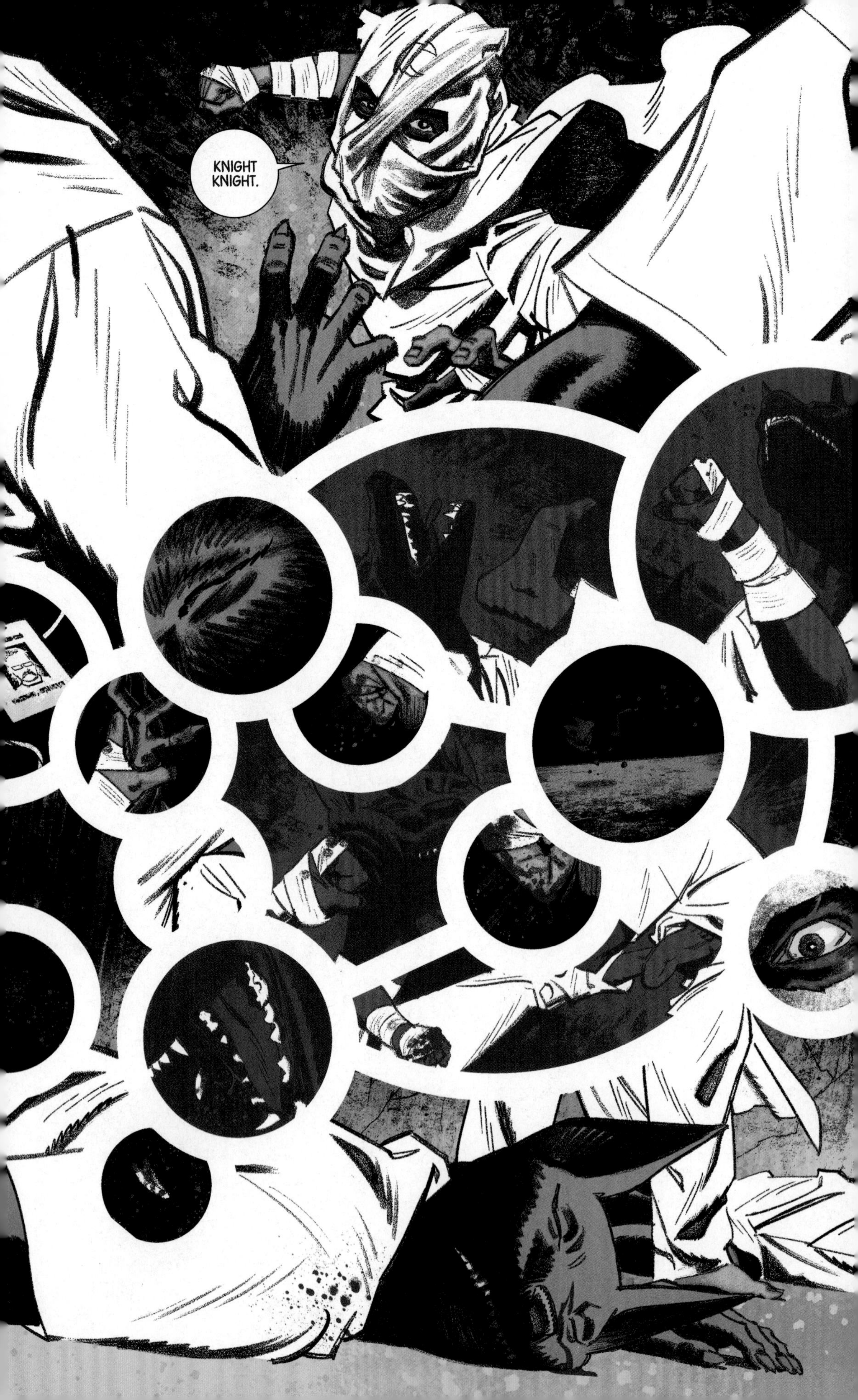
KNIGHT KNIGHT.

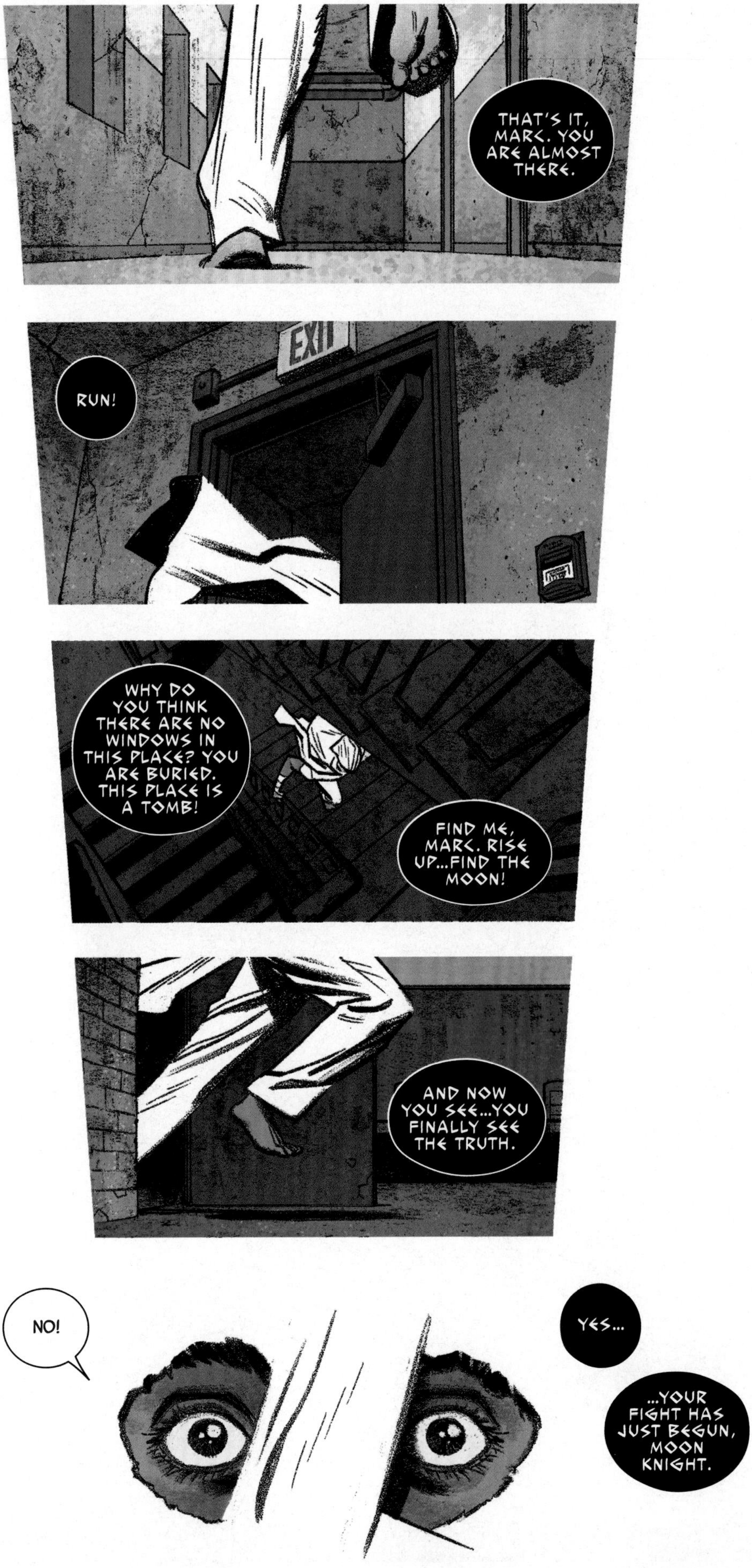
THAT'S IT, MARC. YOU ARE ALMOST THERE.
RUN!
WHY DO YOU THINK THERE ARE NO WINDOWS IN THIS PLACE? YOU ARE BURIED. THIS PLACE IS A TOMB!
FIND ME, MARC. RISE UP...FIND THE MOON!
AND NOW YOU SEE...YOU FINALLY SEE THE TRUTH.
NO!
YES...
...YOUR FIGHT HAS JUST BEGUN, MOON KNIGHT.

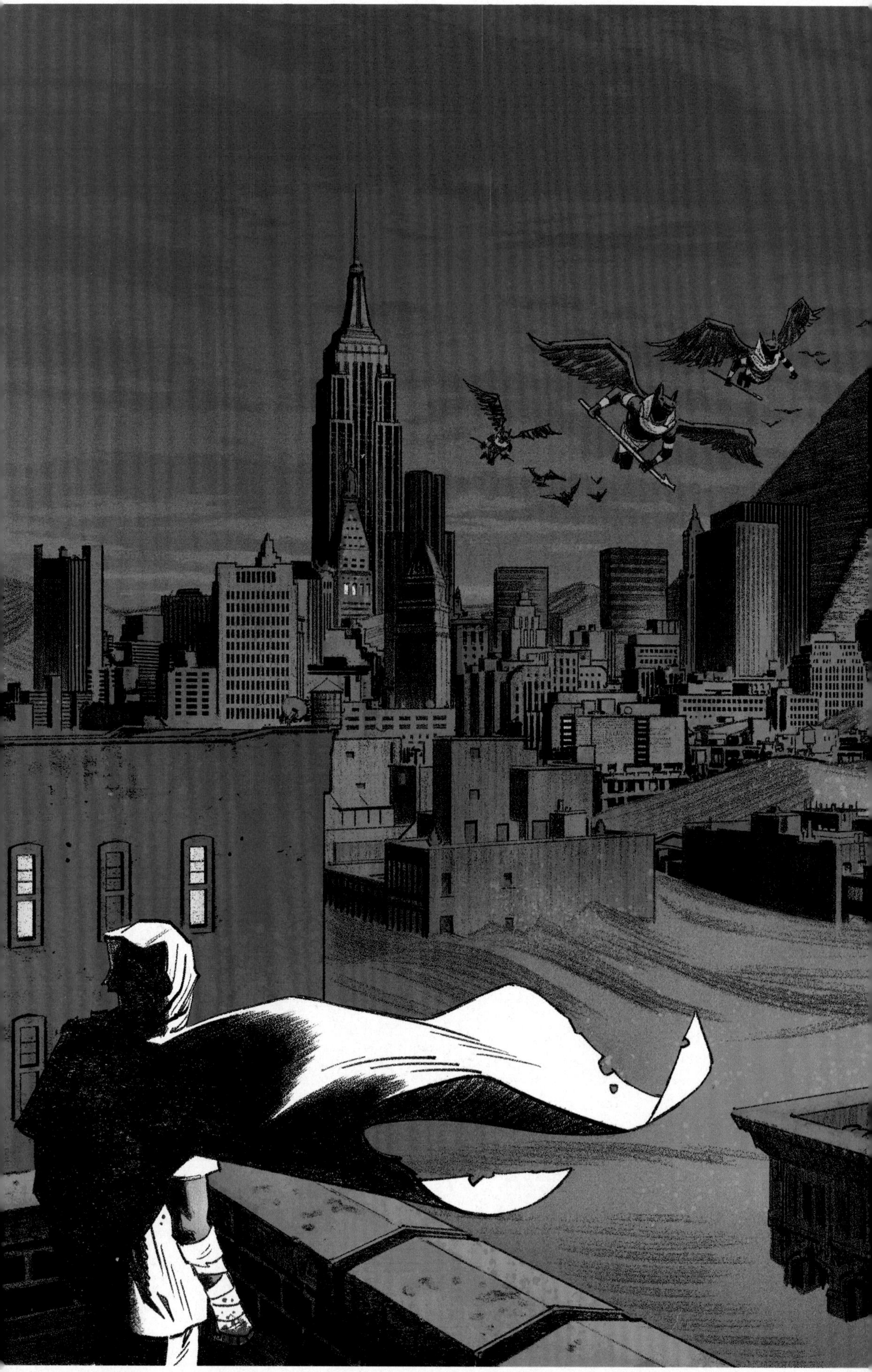

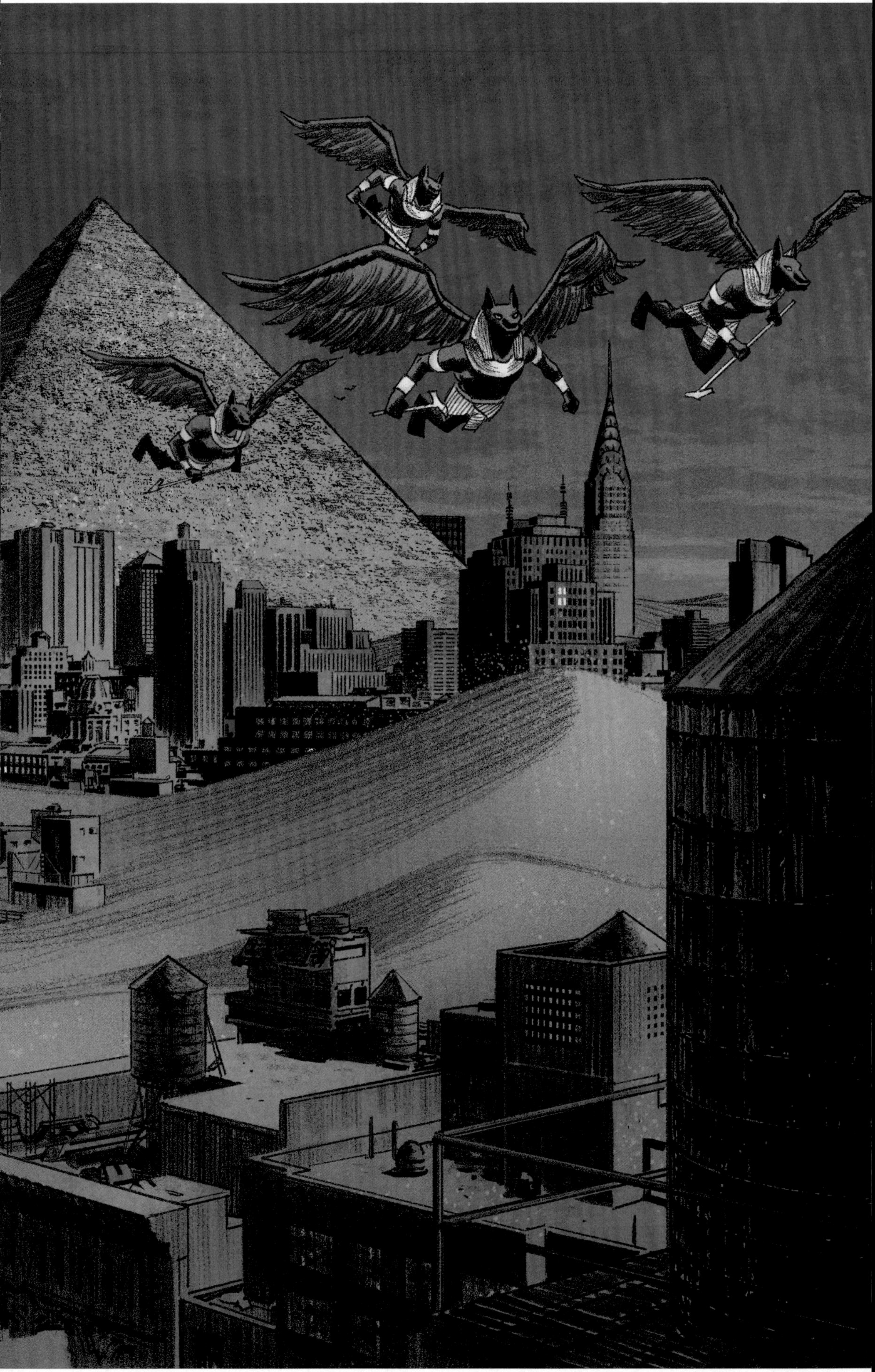

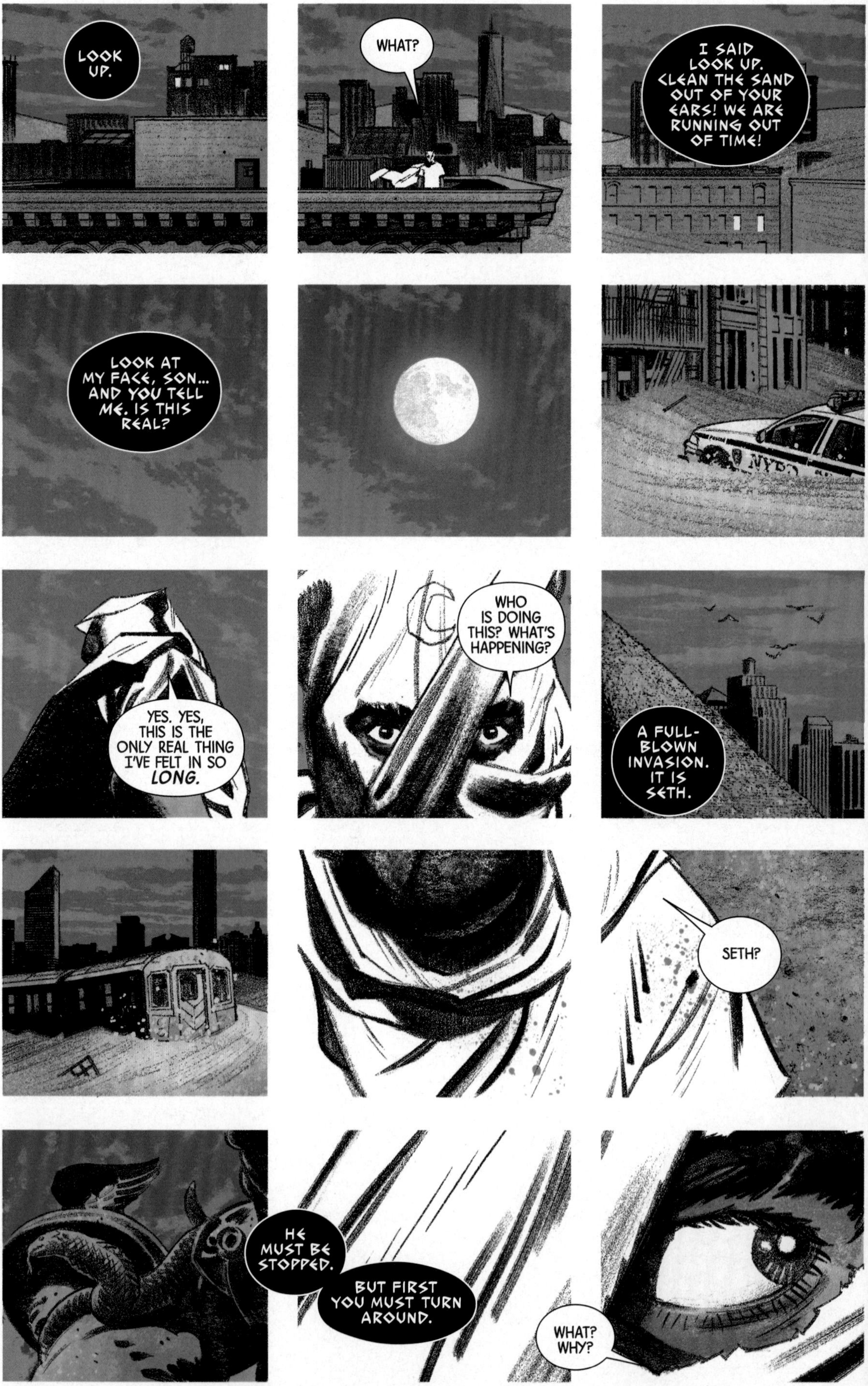
LOOK UP.
WHAT?
I SAID LOOK UP. CLEAN THE SAND OUT OF YOUR EARS! WE ARE RUNNING OUT OF TIME!
LOOK AT MY FACE, SON... AND YOU TELL ME. IS THIS REAL?
YES. YES, THIS IS THE ONLY REAL THING I'VE FELT IN SO LONG.
WHO IS DOING THIS? WHAT'S HAPPENING?
A FULL-BLOWN INVASION. IT IS SETH.
SETH?
HE MUST BE STOPPED.
BUT FIRST YOU MUST TURN AROUND.
WHAT? WHY?

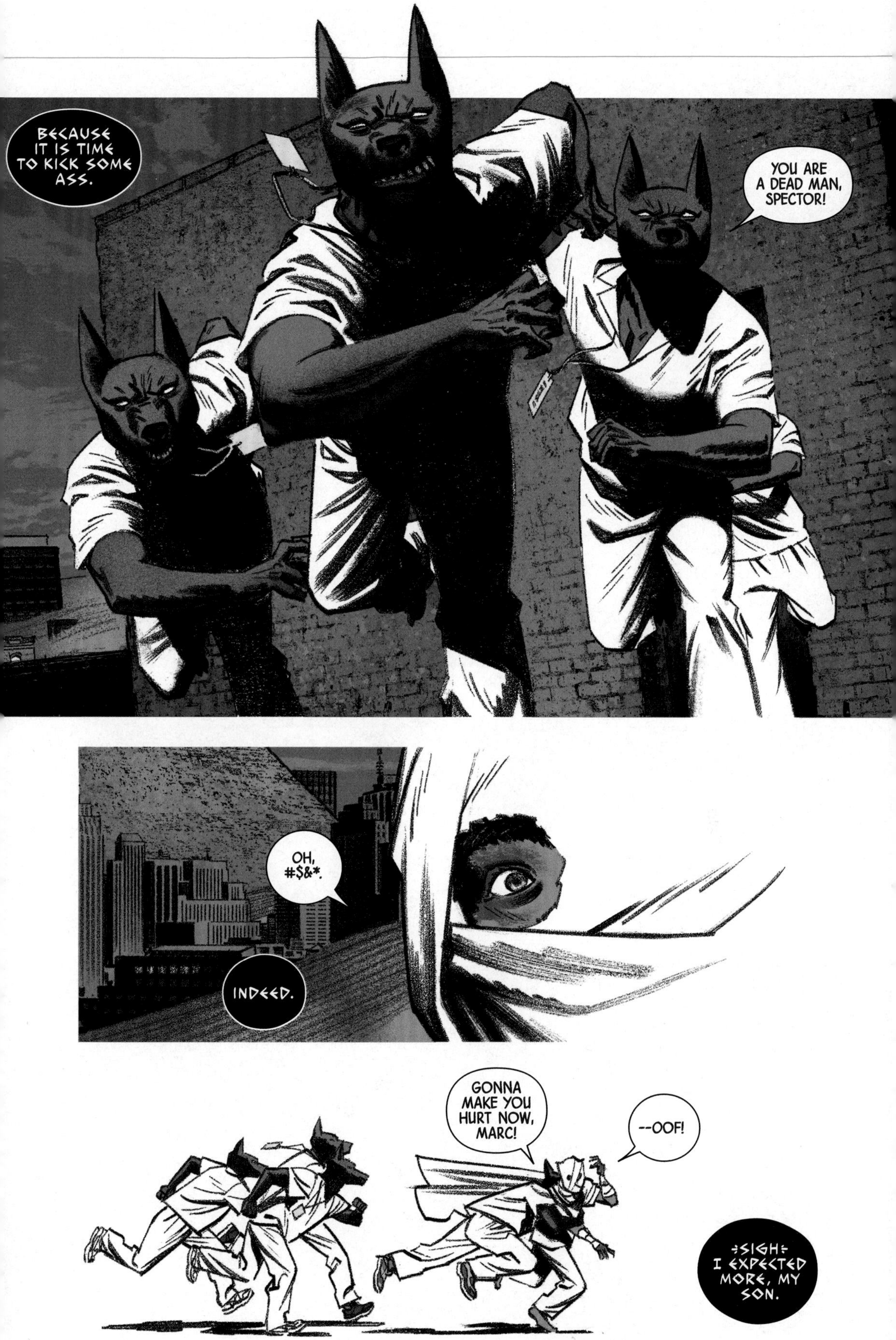
BECAUSE IT IS TIME TO KICK SOME ASS.
YOU ARE A DEAD MAN, SPECTOR!
OH, #$&*.
INDEED.
GONNA MAKE YOU HURT NOW, MARC!
--OOF!
=SIGH= I EXPECTED MORE, MY SON.

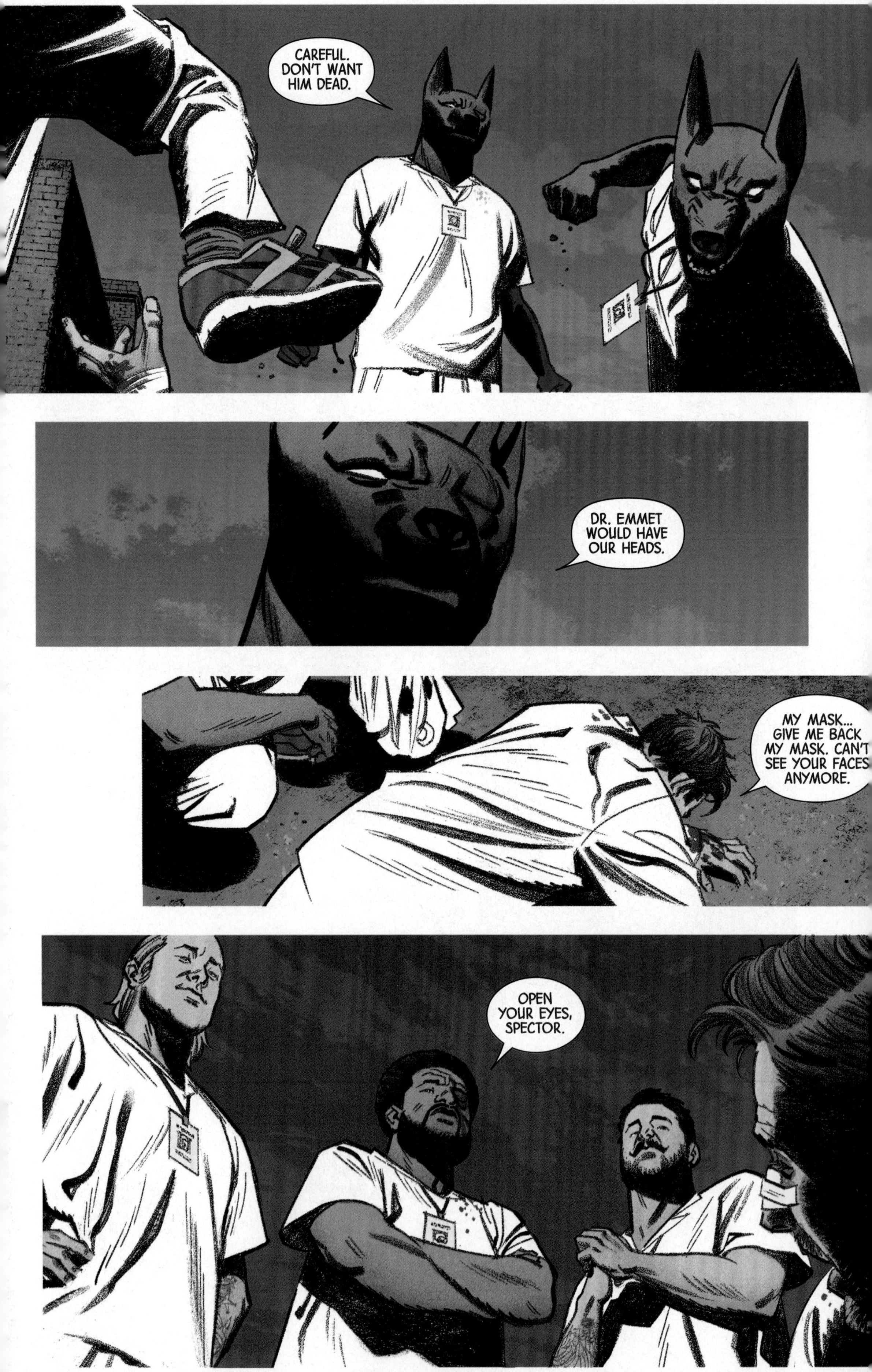
CAREFUL. DON'T WANT HIM DEAD.
DR. EMMET WOULD HAVE OUR HEADS.
MY MASK... GIVE ME BACK MY MASK. CAN'T SEE YOUR FACES ANYMORE.
OPEN YOUR EYES, SPECTOR.

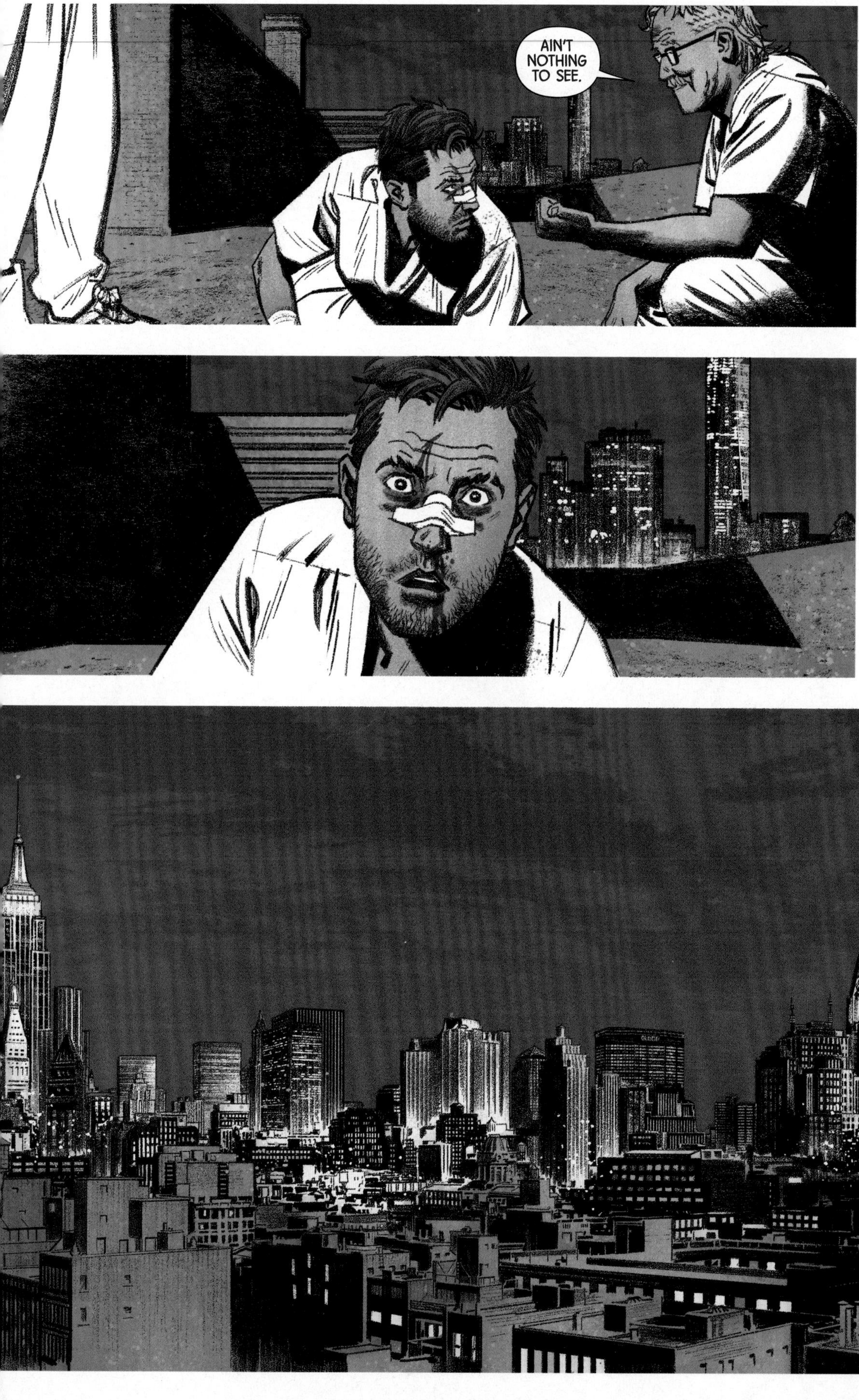
AIN'T NOTHING TO SEE.

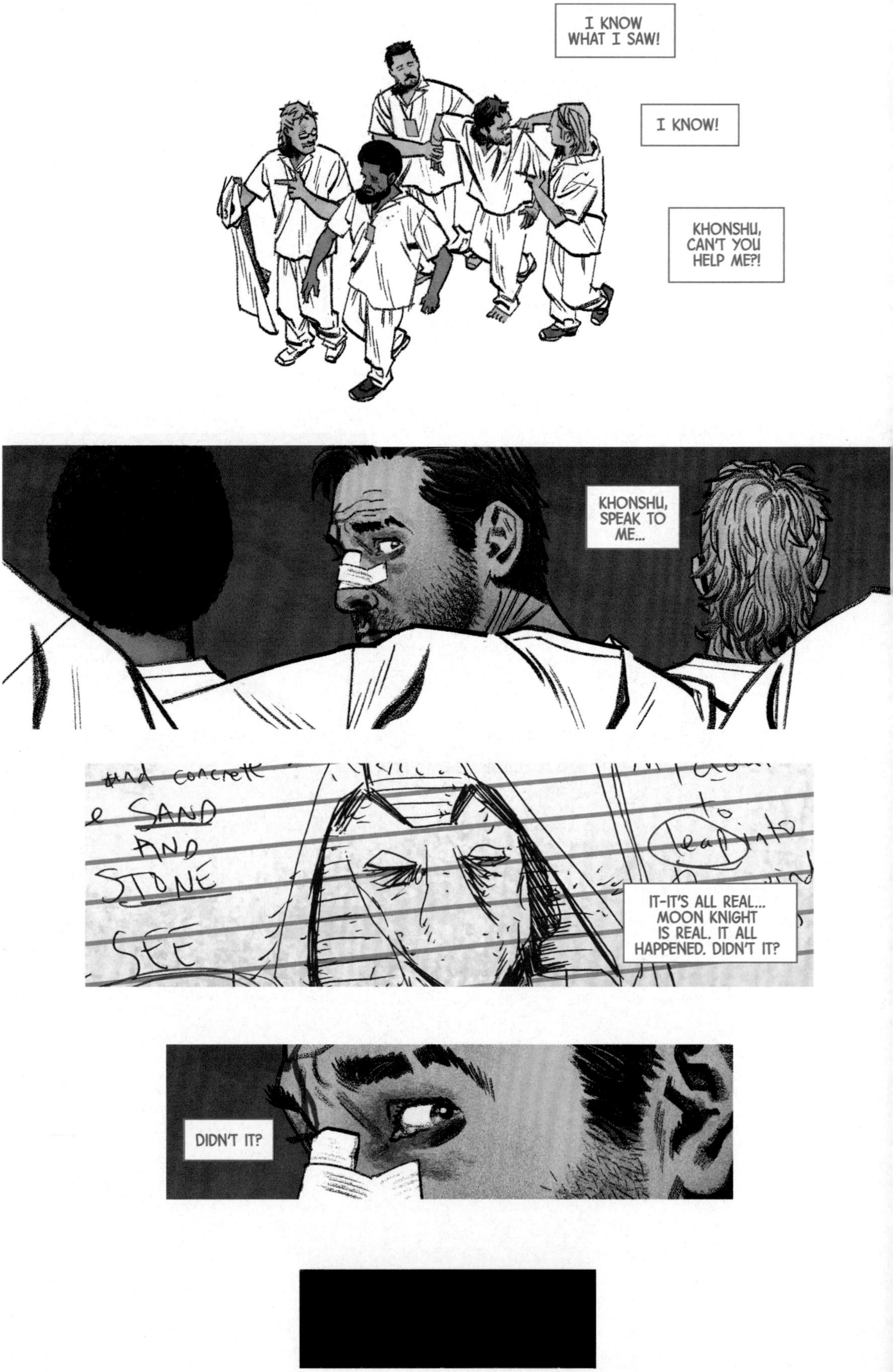
I KNOW WHAT I SAW!
I KNOW!
KHONSHU, CAN'T YOU HELP ME?!
KHONSHU, SPEAK TO ME...
and concrete
SAND
AND
STONE
SEE
IT-IT'S ALL REAL... MOON KNIGHT IS REAL. IT ALL HAPPENED. DIDN'T IT?
DIDN'T IT?

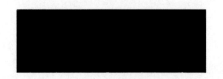

WELCOME TO NEW EGYPT
PART TWO 2

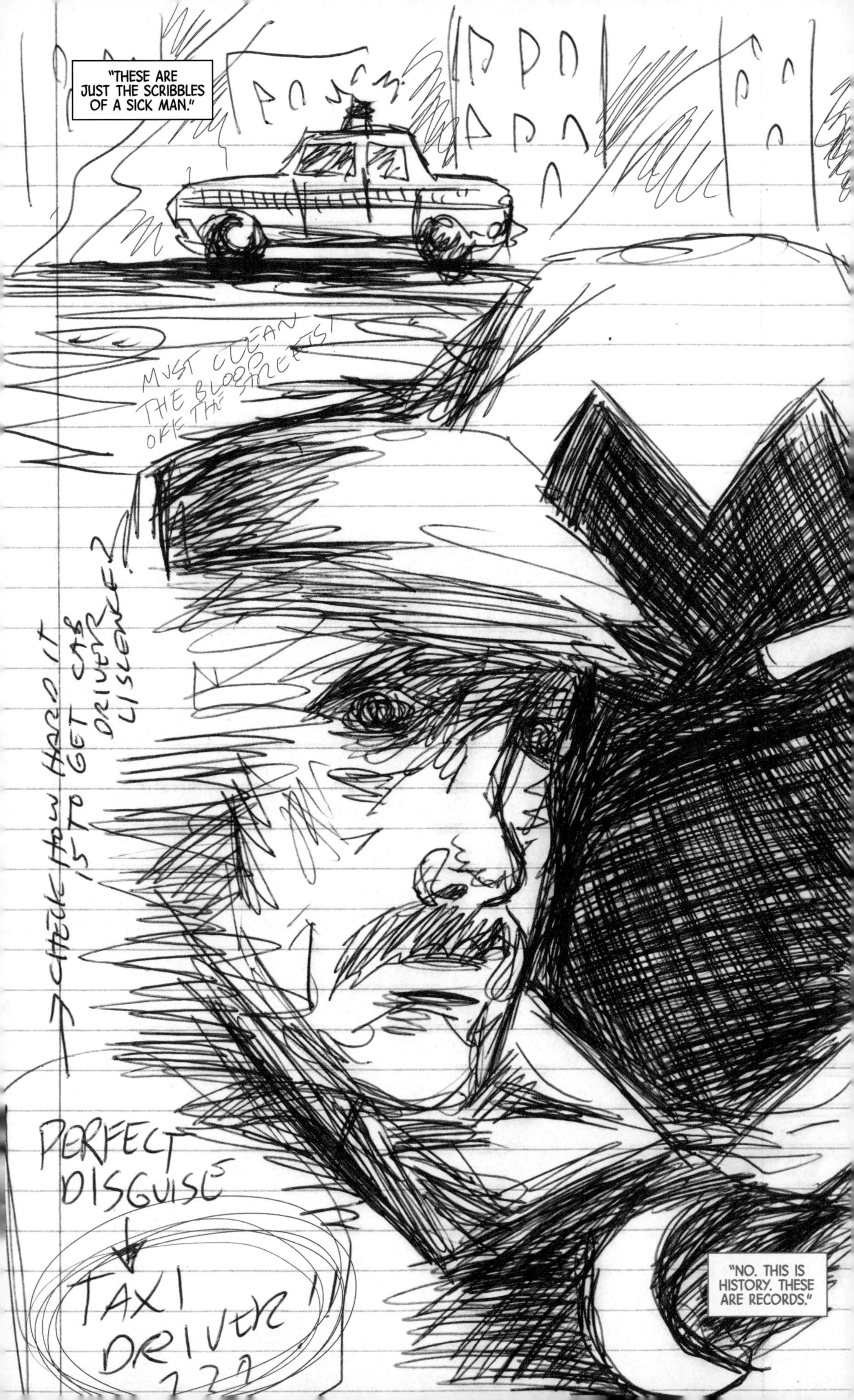
"THESE ARE JUST THE SCRIBBLES OF A SICK MAN."
MUST CLEAN THE BLOOD OFF THE STREETS!
CHECK HOW HARD IT IS TO GET CAB DRIVER
PERFECT DISGUISE
TAXI DRIVER!!
"NO. THIS IS HISTORY. THESE ARE RECORDS."

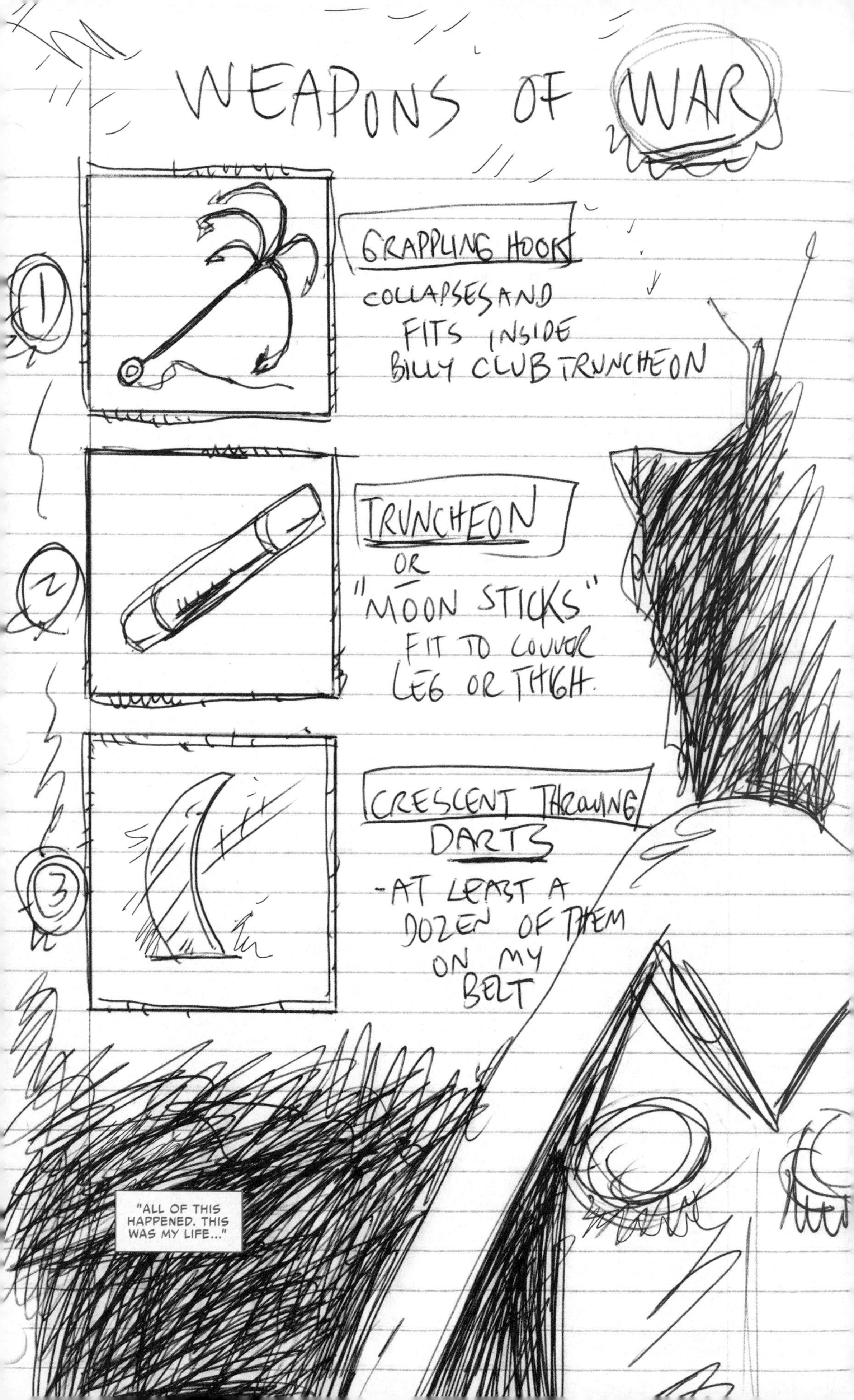

WEAPONS OF WAR
1
GRAPPLING HOOK
COLLAPSES AND FITS INSIDE BILLY CLUB TRUNCHEON
2
TRUNCHEON OR "MOON STICKS" FIT TO COVER LEG OR THIGH.
3
CRESCENT THROWING DARTS
-AT LEAST A DOZEN OF THEM ON MY BELT
"ALL OF THIS HAPPENED. THIS WAS MY LIFE..."

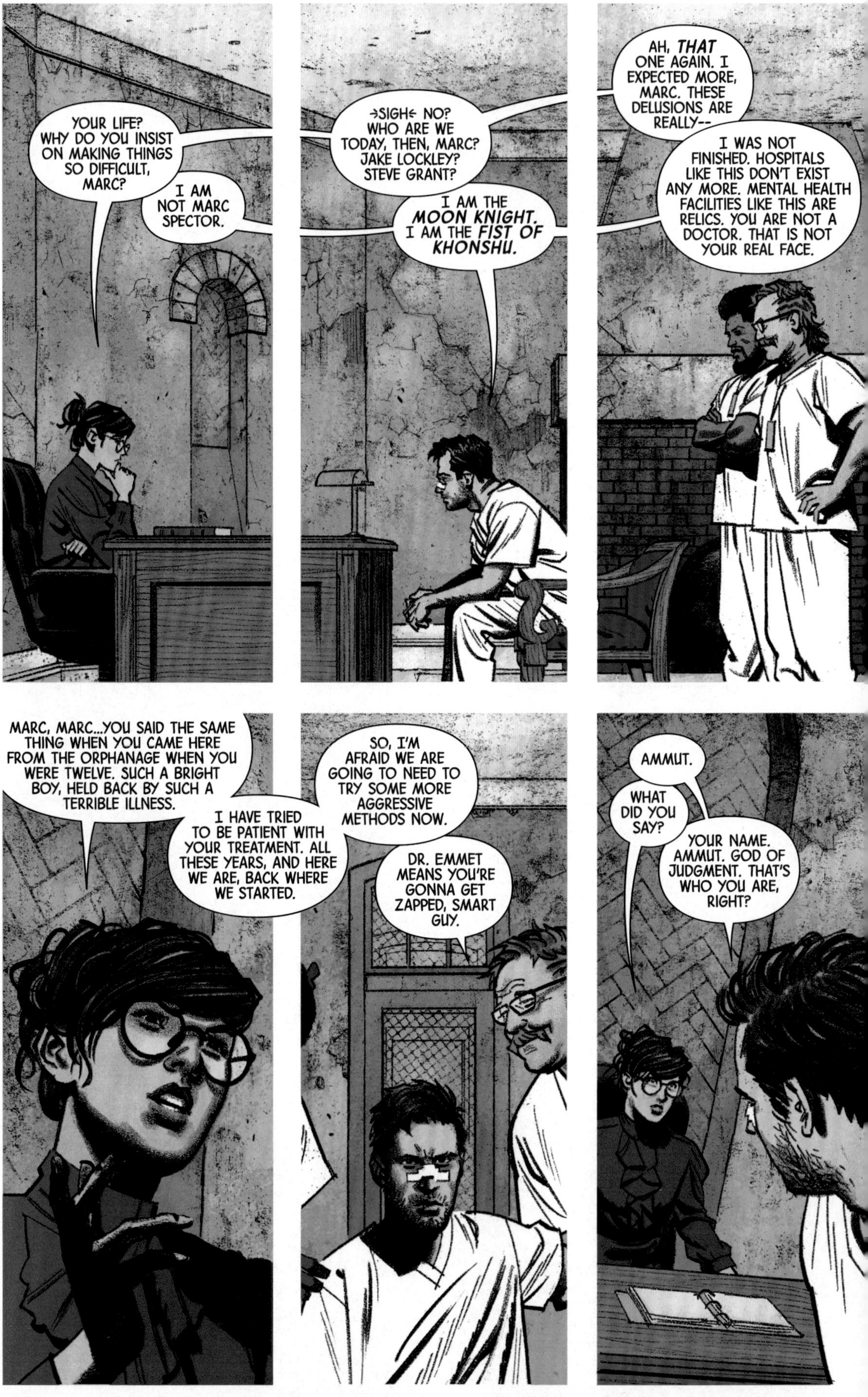
YOUR LIFE? WHY DO YOU INSIST ON MAKING THINGS SO DIFFICULT, MARC?
I AM NOT MARC SPECTOR.
→SIGH← NO? WHO ARE WE TODAY, THEN, MARC? JAKE LOCKLEY? STEVE GRANT?
I AM THE MOON KNIGHT. I AM THE FIST OF KHONSHU.
AH, THAT ONE AGAIN. I EXPECTED MORE, MARC. THESE DELUSIONS ARE REALLY--
I WAS NOT FINISHED. HOSPITALS LIKE THIS DON'T EXIST ANY MORE. MENTAL HEALTH FACILITIES LIKE THIS ARE RELICS. YOU ARE NOT A DOCTOR. THAT IS NOT YOUR REAL FACE.
MARC, MARC...YOU SAID THE SAME THING WHEN YOU CAME HERE FROM THE ORPHANAGE WHEN YOU WERE TWELVE. SUCH A BRIGHT BOY, HELD BACK BY SUCH A TERRIBLE ILLNESS.
I HAVE TRIED TO BE PATIENT WITH YOUR TREATMENT. ALL THESE YEARS, AND HERE WE ARE, BACK WHERE WE STARTED.
SO, I'M AFRAID WE ARE GOING TO NEED TO TRY SOME MORE AGGRESSIVE METHODS NOW.
DR. EMMET MEANS YOU'RE GONNA GET ZAPPED, SMART GUY.
AMMUT.
WHAT DID YOU SAY?
YOUR NAME. AMMUT. GOD OF JUDGMENT. THAT'S WHO YOU ARE, RIGHT?

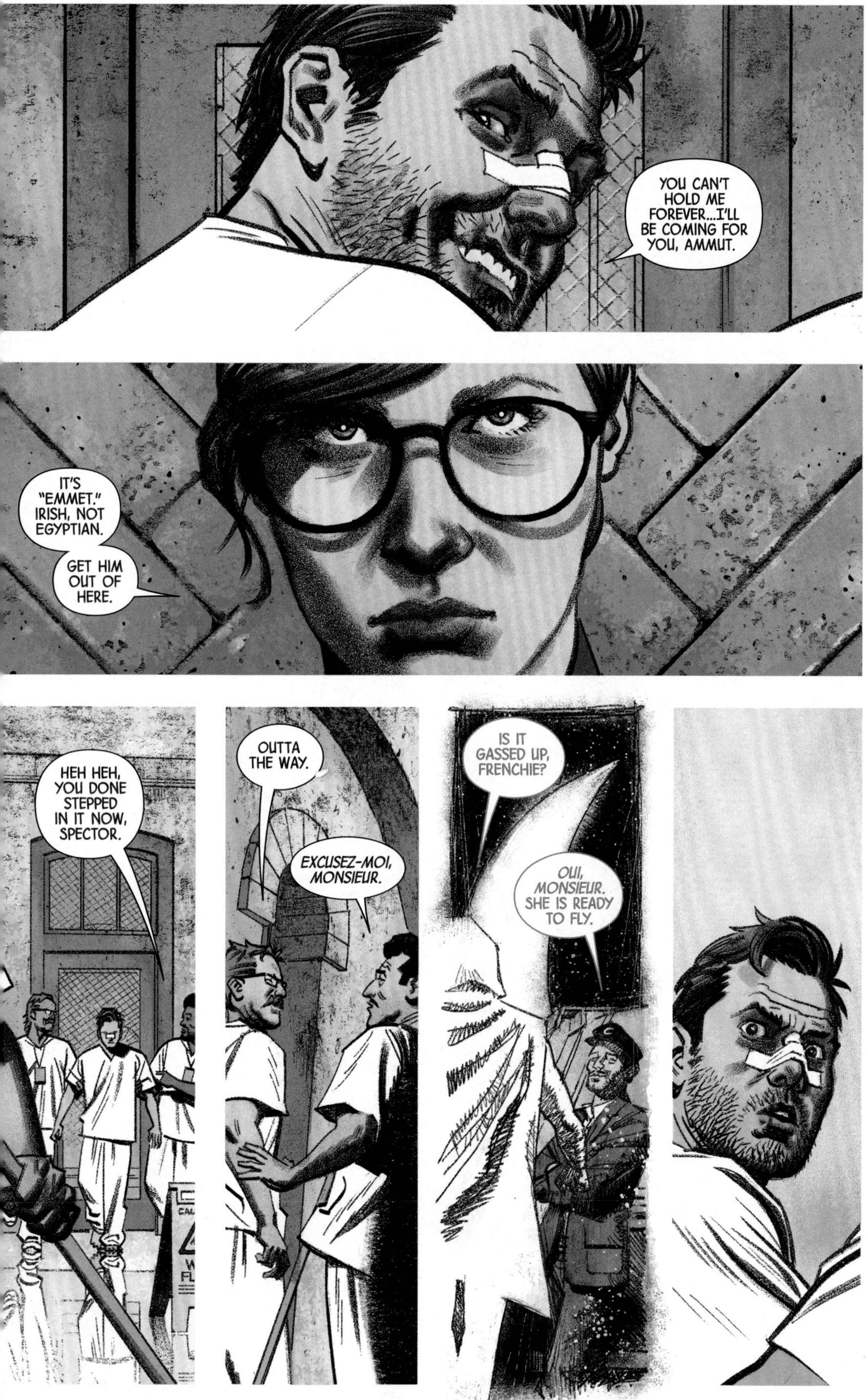
YOU CAN'T HOLD ME FOREVER...I'LL BE COMING FOR YOU, AMMUT.
IT'S "EMMET." IRISH, NOT EGYPTIAN.
GET HIM OUT OF HERE.
HEH HEH, YOU DONE STEPPED IN IT NOW, SPECTOR.
OUTTA THE WAY.
EXCUSEZ-MOI, MONSIEUR.
IS IT GASSED UP, FRENCHIE?
OUI, MONSIEUR. SHE IS READY TO FLY.

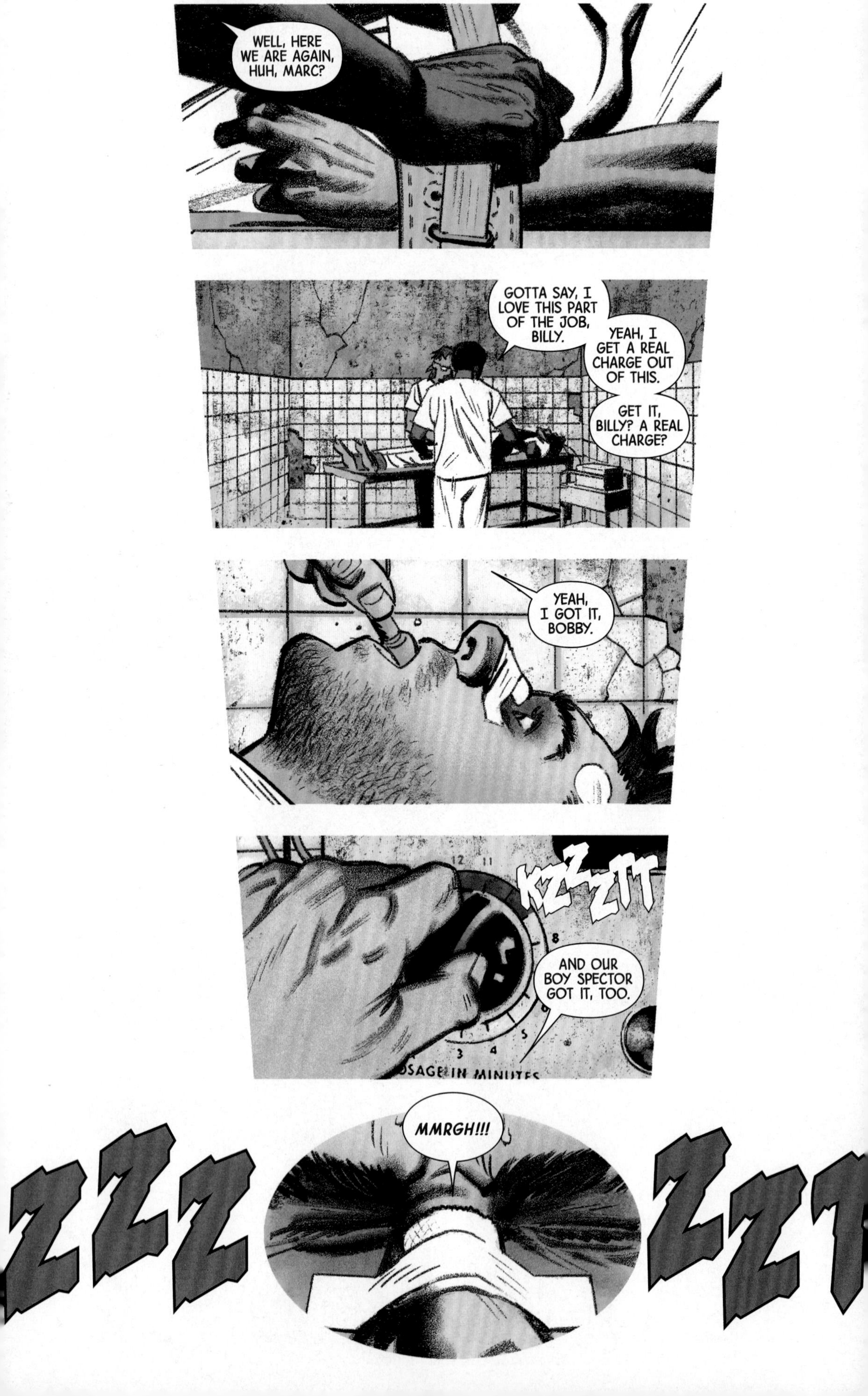
WELL, HERE WE ARE AGAIN, HUH, MARC?
GOTTA SAY, I LOVE THIS PART OF THE JOB, BILLY.
YEAH, I GET A REAL CHARGE OUT OF THIS.
GET IT, BILLY? A REAL CHARGE?
YEAH, I GOT IT, BOBBY.
KZZZTT
AND OUR BOY SPECTOR GOT IT, TOO.
ZZZ
MMRGH!!!
ZZ

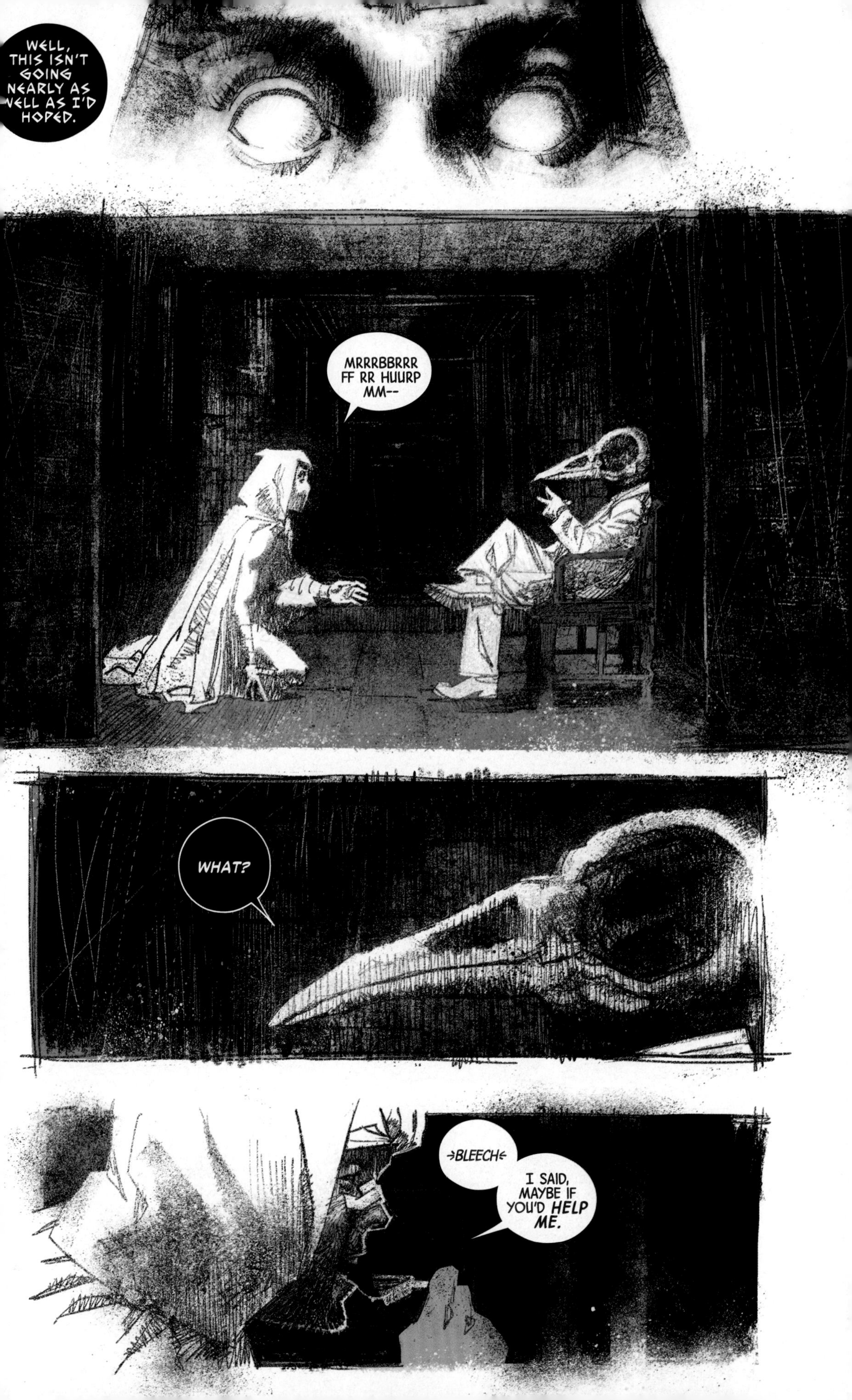
WELL, THIS ISN'T GOING NEARLY AS WELL AS I'D HOPED.
MRRRBBRRR FF RR HUURP MM--
WHAT?
>BLEECH<
I SAID, MAYBE IF YOU'D HELP ME.

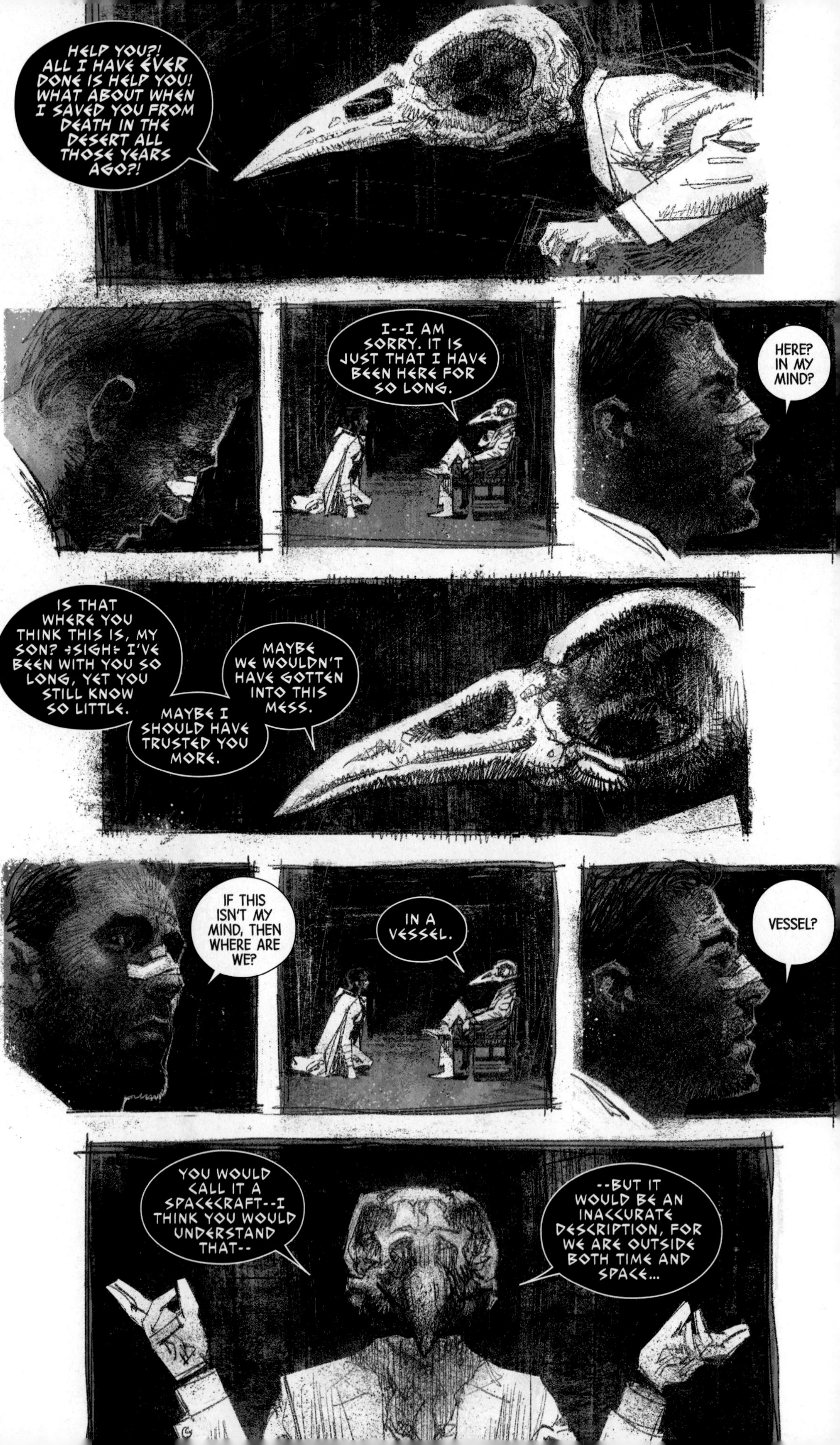
HELP YOU?! ALL I HAVE EVER DONE IS HELP YOU! WHAT ABOUT WHEN I SAVED YOU FROM DEATH IN THE DESERT ALL THOSE YEARS AGO?!
I--I AM SORRY. IT IS JUST THAT I HAVE BEEN HERE FOR SO LONG.
HERE? IN MY MIND?
IS THAT WHERE YOU THINK THIS IS, MY SON? =SIGH= I'VE BEEN WITH YOU SO LONG, YET YOU STILL KNOW SO LITTLE.
MAYBE I SHOULD HAVE TRUSTED YOU MORE.
MAYBE WE WOULDN'T HAVE GOTTEN INTO THIS MESS.
IF THIS ISN'T MY MIND, THEN WHERE ARE WE?
IN A VESSEL.
VESSEL?
YOU WOULD CALL IT A SPACECRAFT--I THINK YOU WOULD UNDERSTAND THAT--
--BUT IT WOULD BE AN INACCURATE DESCRIPTION, FOR WE ARE OUTSIDE BOTH TIME AND SPACE...

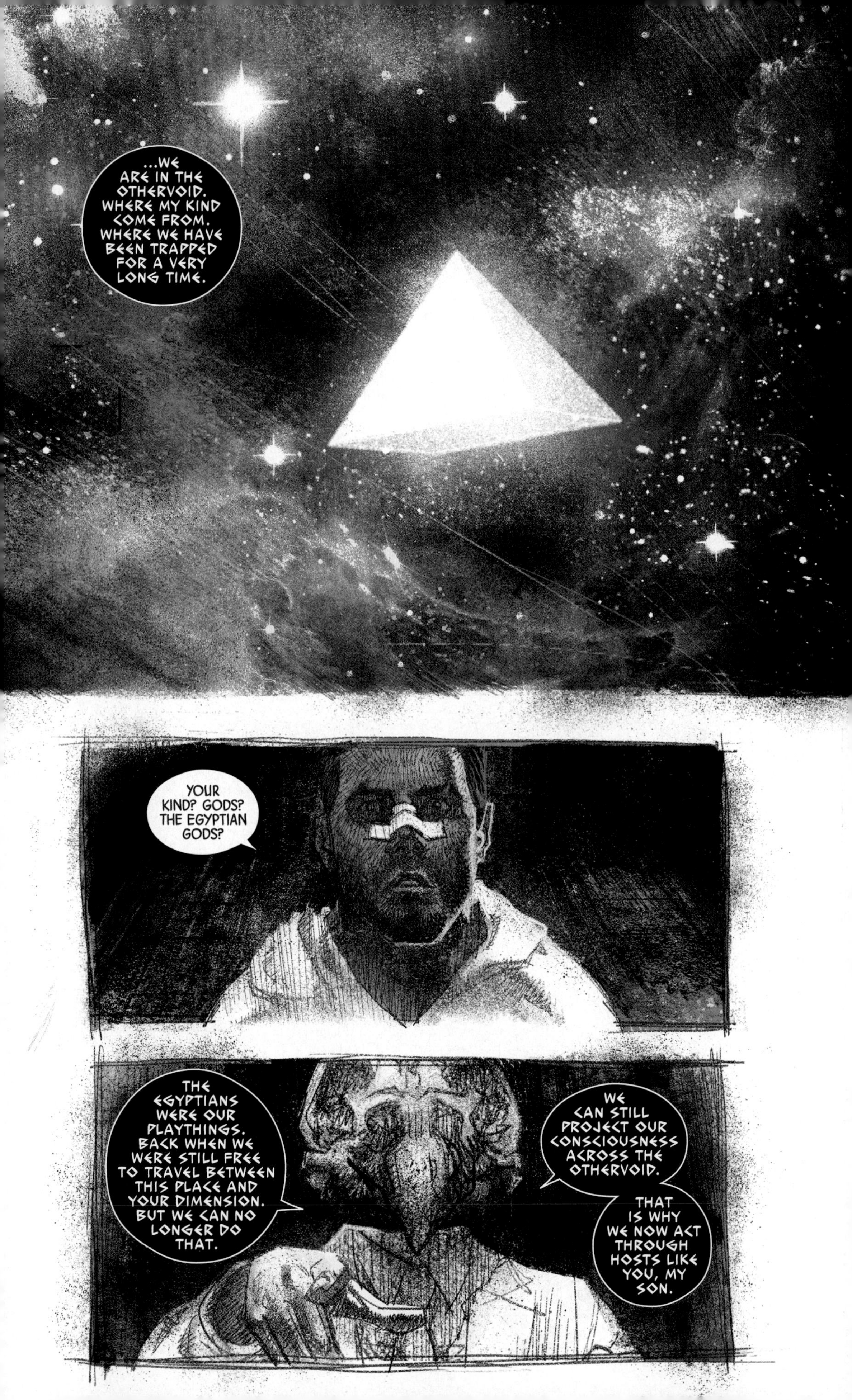
...WE ARE IN THE OTHERVOID. WHERE MY KIND COME FROM. WHERE WE HAVE BEEN TRAPPED FOR A VERY LONG TIME.
YOUR KIND? GODS? THE EGYPTIAN GODS?
THE EGYPTIANS WERE OUR PLAYTHINGS. BACK WHEN WE WERE STILL FREE TO TRAVEL BETWEEN THIS PLACE AND YOUR DIMENSION. BUT WE CAN NO LONGER DO THAT.
WE CAN STILL PROJECT OUR CONSCIOUSNESS ACROSS THE OTHERVOID.
THAT IS WHY WE NOW ACT THROUGH HOSTS LIKE YOU, MY SON.

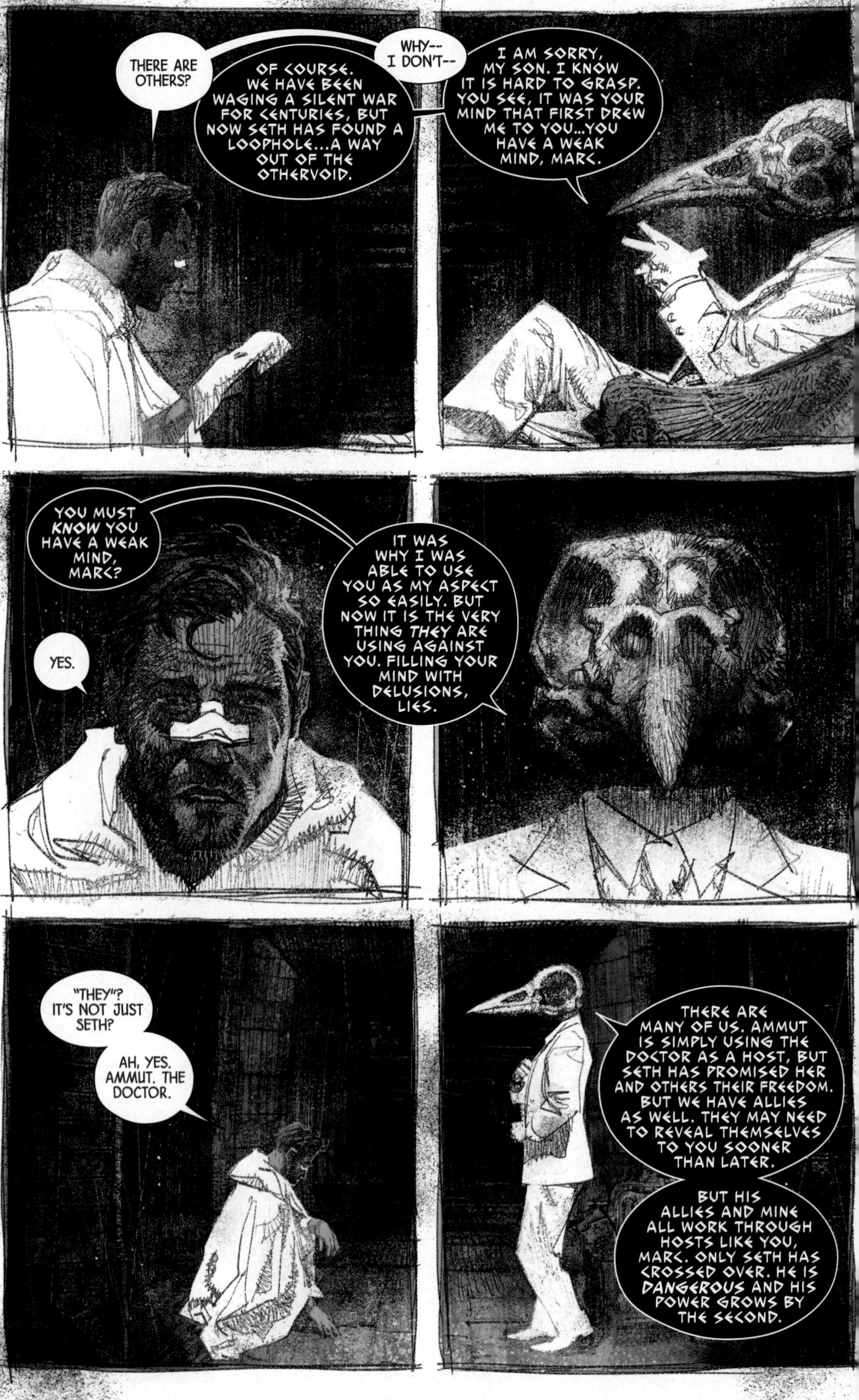
THERE ARE OTHERS?
OF COURSE. WE HAVE BEEN WAGING A SILENT WAR FOR CENTURIES, BUT NOW SETH HAS FOUND A LOOPHOLE...A WAY OUT OF THE OTHERVOID.
WHY-- I DON'T--
I AM SORRY, MY SON. I KNOW IT IS HARD TO GRASP. YOU SEE, IT WAS YOUR MIND THAT FIRST DREW ME TO YOU...YOU HAVE A WEAK MIND, MARC.
YOU MUST KNOW YOU HAVE A WEAK MIND, MARC?
YES.
IT WAS WHY I WAS ABLE TO USE YOU AS MY ASPECT SO EASILY. BUT NOW IT IS THE VERY THING THEY ARE USING AGAINST YOU. FILLING YOUR MIND WITH DELUSIONS, LIES.
"THEY"? IT'S NOT JUST SETH?
AH, YES. AMMUT. THE DOCTOR.
THERE ARE MANY OF US. AMMUT IS SIMPLY USING THE DOCTOR AS A HOST, BUT SETH HAS PROMISED HER AND OTHERS THEIR FREEDOM. BUT WE HAVE ALLIES AS WELL. THEY MAY NEED TO REVEAL THEMSELVES TO YOU SOONER THAN LATER.
BUT HIS ALLIES AND MINE ALL WORK THROUGH HOSTS LIKE YOU, MARC. ONLY SETH HAS CROSSED OVER. HE IS DANGEROUS AND HIS POWER GROWS BY THE SECOND.

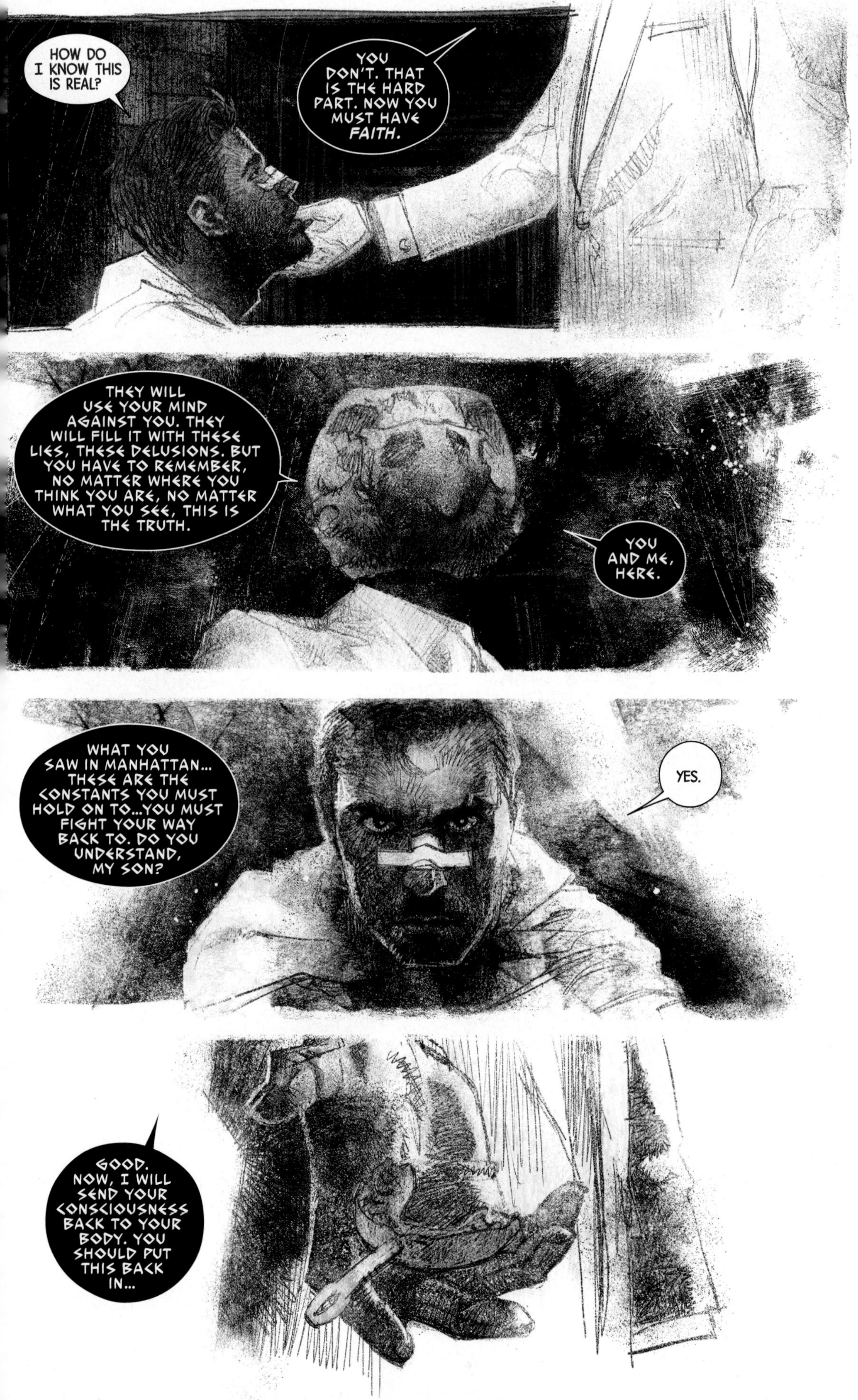
HOW DO I KNOW THIS IS REAL?
YOU DON'T. THAT IS THE HARD PART. NOW YOU MUST HAVE *FAITH*.
THEY WILL USE YOUR MIND AGAINST YOU. THEY WILL FILL IT WITH THESE LIES, THESE DELUSIONS. BUT YOU HAVE TO REMEMBER, NO MATTER WHERE YOU THINK YOU ARE, NO MATTER WHAT YOU SEE, THIS IS THE TRUTH.
YOU AND ME, HERE.
WHAT YOU SAW IN MANHATTAN... THESE ARE THE CONSTANTS YOU MUST HOLD ON TO...YOU MUST FIGHT YOUR WAY BACK TO. DO YOU UNDERSTAND, MY SON?
YES.
GOOD. NOW, I WILL SEND YOUR CONSCIOUSNESS BACK TO YOUR BODY. YOU SHOULD PUT THIS BACK IN...

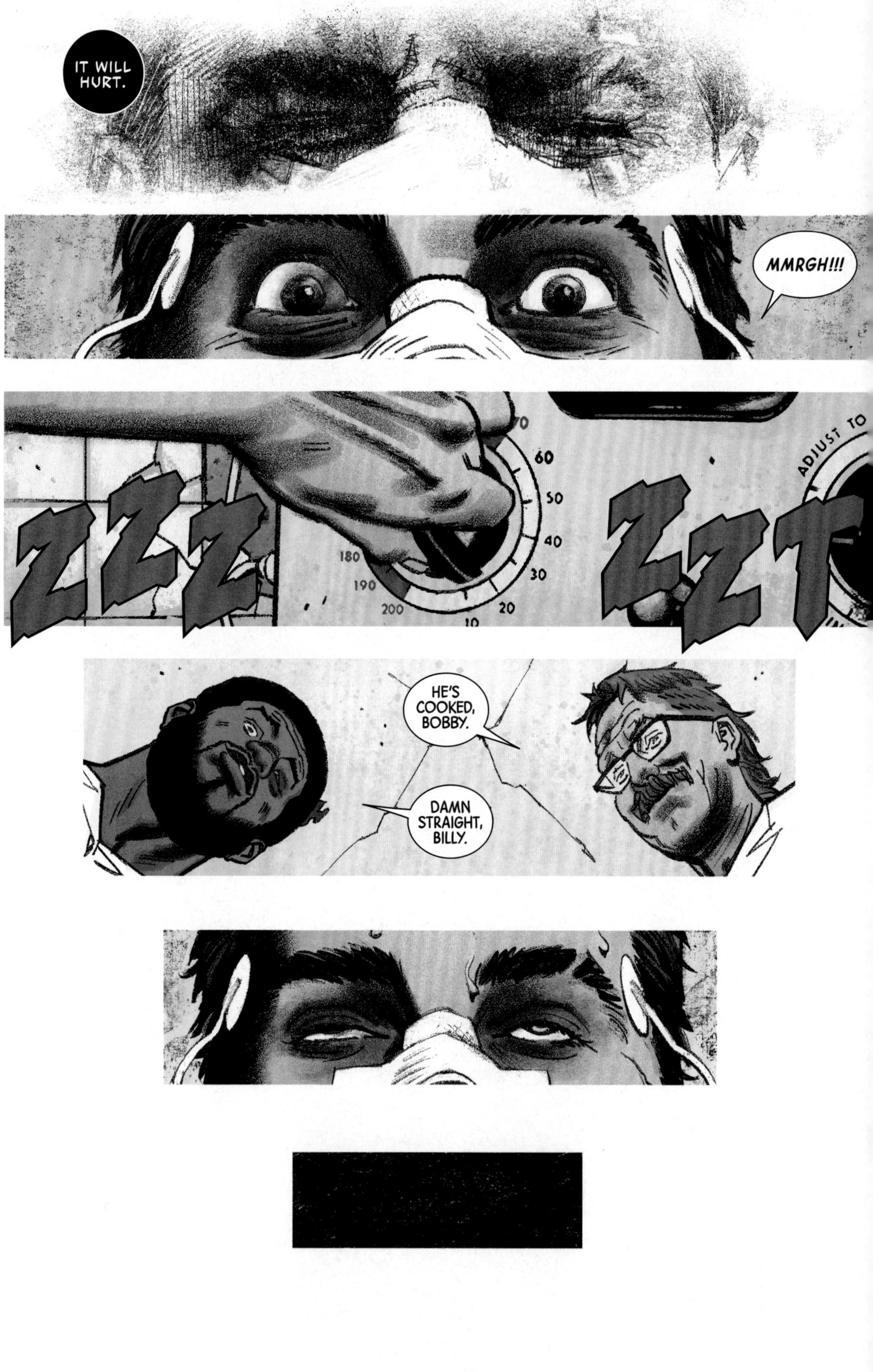
IT WILL HURT.
MMRGH!!!
ZZZ
ADJUST TO
ZZT
HE'S COOKED, BOBBY.
DAMN STRAIGHT, BILLY.

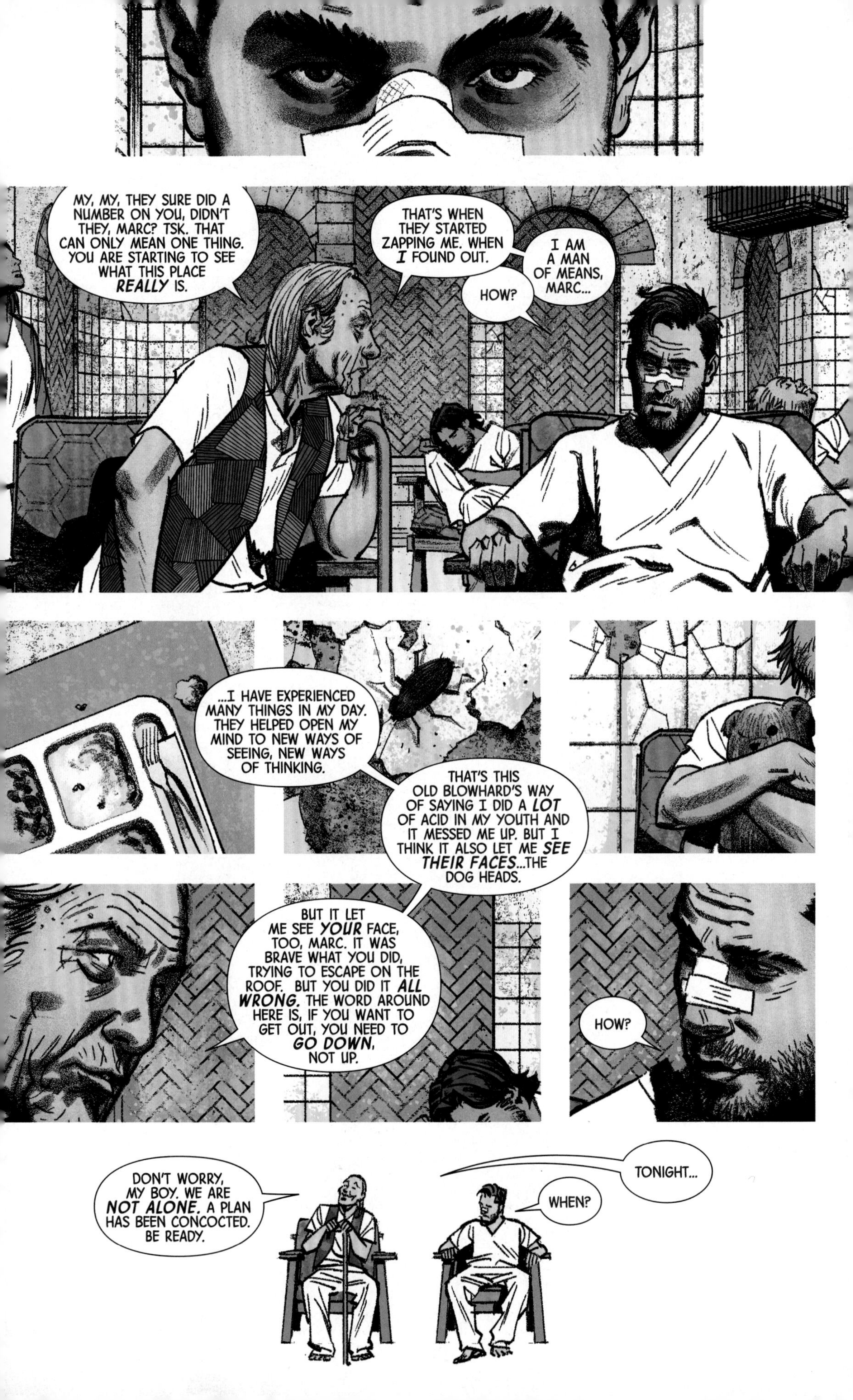
MY, MY, THEY SURE DID A NUMBER ON YOU, DIDN'T THEY, MARC? TSK. THAT CAN ONLY MEAN ONE THING. YOU ARE STARTING TO SEE WHAT THIS PLACE REALLY IS.
THAT'S WHEN THEY STARTED ZAPPING ME. WHEN I FOUND OUT.
HOW?
I AM A MAN OF MEANS, MARC...
...I HAVE EXPERIENCED MANY THINGS IN MY DAY. THEY HELPED OPEN MY MIND TO NEW WAYS OF SEEING, NEW WAYS OF THINKING.
THAT'S THIS OLD BLOWHARD'S WAY OF SAYING I DID A LOT OF ACID IN MY YOUTH AND IT MESSED ME UP. BUT I THINK IT ALSO LET ME SEE THEIR FACES...THE DOG HEADS.
BUT IT LET ME SEE YOUR FACE, TOO, MARC. IT WAS BRAVE WHAT YOU DID, TRYING TO ESCAPE ON THE ROOF. BUT YOU DID IT ALL WRONG. THE WORD AROUND HERE IS, IF YOU WANT TO GET OUT, YOU NEED TO GO DOWN, NOT UP.
HOW?
DON'T WORRY, MY BOY. WE ARE NOT ALONE. A PLAN HAS BEEN CONCOCTED. BE READY.
WHEN?
TONIGHT...

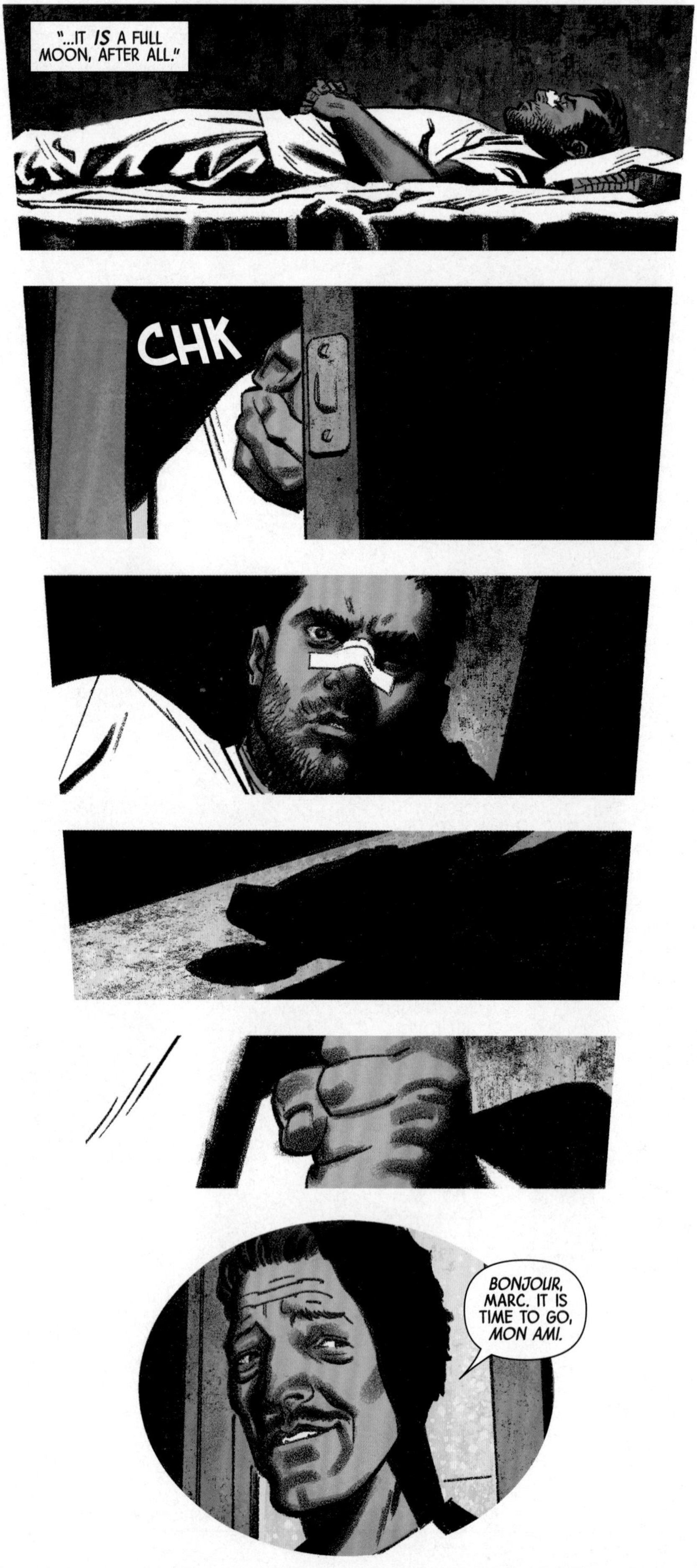
"...IT IS A FULL MOON, AFTER ALL."
CHK
BONJOUR, MARC. IT IS TIME TO GO, MON AMI.

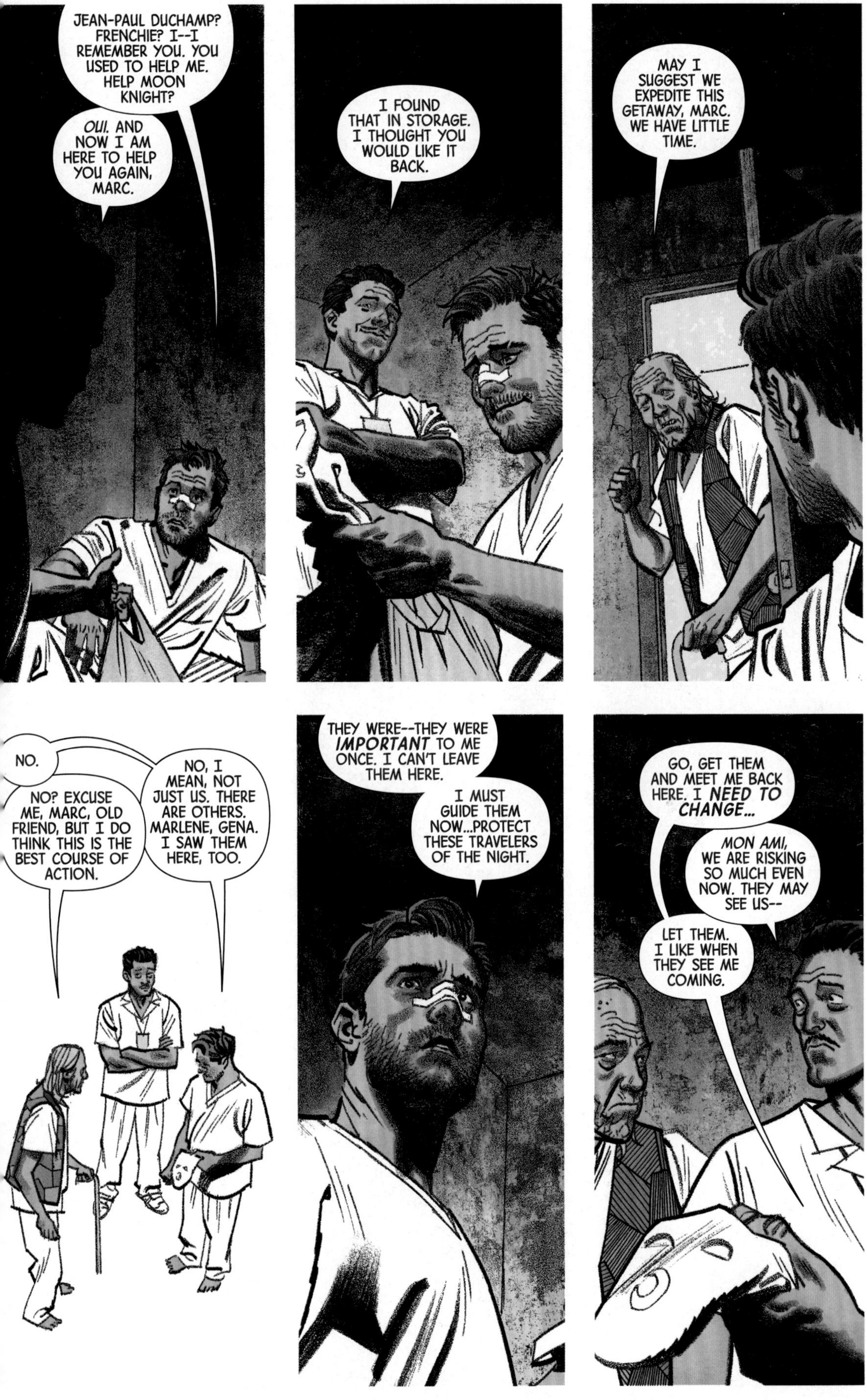

JEAN-PAUL DUCHAMP? FRENCHIE? I--I REMEMBER YOU. YOU USED TO HELP ME. HELP MOON KNIGHT?
OUI. AND NOW I AM HERE TO HELP YOU AGAIN, MARC.
I FOUND THAT IN STORAGE. I THOUGHT YOU WOULD LIKE IT BACK.
MAY I SUGGEST WE EXPEDITE THIS GETAWAY, MARC. WE HAVE LITTLE TIME.
NO.
NO? EXCUSE ME, MARC, OLD FRIEND, BUT I DO THINK THIS IS THE BEST COURSE OF ACTION.
NO, I MEAN, NOT JUST US. THERE ARE OTHERS. MARLENE, GENA. I SAW THEM HERE, TOO.
THEY WERE--THEY WERE IMPORTANT TO ME ONCE. I CAN'T LEAVE THEM HERE.
I MUST GUIDE THEM NOW...PROTECT THESE TRAVELERS OF THE NIGHT.
GO, GET THEM AND MEET ME BACK HERE. I NEED TO CHANGE...
MON AMI, WE ARE RISKING SO MUCH EVEN NOW. THEY MAY SEE US--
LET THEM. I LIKE WHEN THEY SEE ME COMING.

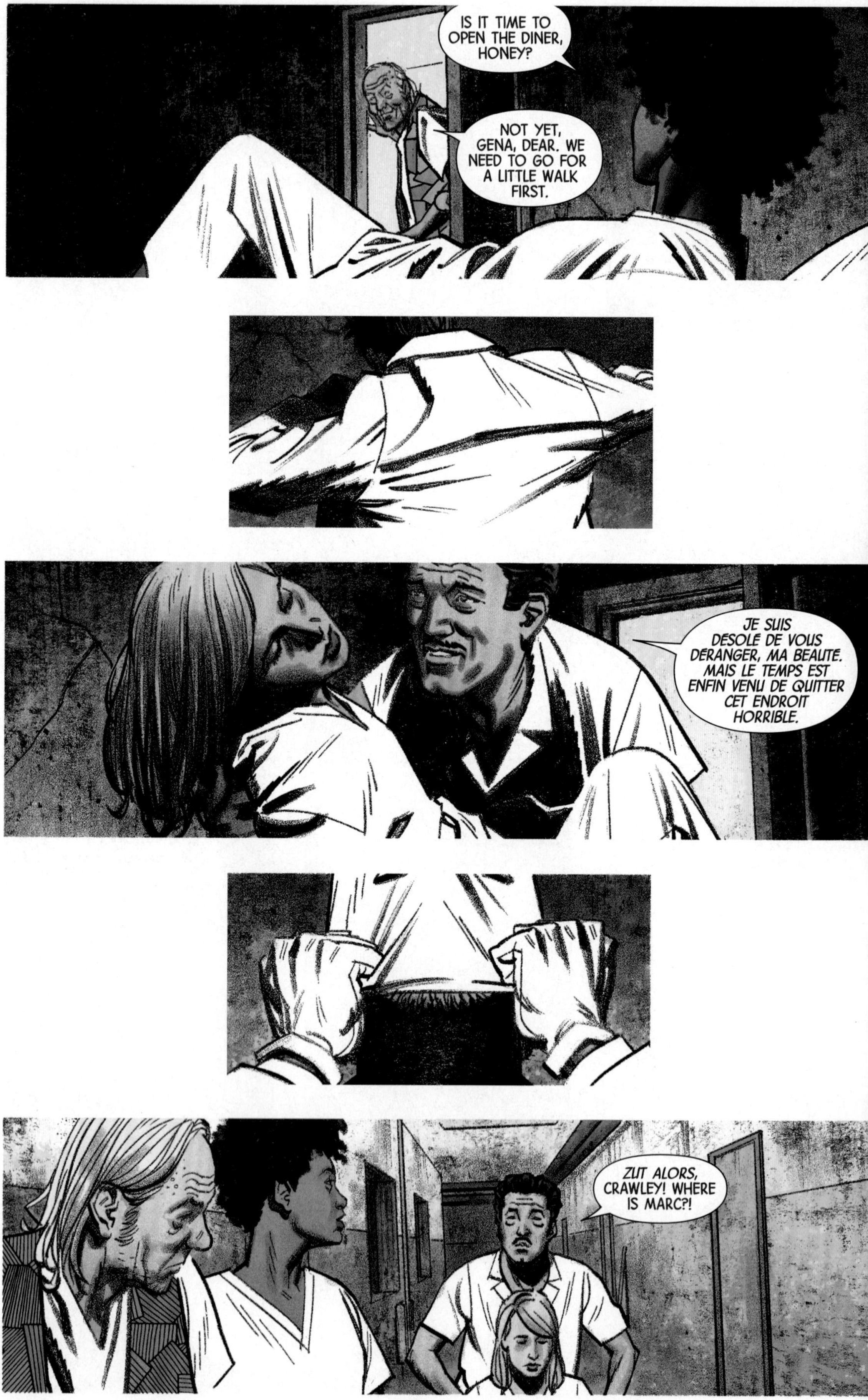
IS IT TIME TO OPEN THE DINER, HONEY?
NOT YET, GENA, DEAR. WE NEED TO GO FOR A LITTLE WALK FIRST.
JE SUIS DÉSOLÉ DE VOUS DÉRANGER, MA BEAUTÉ. MAIS LE TEMPS EST ENFIN VENU DE QUITTER CET ENDROIT HORRIBLE.
ZUT ALORS, CRAWLEY! WHERE IS MARC?!

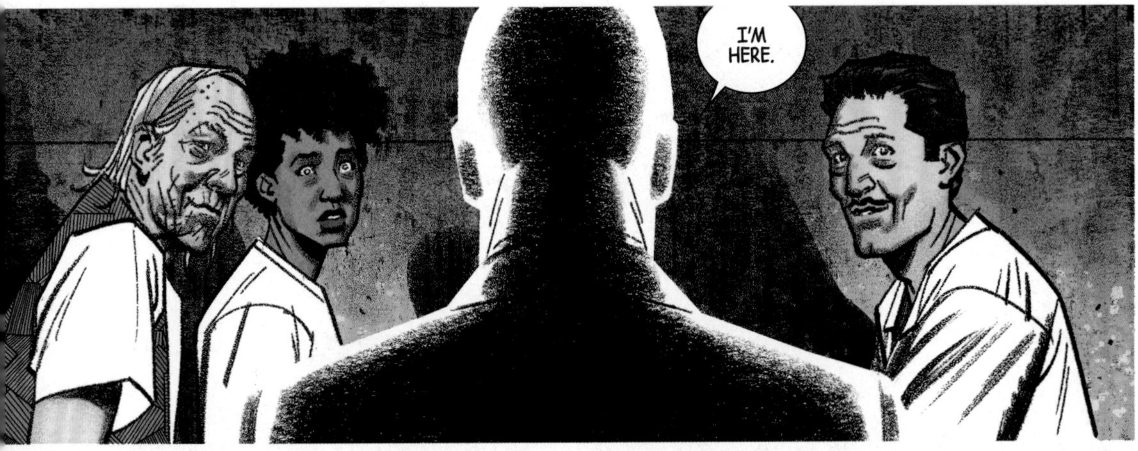
I'M HERE.

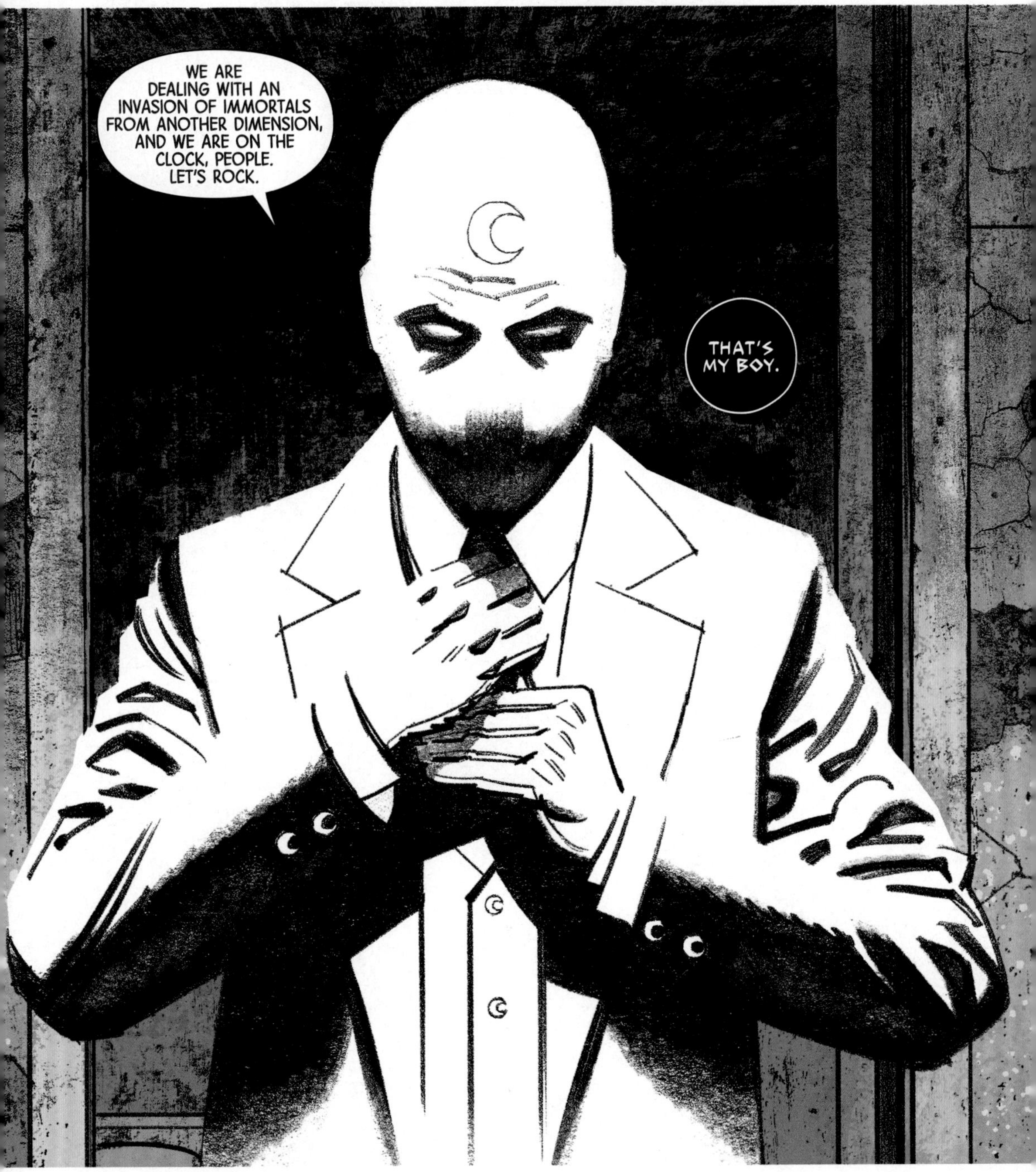
WE ARE DEALING WITH AN INVASION OF IMMORTALS FROM ANOTHER DIMENSION, AND WE ARE ON THE CLOCK, PEOPLE. LET'S ROCK.
THAT'S MY BOY.

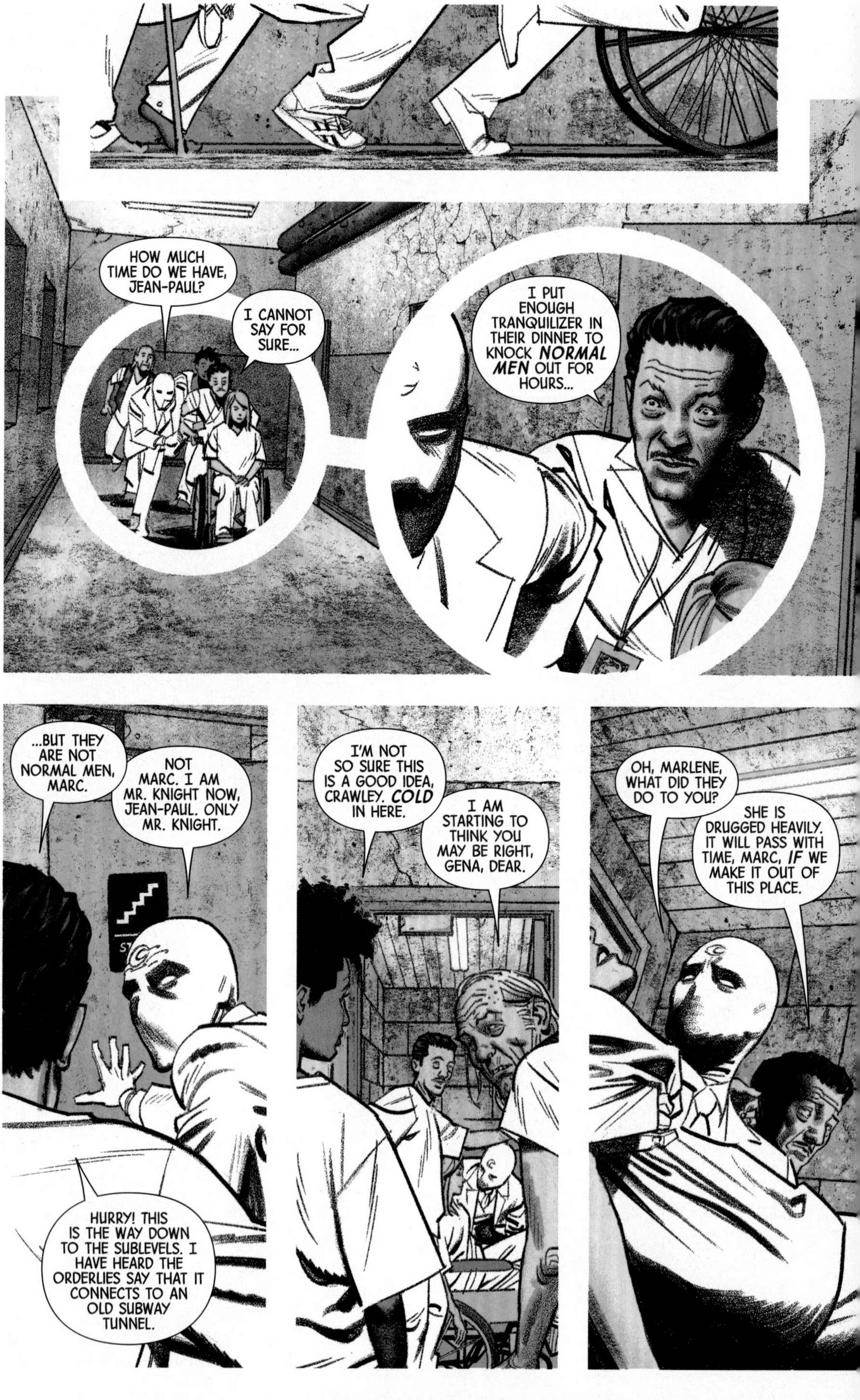
HOW MUCH TIME DO WE HAVE, JEAN-PAUL?
I CANNOT SAY FOR SURE...
I PUT ENOUGH TRANQUILIZER IN THEIR DINNER TO KNOCK NORMAL MEN OUT FOR HOURS...
...BUT THEY ARE NOT NORMAL MEN, MARC.
NOT MARC. I AM MR. KNIGHT NOW, JEAN-PAUL. ONLY MR. KNIGHT.
HURRY! THIS IS THE WAY DOWN TO THE SUBLEVELS. I HAVE HEARD THE ORDERLIES SAY THAT IT CONNECTS TO AN OLD SUBWAY TUNNEL.
I'M NOT SO SURE THIS IS A GOOD IDEA, CRAWLEY. COLD IN HERE.
I AM STARTING TO THINK YOU MAY BE RIGHT, GENA, DEAR.
OH, MARLENE, WHAT DID THEY DO TO YOU?
SHE IS DRUGGED HEAVILY. IT WILL PASS WITH TIME, MARC, IF WE MAKE IT OUT OF THIS PLACE.

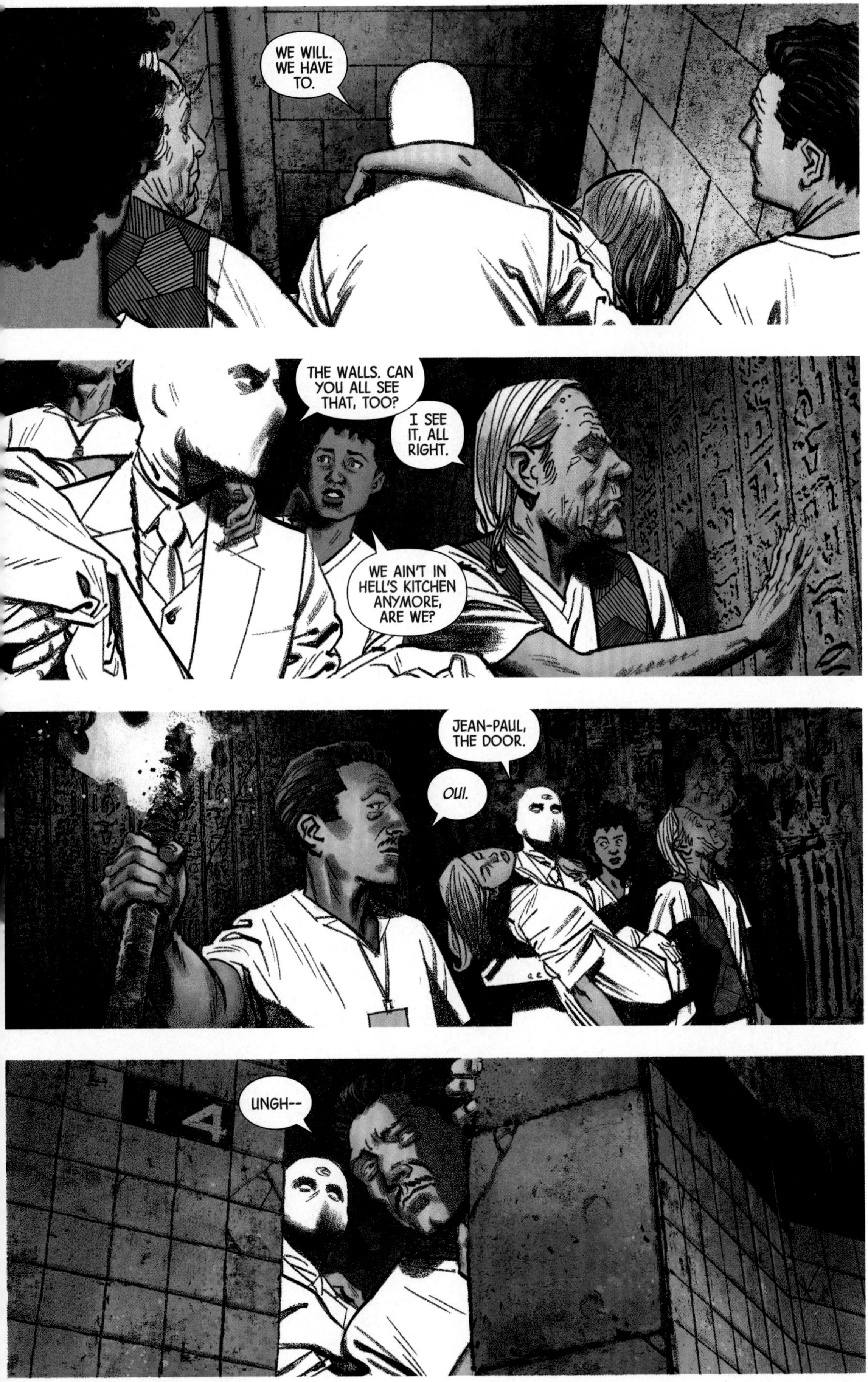
WE WILL. WE HAVE TO.
THE WALLS. CAN YOU ALL SEE THAT, TOO?
I SEE IT, ALL RIGHT.
WE AIN'T IN HELL'S KITCHEN ANYMORE, ARE WE?
JEAN-PAUL, THE DOOR.
OUI.
UNGH--

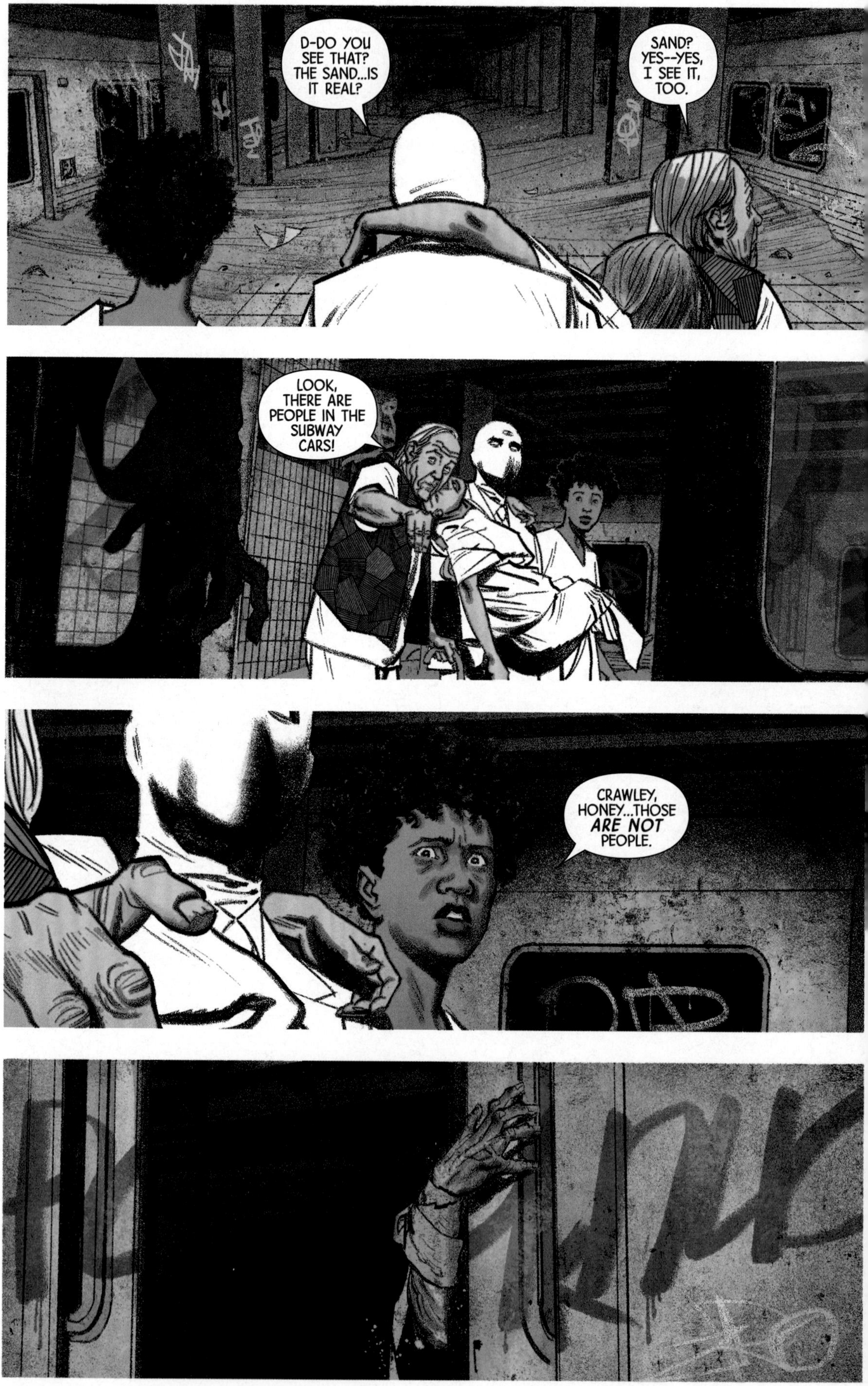
D-DO YOU SEE THAT? THE SAND...IS IT REAL?
SAND? YES--YES, I SEE IT, TOO.
LOOK, THERE ARE PEOPLE IN THE SUBWAY CARS!
CRAWLEY, HONEY...THOSE *ARE NOT* PEOPLE.

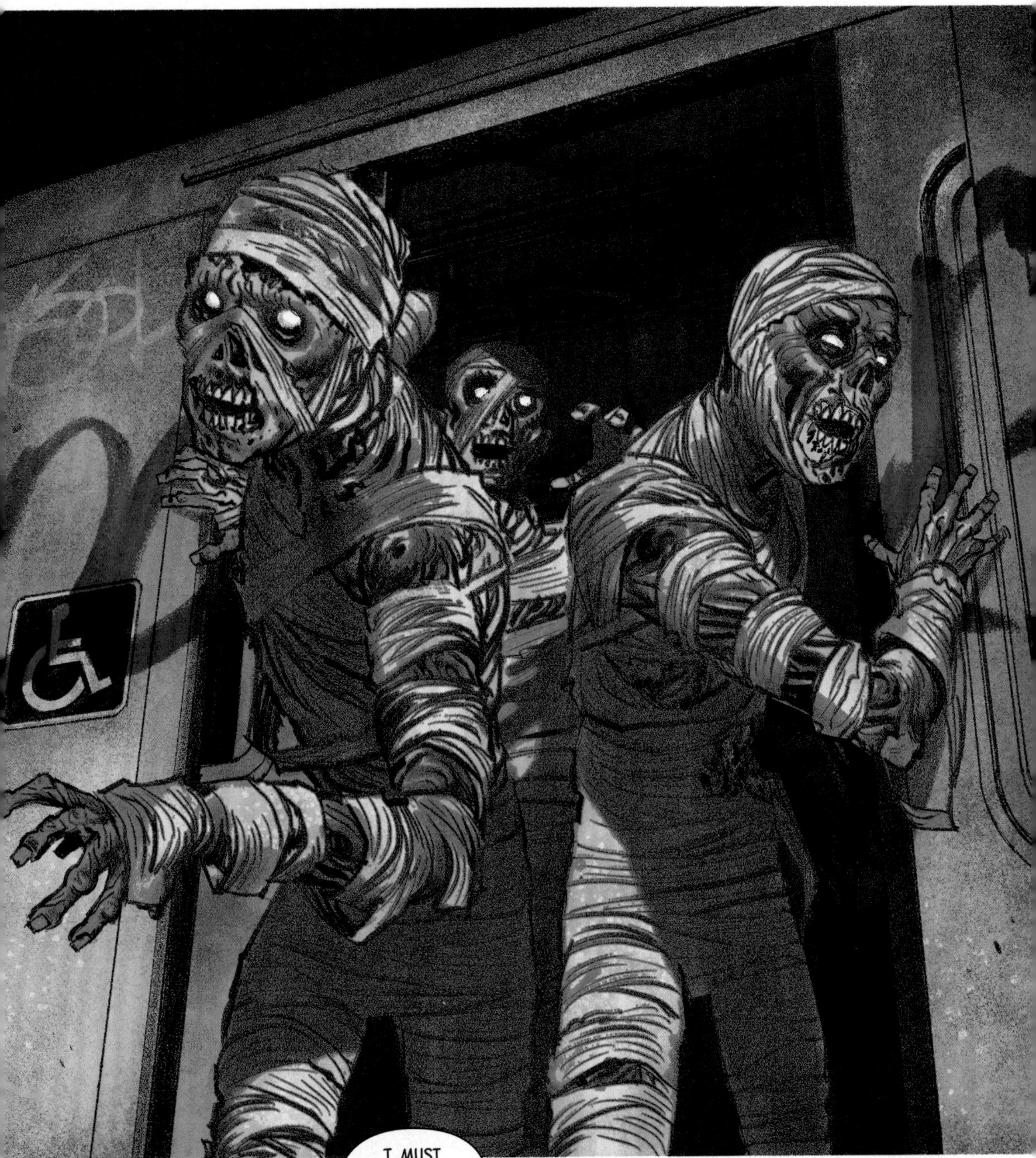

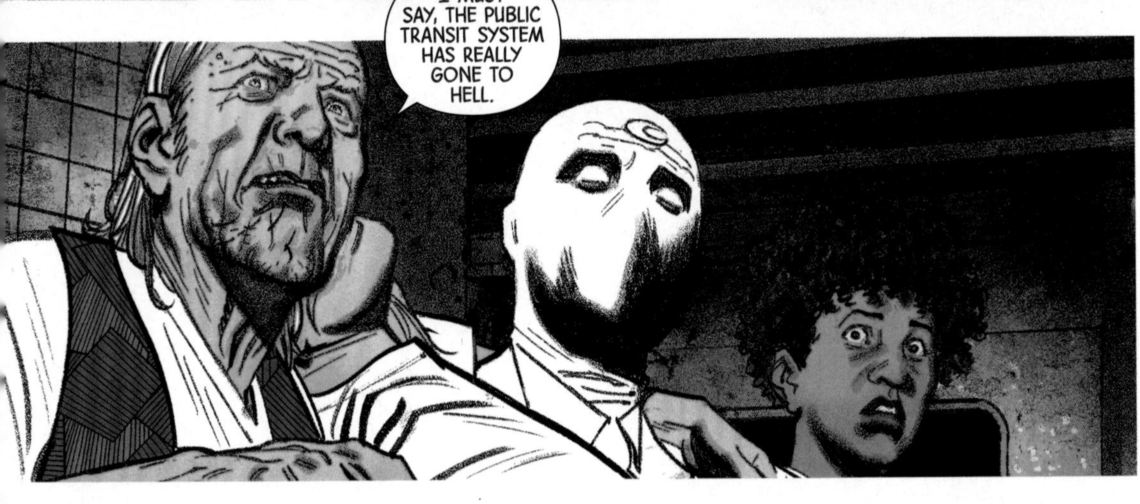
I MUST SAY, THE PUBLIC TRANSIT SYSTEM HAS REALLY GONE TO HELL.

WELCOME TO NEW EGYPT

PART THREE

3

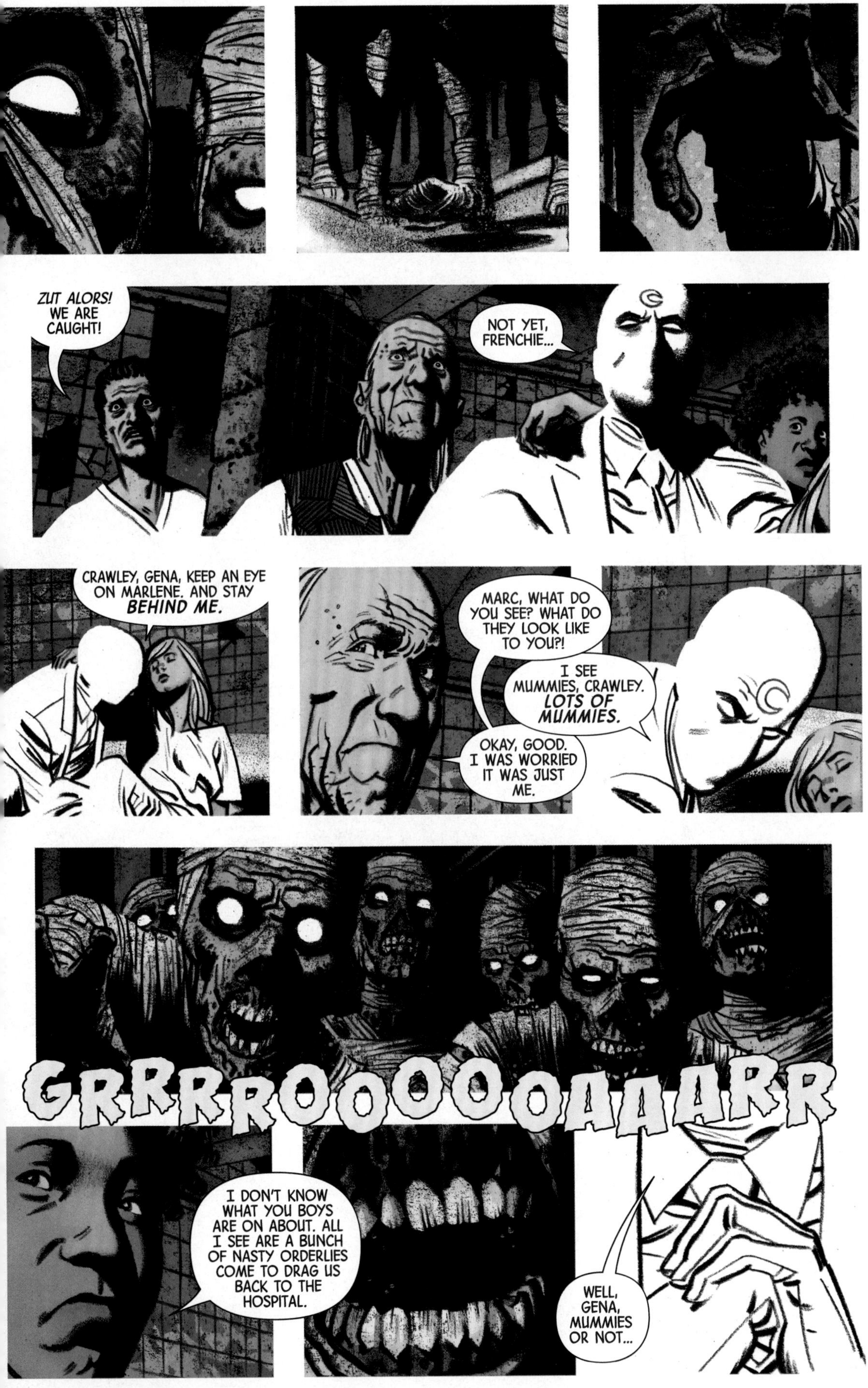
ZUT ALORS! WE ARE CAUGHT!
NOT YET, FRENCHIE...
CRAWLEY, GENA, KEEP AN EYE ON MARLENE. AND STAY *BEHIND ME.*
MARC, WHAT DO YOU SEE? WHAT DO THEY LOOK LIKE TO YOU?!
I SEE MUMMIES, CRAWLEY. *LOTS OF MUMMIES.*
OKAY, GOOD. I WAS WORRIED IT WAS JUST ME.
GRRRROOOOOAAARR
I DON'T KNOW WHAT YOU BOYS ARE ON ABOUT. ALL I SEE ARE A BUNCH OF NASTY ORDERLIES COME TO DRAG US BACK TO THE HOSPITAL.
WELL, GENA, MUMMIES OR NOT...

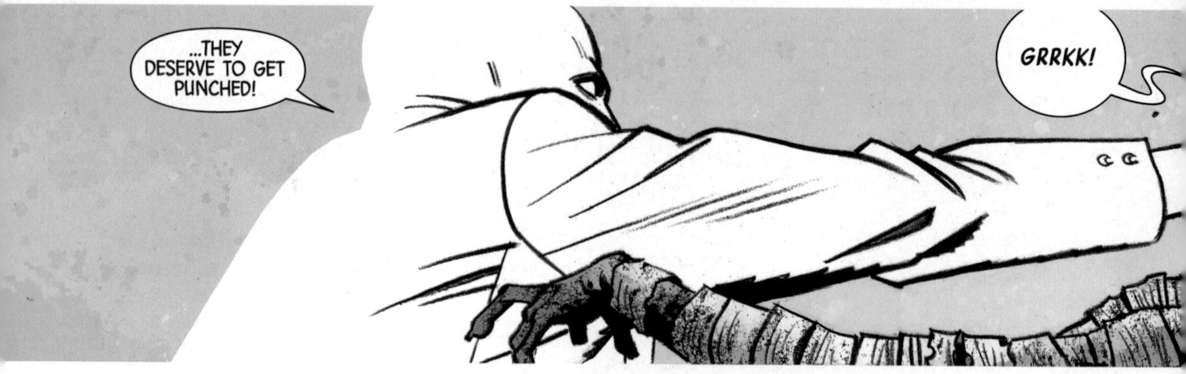
...THEY DESERVE TO GET PUNCHED!
GRRKK!

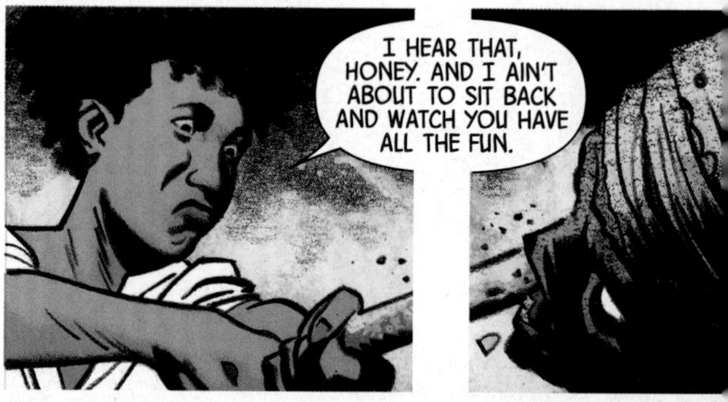
I HEAR THAT, HONEY. AND I AIN'T ABOUT TO SIT BACK AND WATCH YOU HAVE ALL THE FUN.

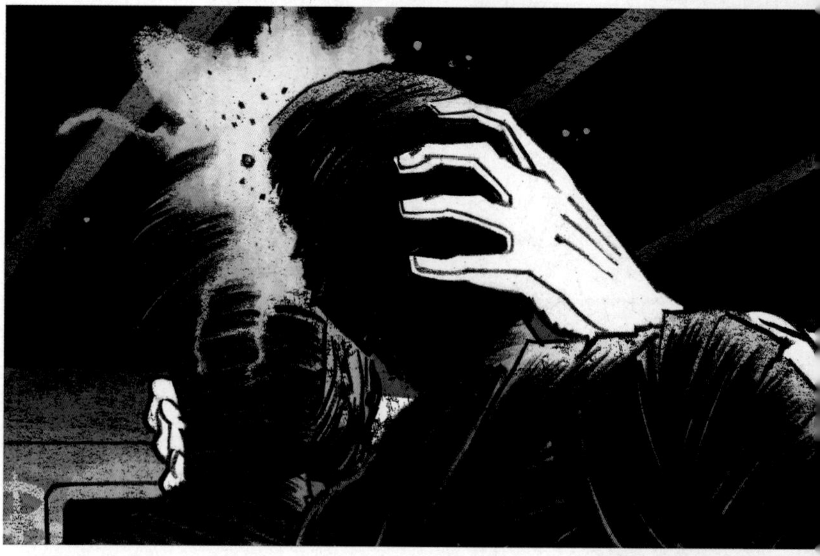

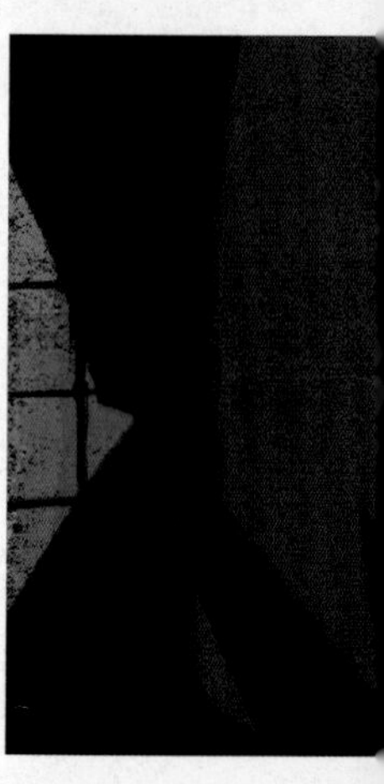

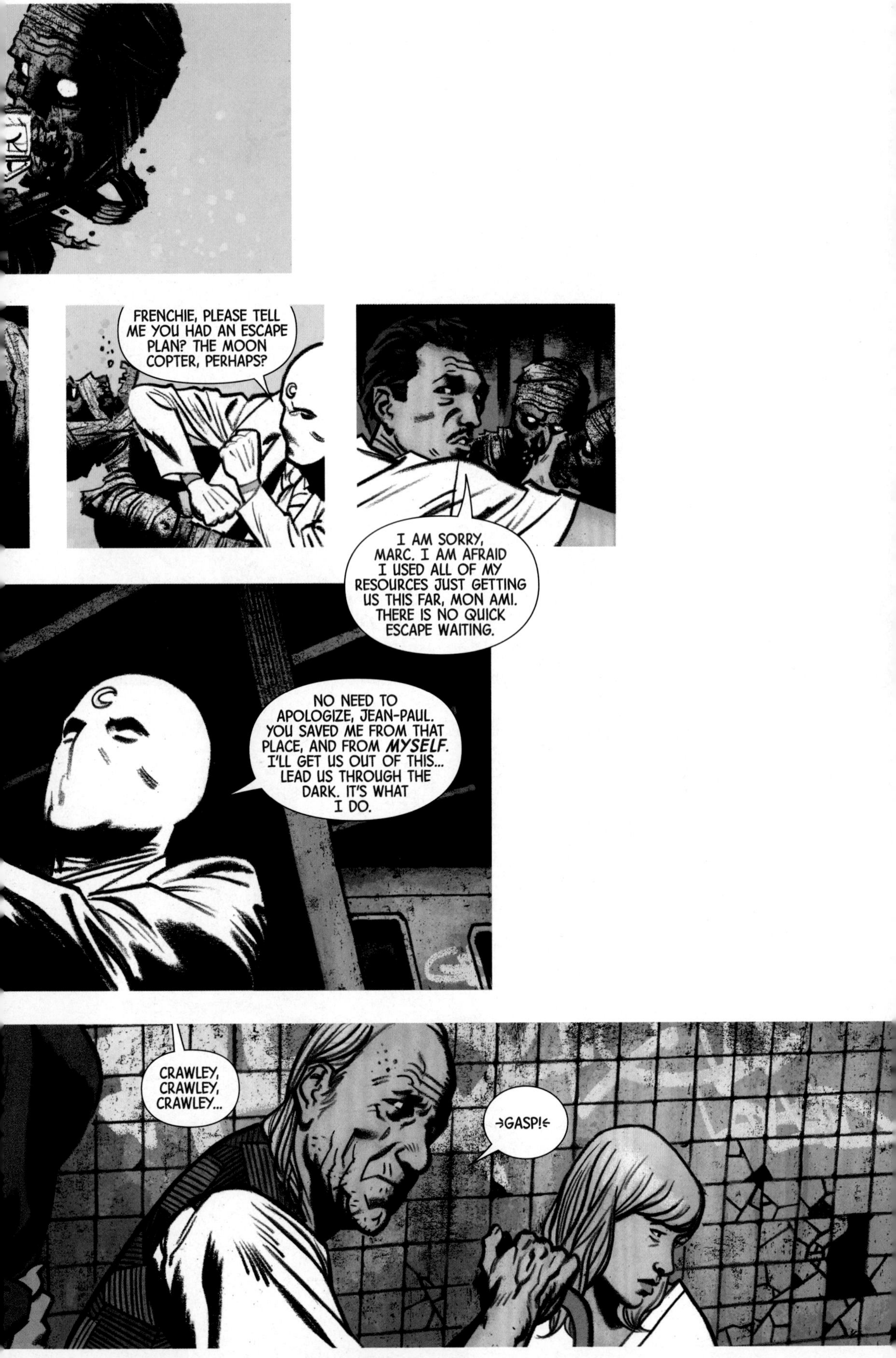
FRENCHIE, PLEASE TELL ME YOU HAD AN ESCAPE PLAN? THE MOON COPTER, PERHAPS?
I AM SORRY, MARC. I AM AFRAID I USED ALL OF MY RESOURCES JUST GETTING US THIS FAR, MON AMI. THERE IS NO QUICK ESCAPE WAITING.
NO NEED TO APOLOGIZE, JEAN-PAUL. YOU SAVED ME FROM THAT PLACE, AND FROM *MYSELF*. I'LL GET US OUT OF THIS... LEAD US THROUGH THE DARK. IT'S WHAT I DO.
CRAWLEY, CRAWLEY, CRAWLEY...
→GASP!←

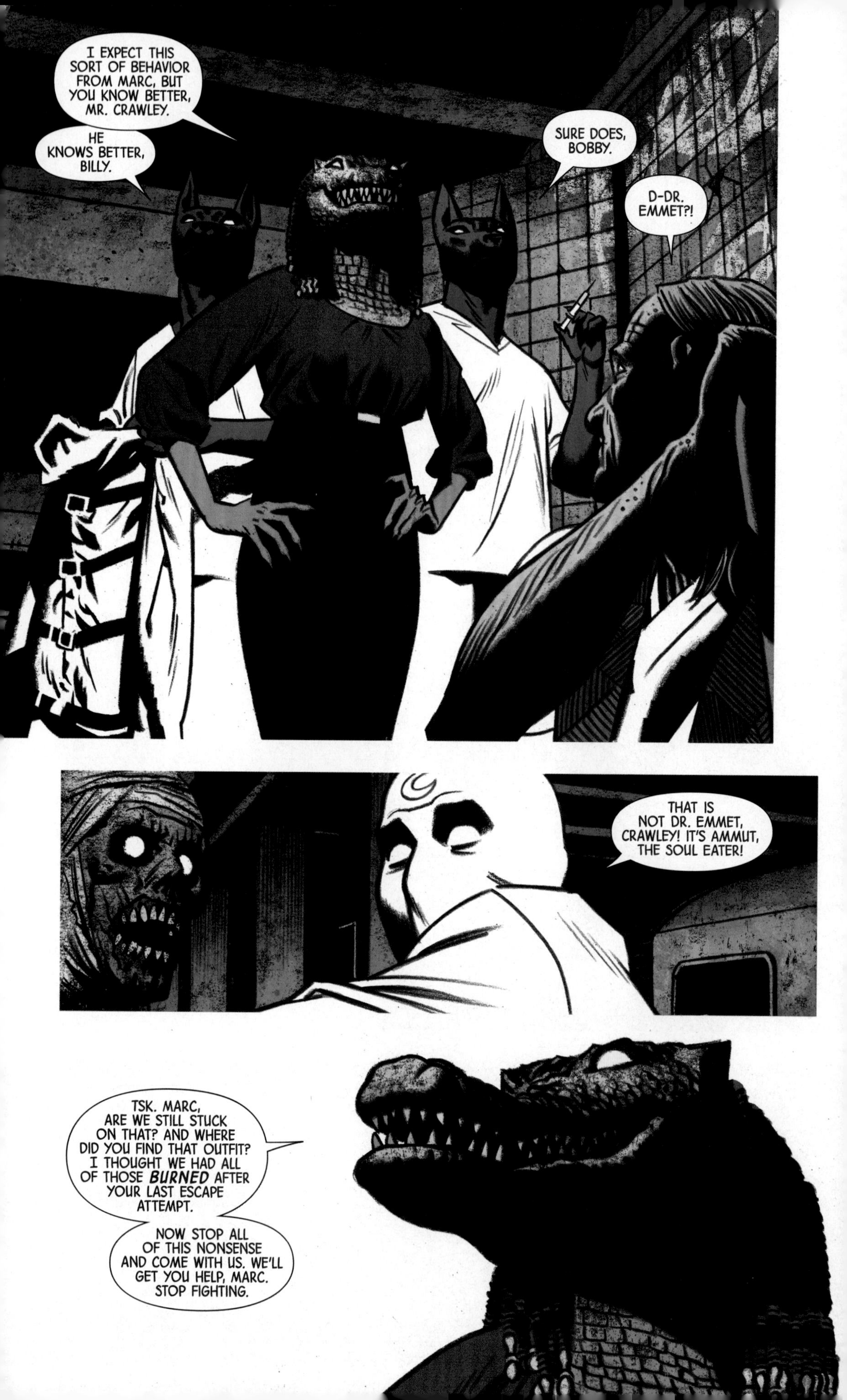

I EXPECT THIS SORT OF BEHAVIOR FROM MARC, BUT YOU KNOW BETTER, MR. CRAWLEY.
HE KNOWS BETTER, BILLY.
SURE DOES, BOBBY.
D-DR. EMMET?!
THAT IS NOT DR. EMMET, CRAWLEY! IT'S AMMUT, THE SOUL EATER!
TSK. MARC, ARE WE STILL STUCK ON THAT? AND WHERE DID YOU FIND THAT OUTFIT? I THOUGHT WE HAD ALL OF THOSE BURNED AFTER YOUR LAST ESCAPE ATTEMPT.
NOW STOP ALL OF THIS NONSENSE AND COME WITH US. WE'LL GET YOU HELP, MARC. STOP FIGHTING.

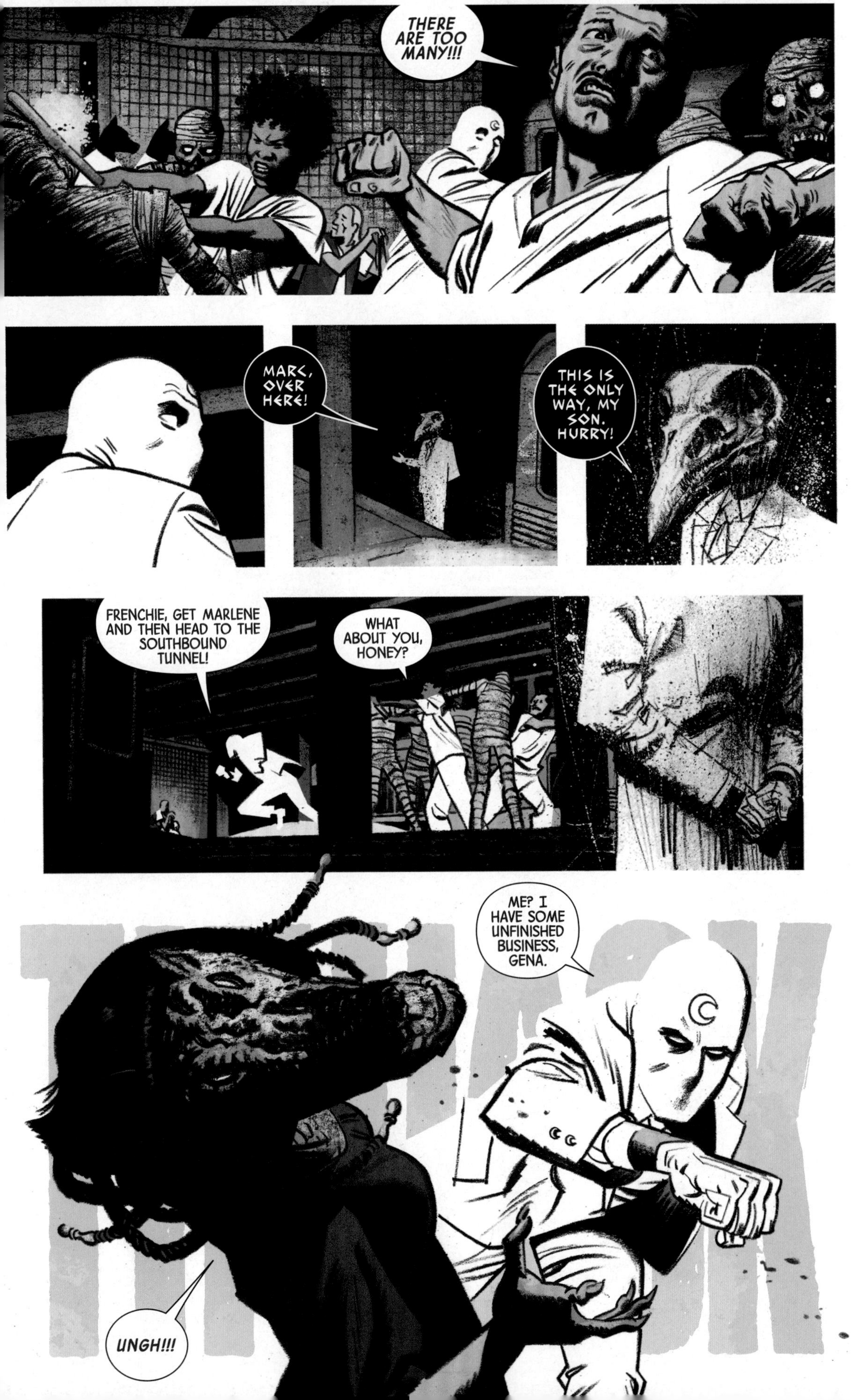

THERE ARE TOO MANY!!!
MARC, OVER HERE!
THIS IS THE ONLY WAY, MY SON. HURRY!
FRENCHIE, GET MARLENE AND THEN HEAD TO THE SOUTHBOUND TUNNEL!
WHAT ABOUT YOU, HONEY?
ME? I HAVE SOME UNFINISHED BUSINESS, GENA.
UNGH!!!

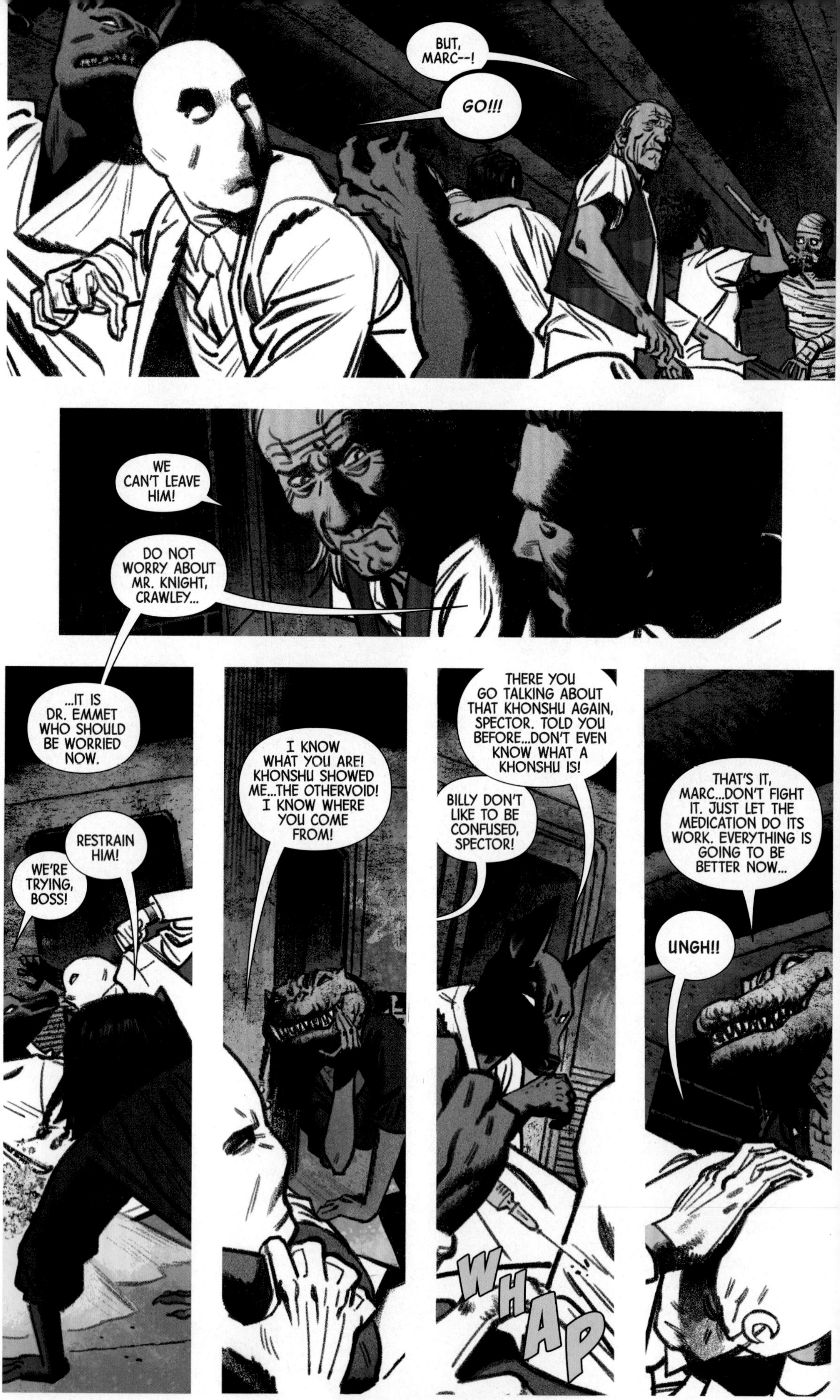
BUT, MARC--!
GO!!!
WE CAN'T LEAVE HIM!
DO NOT WORRY ABOUT MR. KNIGHT, CRAWLEY...
...IT IS DR. EMMET WHO SHOULD BE WORRIED NOW.
RESTRAIN HIM!
WE'RE TRYING, BOSS!
I KNOW WHAT YOU ARE! KHONSHU SHOWED ME...THE OTHERVOID! I KNOW WHERE YOU COME FROM!
THERE YOU GO TALKING ABOUT THAT KHONSHU AGAIN, SPECTOR. TOLD YOU BEFORE...DON'T EVEN KNOW WHAT A KHONSHU IS!
BILLY DON'T LIKE TO BE CONFUSED, SPECTOR!
WHAP
THAT'S IT, MARC...DON'T FIGHT IT. JUST LET THE MEDICATION DO ITS WORK. EVERYTHING IS GOING TO BE BETTER NOW...
UNGH!!

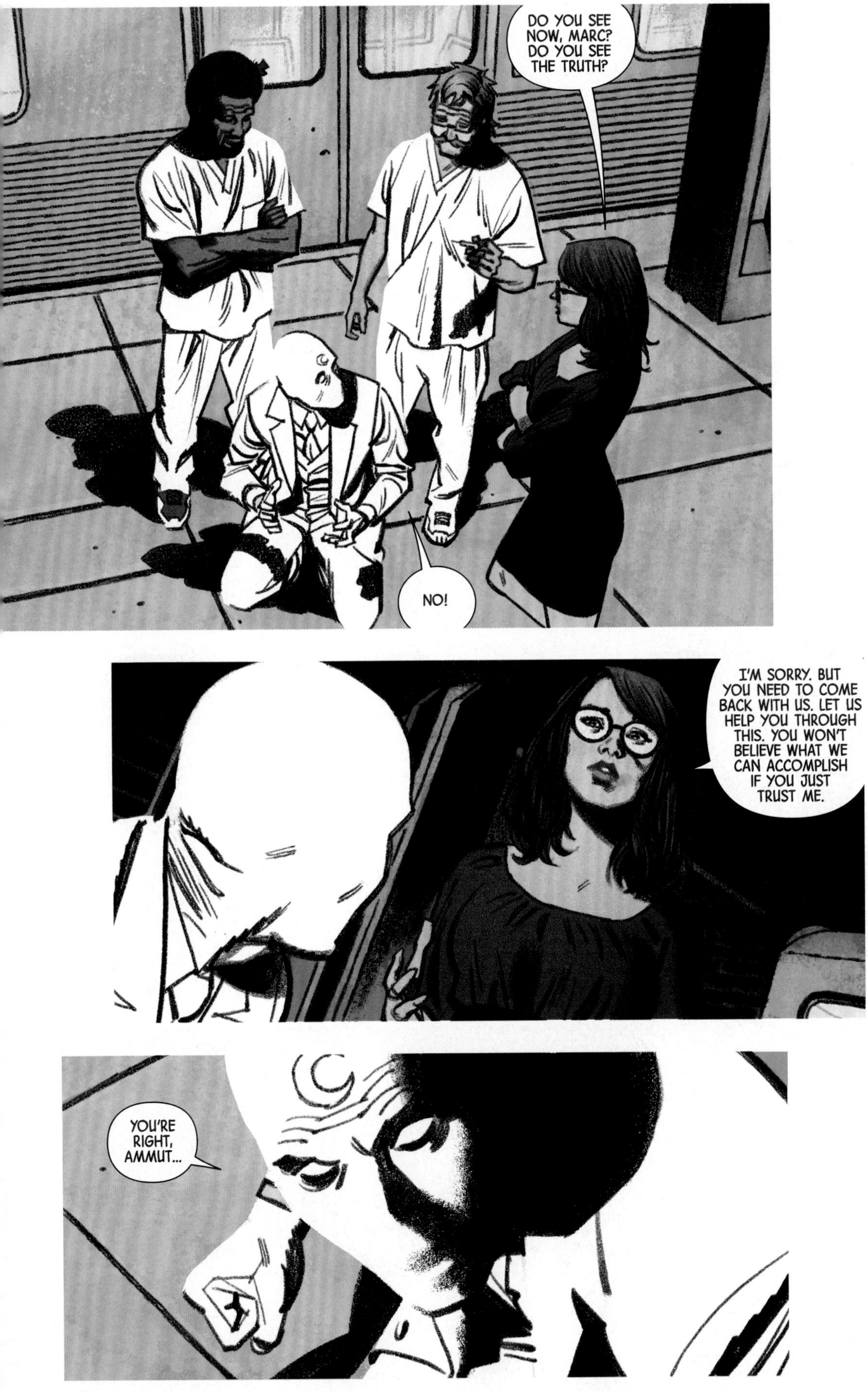
DO YOU SEE NOW, MARC? DO YOU SEE THE TRUTH?
NO!
I'M SORRY. BUT YOU NEED TO COME BACK WITH US. LET US HELP YOU THROUGH THIS. YOU WON'T BELIEVE WHAT WE CAN ACCOMPLISH IF YOU JUST TRUST ME.
YOU'RE RIGHT, AMMUT...

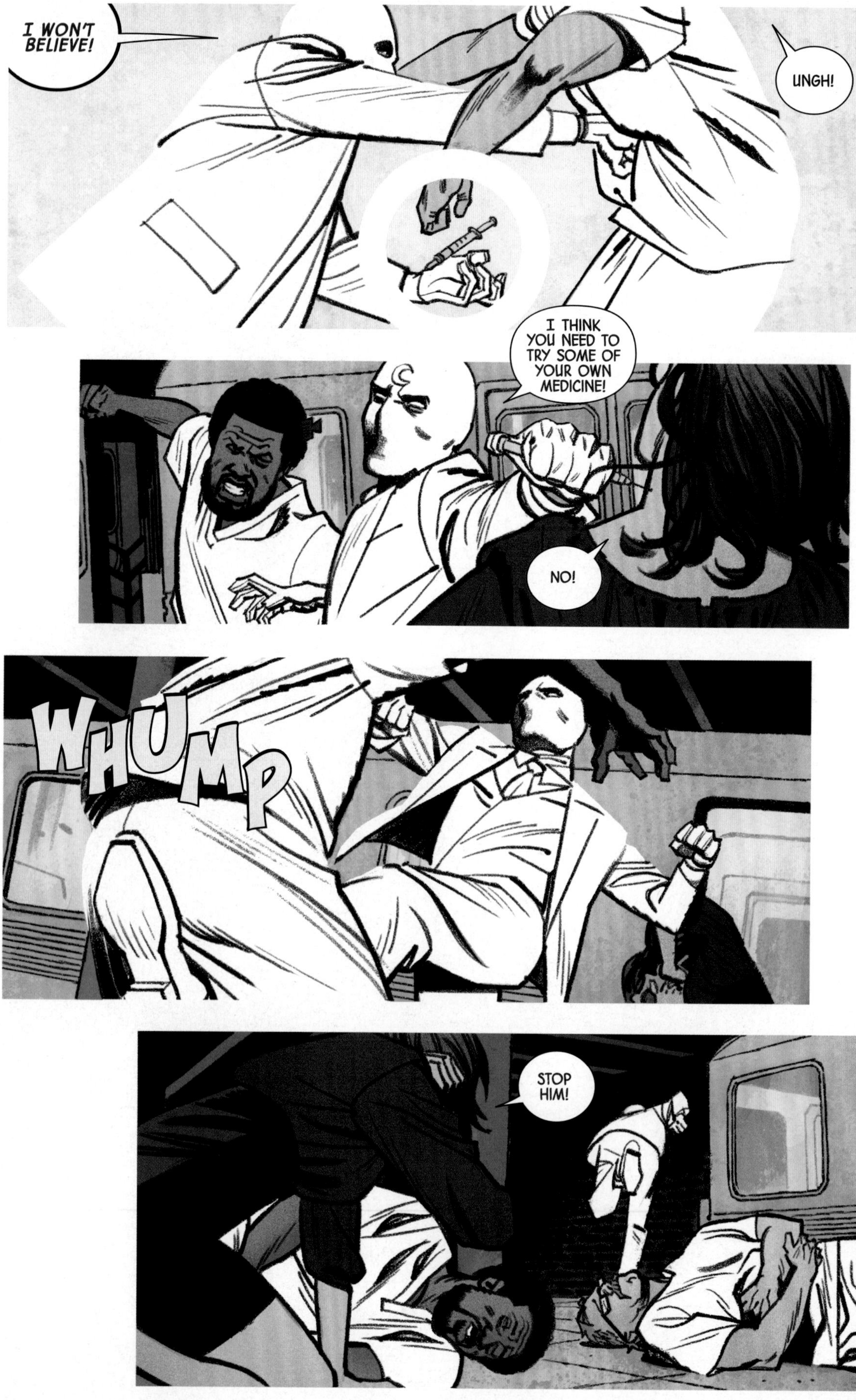
I WON'T BELIEVE!
UNGH!
I THINK YOU NEED TO TRY SOME OF YOUR OWN MEDICINE!
NO!
WHUMP
STOP HIM!

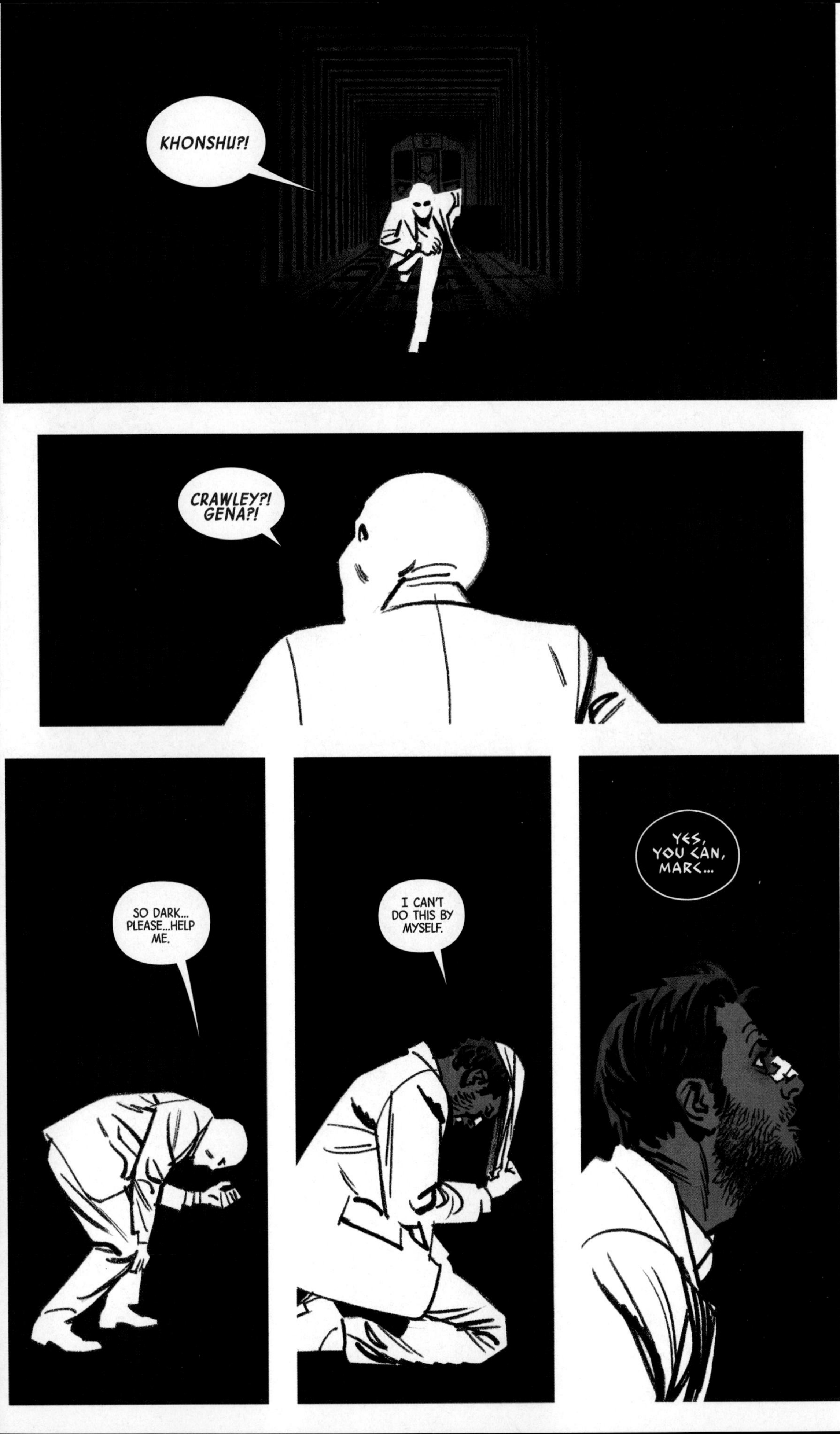
KHONSHU?!
CRAWLEY?! GENA?!
SO DARK... PLEASE...HELP ME.
I CAN'T DO THIS BY MYSELF.
YES, YOU CAN, MARC...

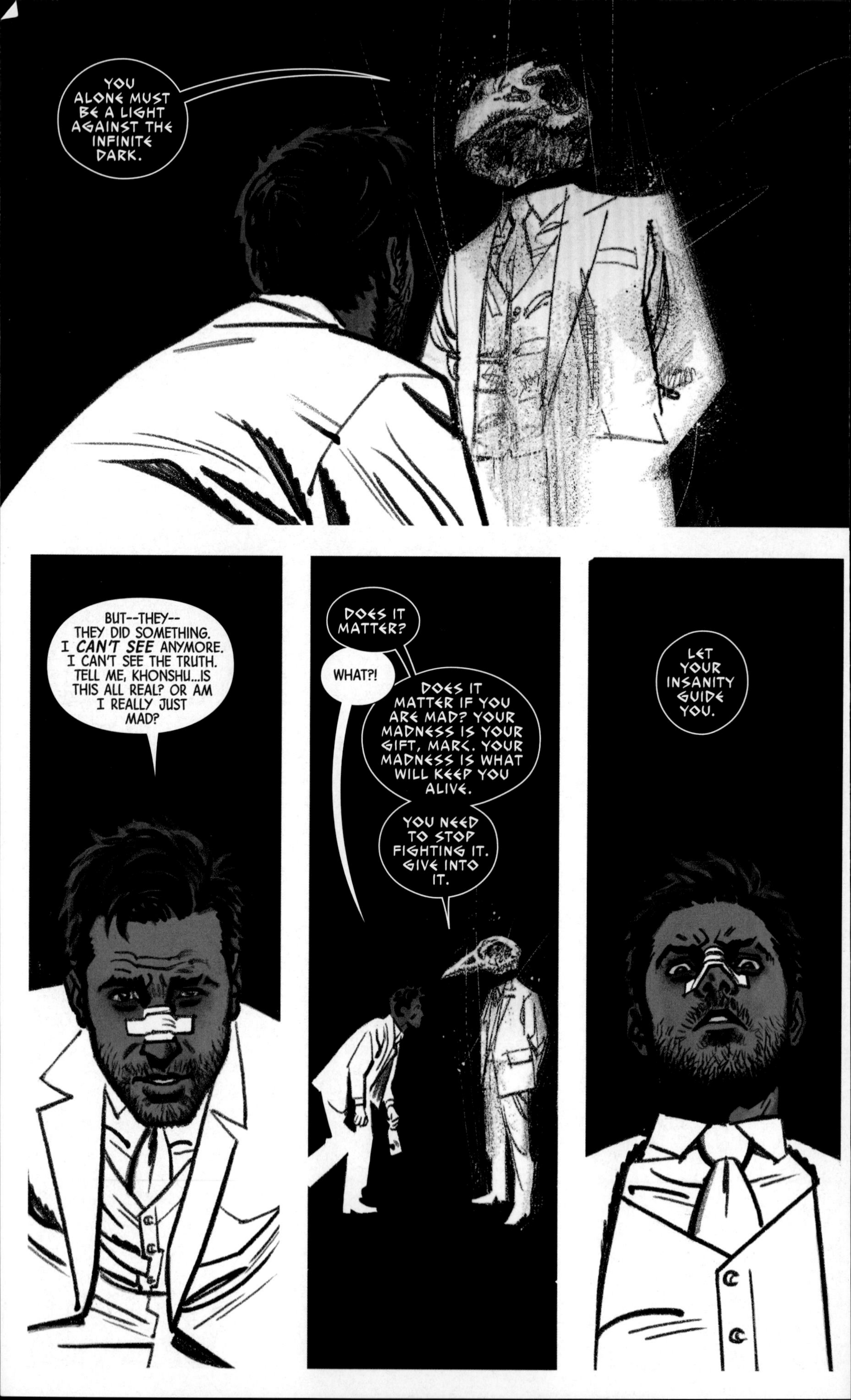
YOU ALONE MUST BE A LIGHT AGAINST THE INFINITE DARK.
BUT--THEY-- THEY DID SOMETHING. I CAN'T SEE ANYMORE. I CAN'T SEE THE TRUTH. TELL ME, KHONSHU...IS THIS ALL REAL? OR AM I REALLY JUST MAD?
DOES IT MATTER?
WHAT?!
DOES IT MATTER IF YOU ARE MAD? YOUR MADNESS IS YOUR GIFT, MARC. YOUR MADNESS IS WHAT WILL KEEP YOU ALIVE.
YOU NEED TO STOP FIGHTING IT. GIVE INTO IT.
LET YOUR INSANITY GUIDE YOU.

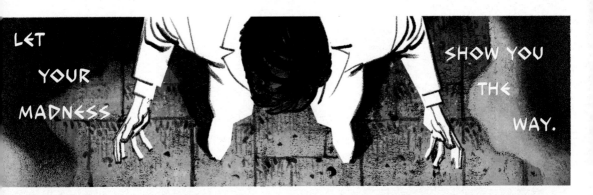

LET YOUR MADNESS

SHOW YOU THE WAY.

SPECTOR!

I DON'T SEE HIM, BOBBY!

UP AHEAD, BILLY. ONCE WE CATCH HIM, HE AIN'T EVER GETTING OFF THAT SHOCK TABLE.

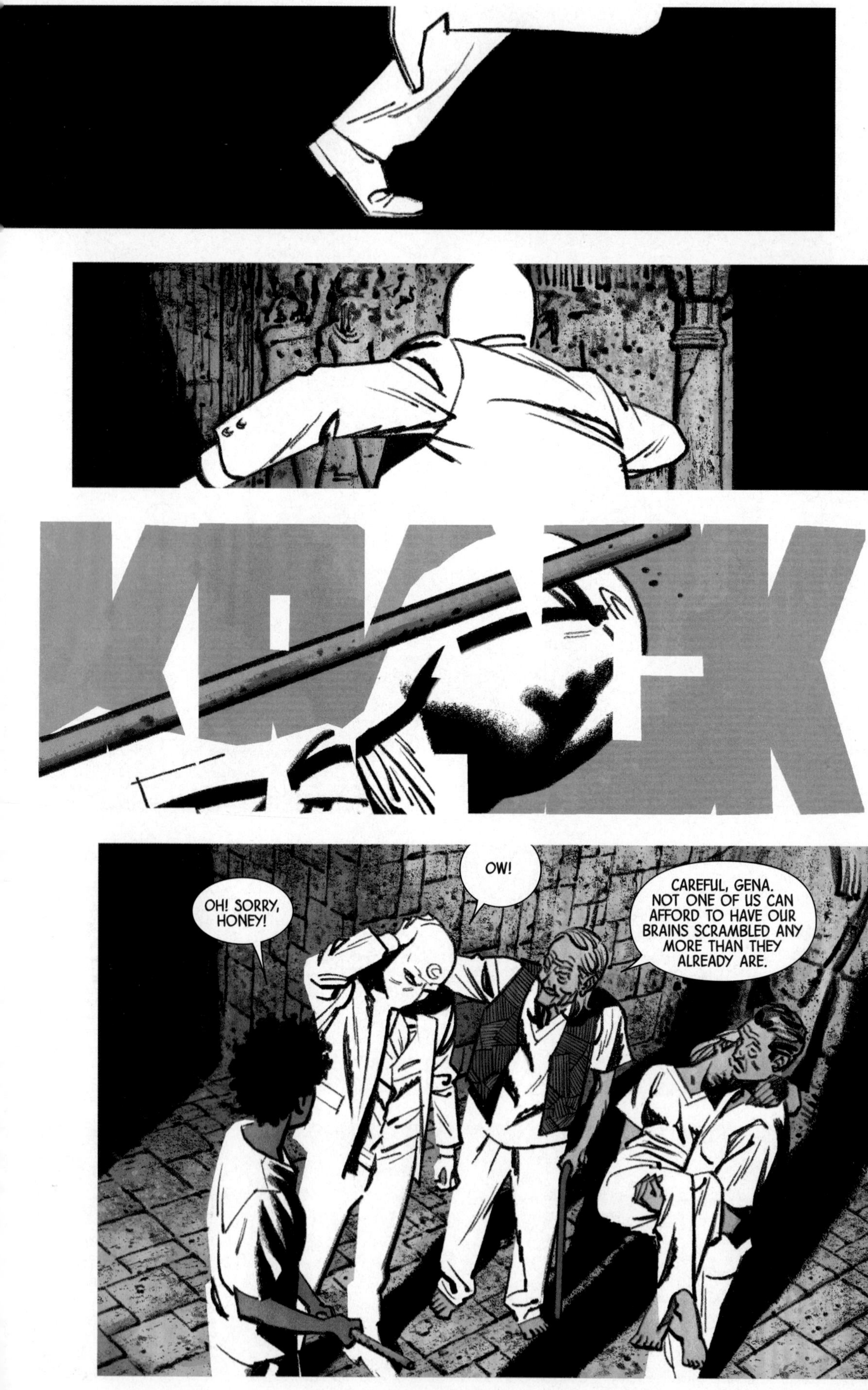
OW!
OH! SORRY, HONEY!
CAREFUL, GENA. NOT ONE OF US CAN AFFORD TO HAVE OUR BRAINS SCRAMBLED ANY MORE THAN THEY ALREADY ARE.

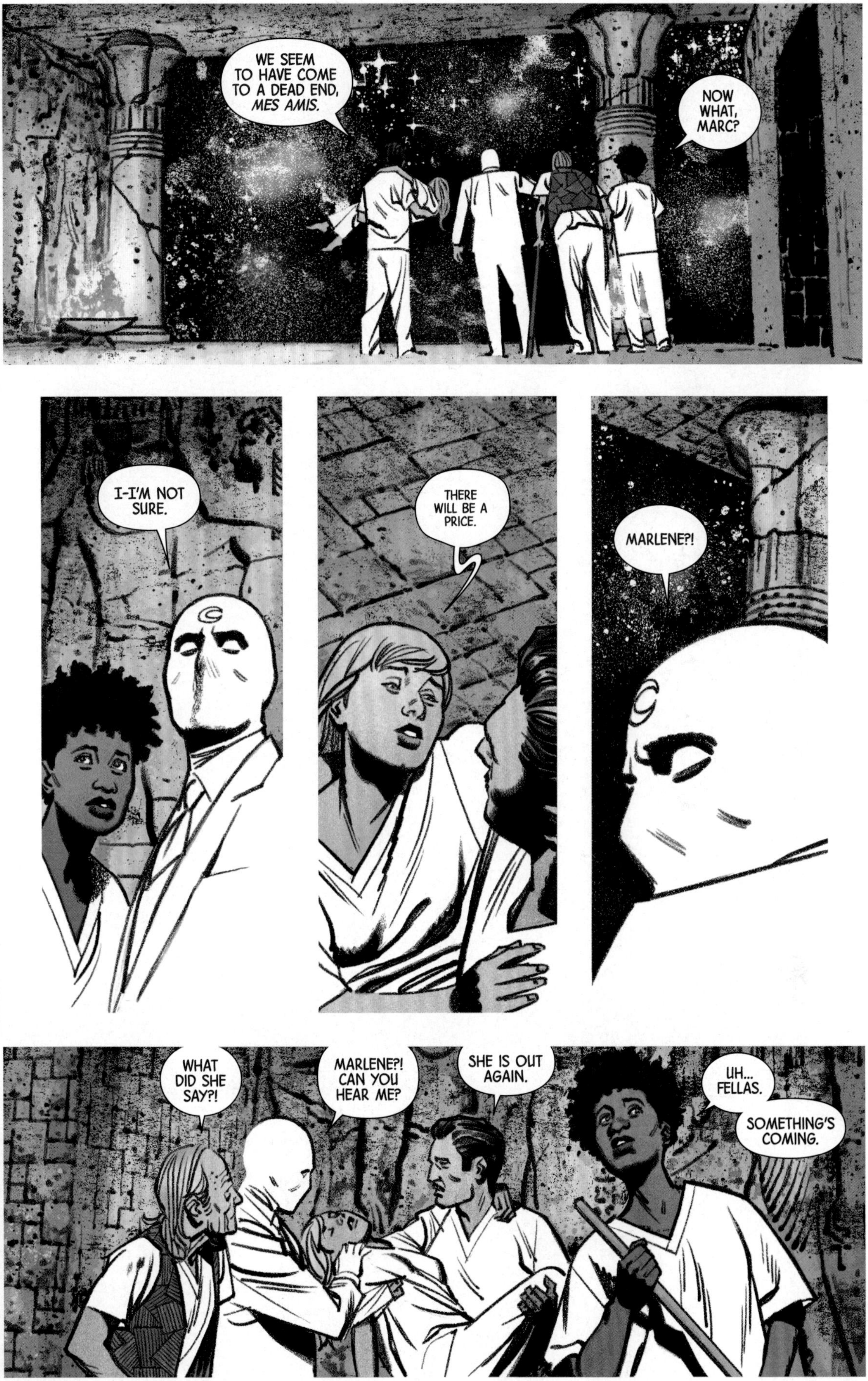

WE SEEM TO HAVE COME TO A DEAD END, *MES AMIS.*
NOW WHAT, MARC?
I-I'M NOT SURE.
THERE WILL BE A PRICE.
MARLENE?!
WHAT DID SHE SAY?!
MARLENE?! CAN YOU HEAR ME?
SHE IS OUT AGAIN.
UH... FELLAS.
SOMETHING'S COMING.

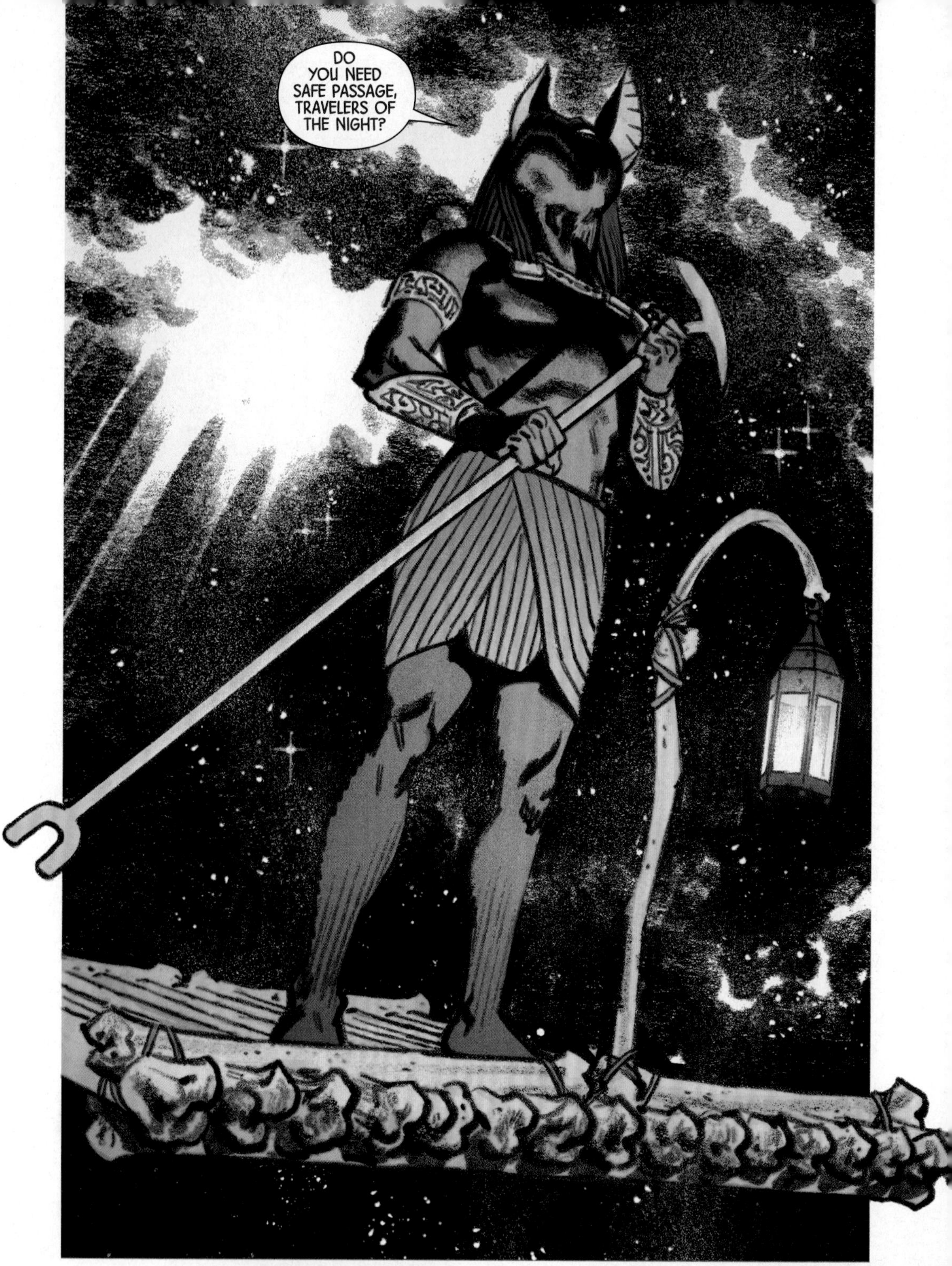
DO YOU NEED SAFE PASSAGE, TRAVELERS OF THE NIGHT?

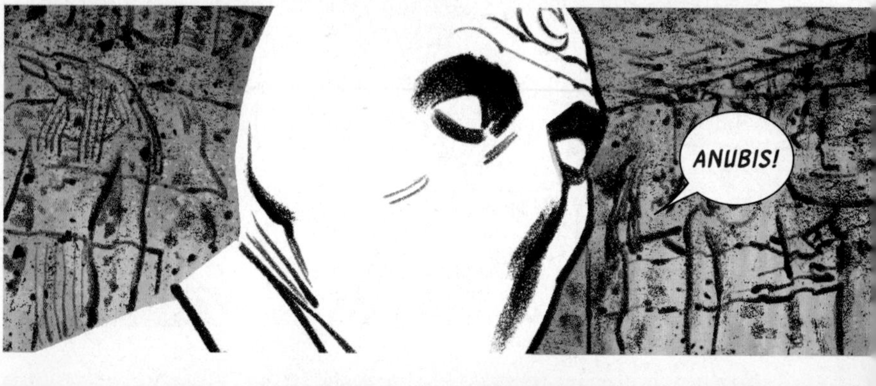
ANUBIS!

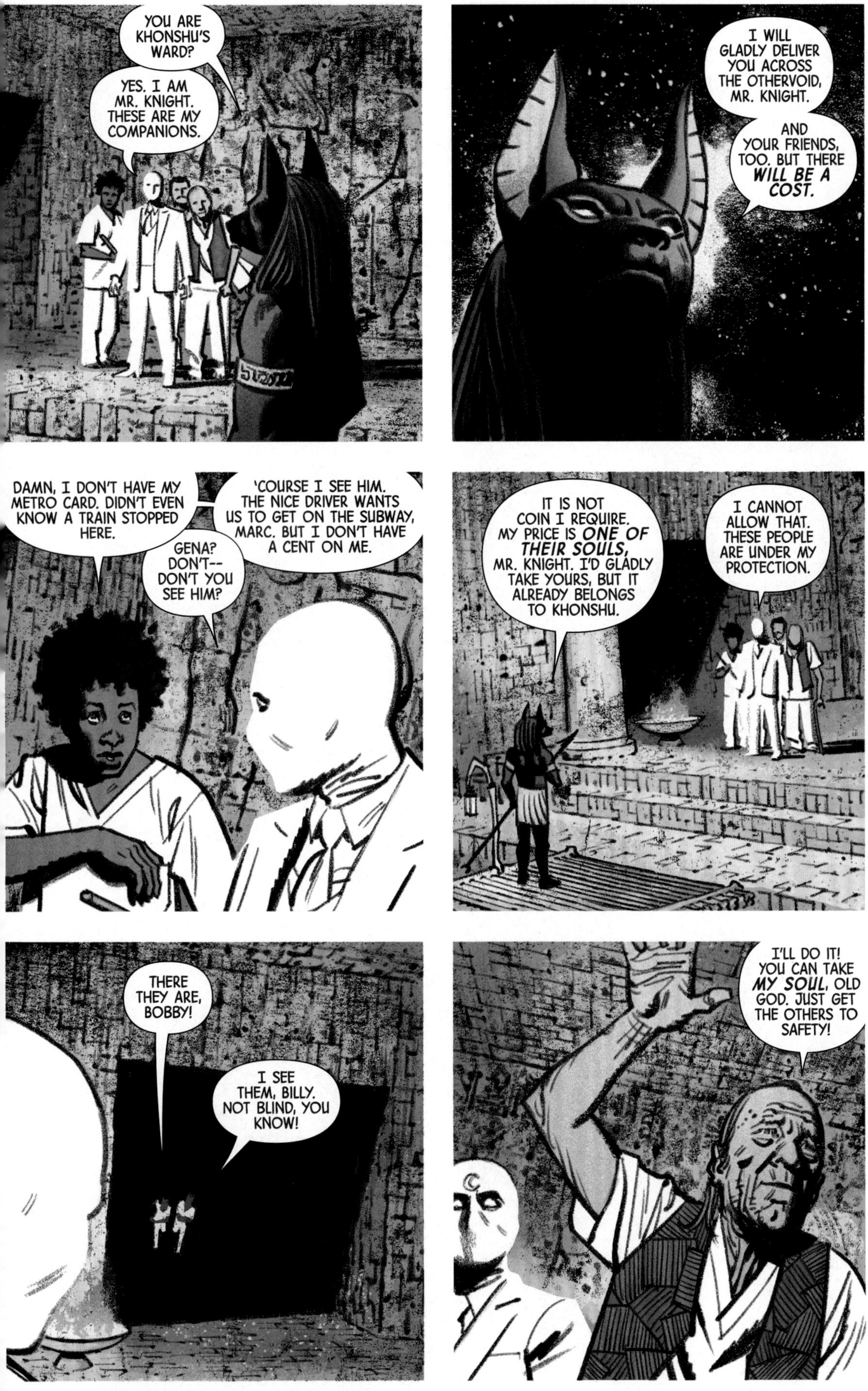
YOU ARE KHONSHU'S WARD?
YES. I AM MR. KNIGHT. THESE ARE MY COMPANIONS.
I WILL GLADLY DELIVER YOU ACROSS THE OTHERVOID, MR. KNIGHT.
AND YOUR FRIENDS, TOO. BUT THERE *WILL BE A COST.*
DAMN, I DON'T HAVE MY METRO CARD. DIDN'T EVEN KNOW A TRAIN STOPPED HERE.
GENA? DON'T-- DON'T YOU SEE HIM?
'COURSE I SEE HIM. THE NICE DRIVER WANTS US TO GET ON THE SUBWAY, MARC. BUT I DON'T HAVE A CENT ON ME.
IT IS NOT COIN I REQUIRE. MY PRICE IS *ONE OF THEIR SOULS,* MR. KNIGHT. I'D GLADLY TAKE YOURS, BUT IT ALREADY BELONGS TO KHONSHU.
I CANNOT ALLOW THAT. THESE PEOPLE ARE UNDER MY PROTECTION.
THERE THEY ARE, BOBBY!
I SEE THEM, BILLY. NOT BLIND, YOU KNOW!
I'LL DO IT! YOU CAN TAKE *MY SOUL*, OLD GOD. JUST GET THE OTHERS TO SAFETY!

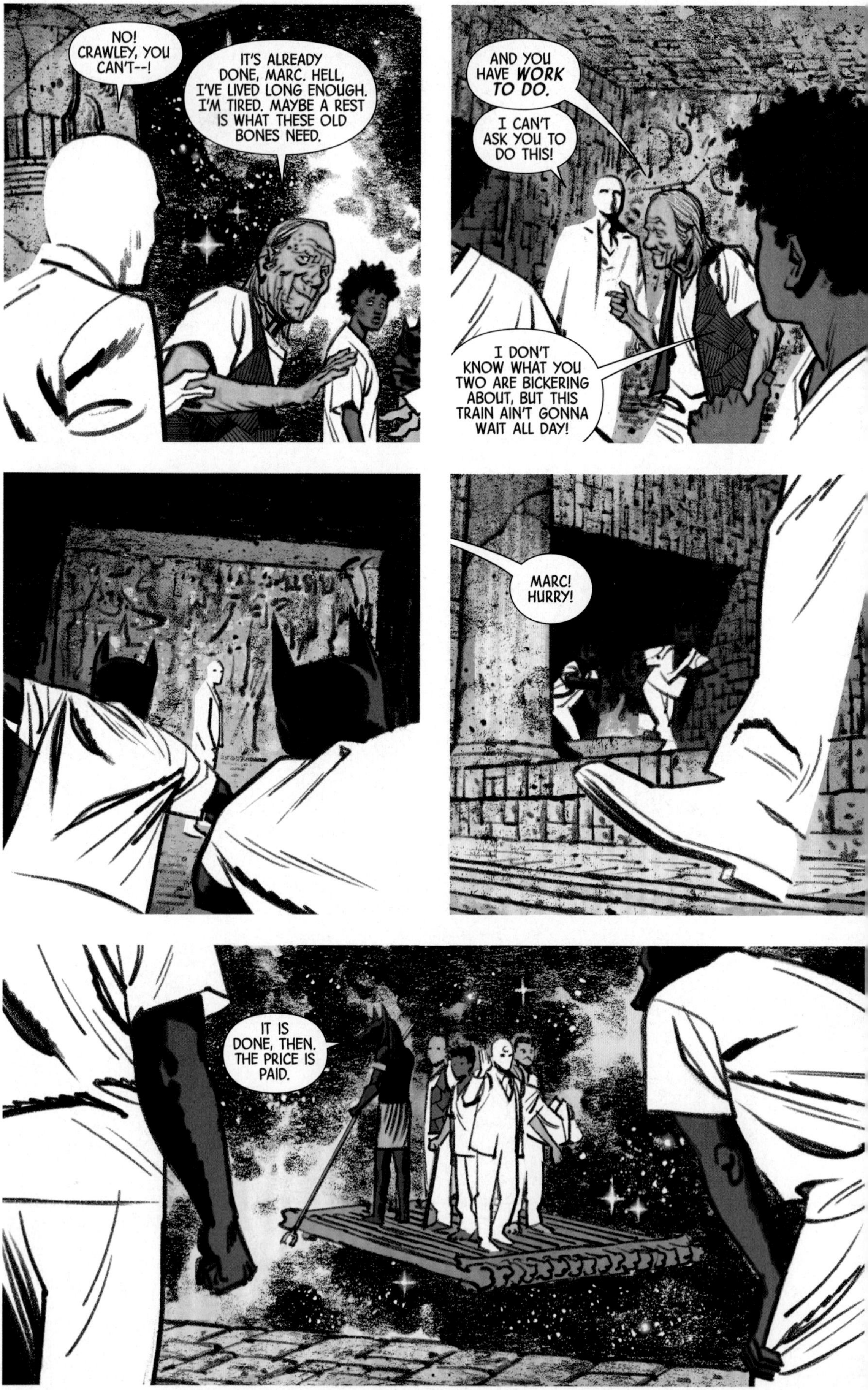
NO! CRAWLEY, YOU CAN'T--!
IT'S ALREADY DONE, MARC. HELL, I'VE LIVED LONG ENOUGH. I'M TIRED. MAYBE A REST IS WHAT THESE OLD BONES NEED.
AND YOU HAVE WORK TO DO.
I CAN'T ASK YOU TO DO THIS!
I DON'T KNOW WHAT YOU TWO ARE BICKERING ABOUT, BUT THIS TRAIN AIN'T GONNA WAIT ALL DAY!
MARC! HURRY!
IT IS DONE, THEN. THE PRICE IS PAID.

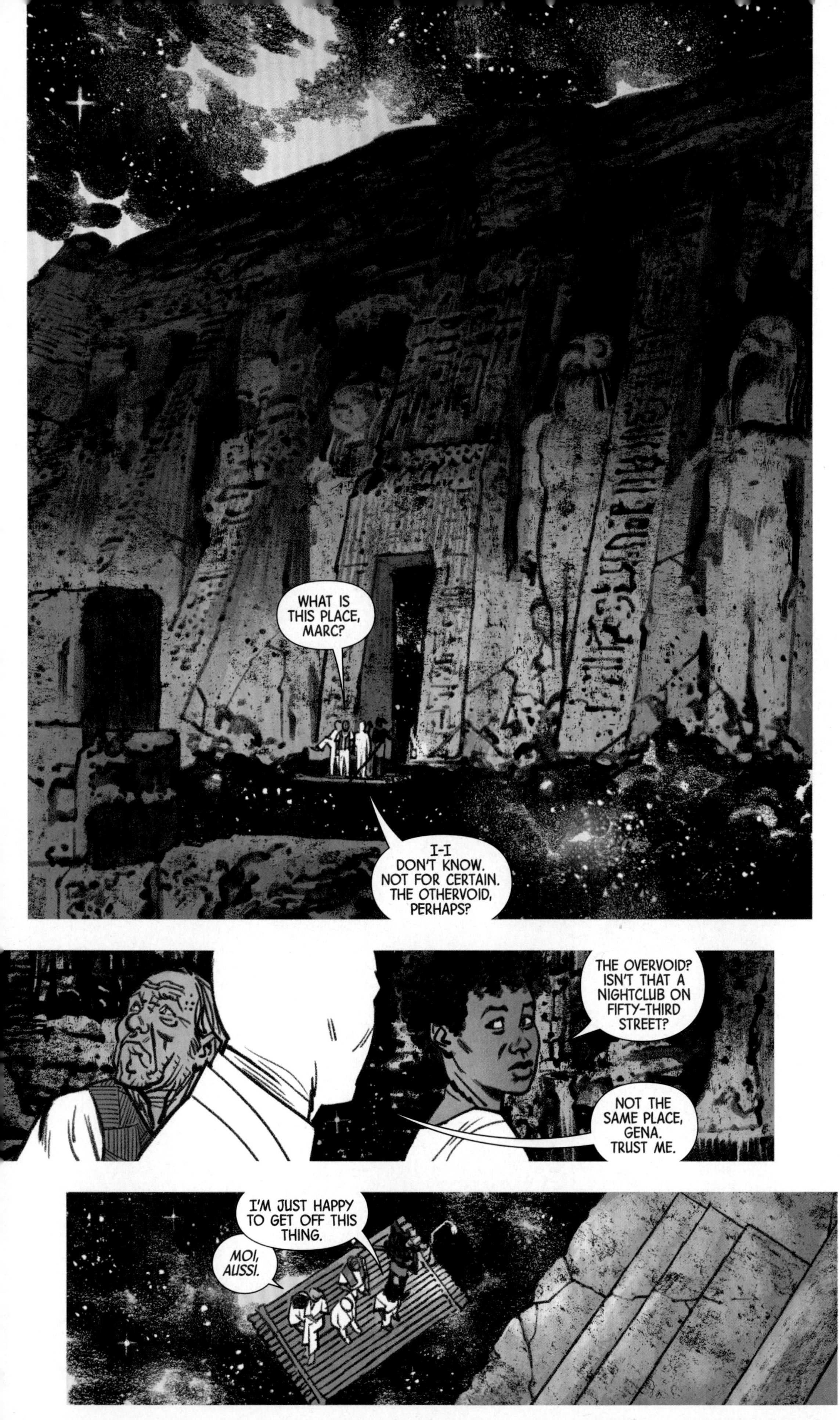
WHAT IS THIS PLACE, MARC?
I-I DON'T KNOW. NOT FOR CERTAIN. THE OTHERVOID, PERHAPS?
THE OVERVOID? ISN'T THAT A NIGHTCLUB ON FIFTY-THIRD STREET?
NOT THE SAME PLACE, GENA. TRUST ME.
I'M JUST HAPPY TO GET OFF THIS THING.
MOI, AUSSI.

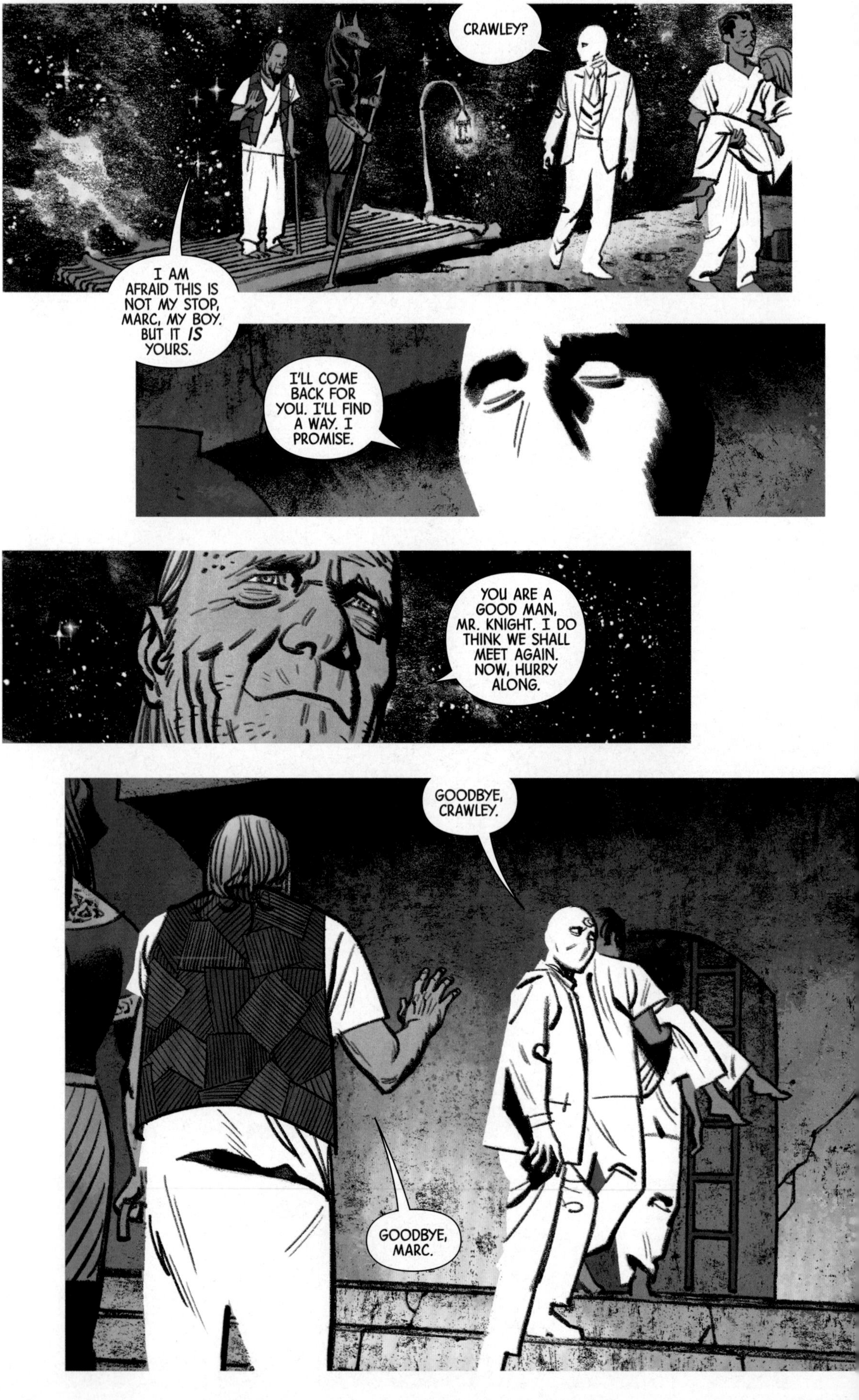
CRAWLEY?
I AM AFRAID THIS IS NOT MY STOP, MARC, MY BOY. BUT IT IS YOURS.
I'LL COME BACK FOR YOU. I'LL FIND A WAY. I PROMISE.
YOU ARE A GOOD MAN, MR. KNIGHT. I DO THINK WE SHALL MEET AGAIN. NOW, HURRY ALONG.
GOODBYE, CRAWLEY.
GOODBYE, MARC.

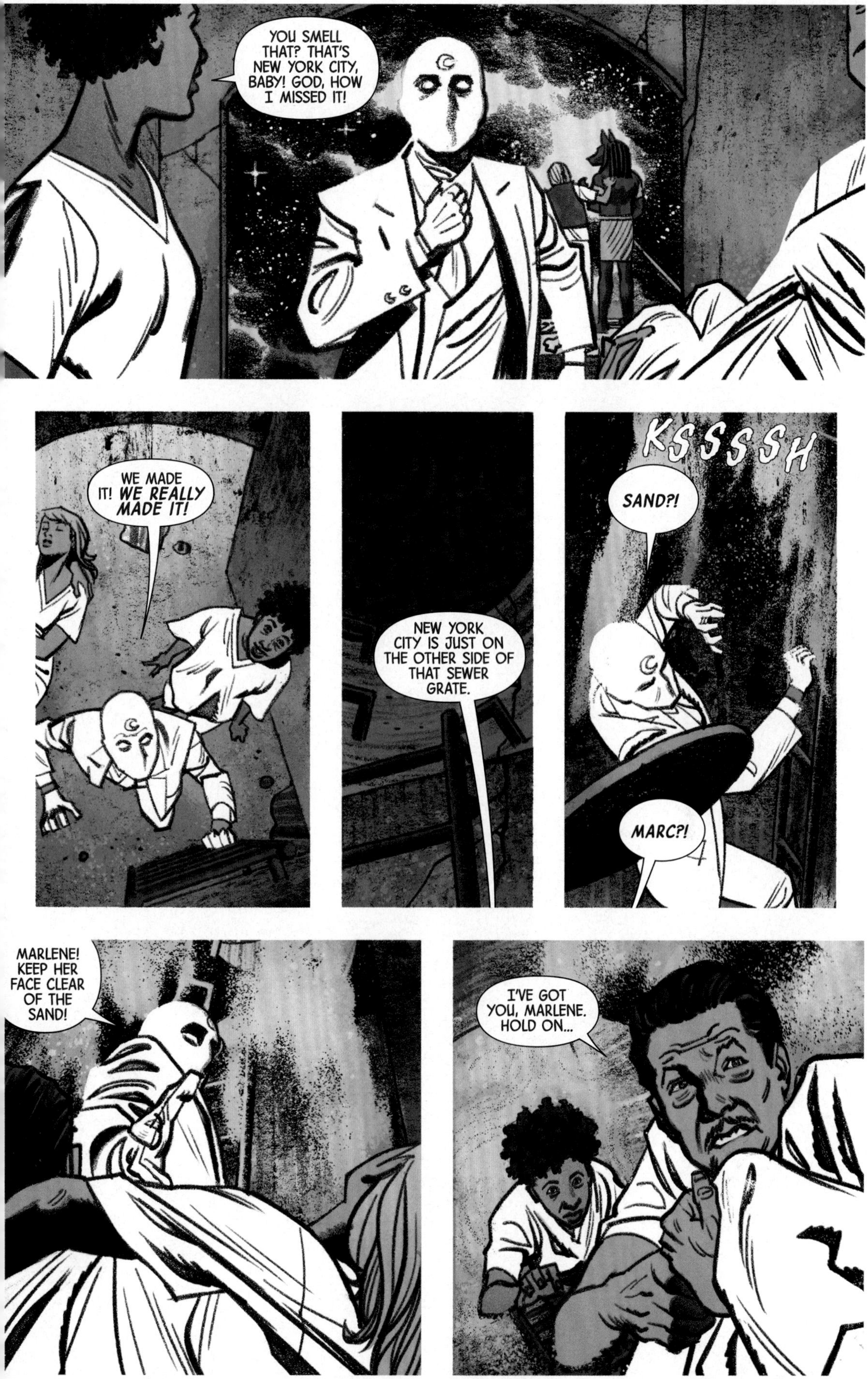
YOU SMELL THAT? THAT'S NEW YORK CITY, BABY! GOD, HOW I MISSED IT!
WE MADE IT! WE REALLY MADE IT!
NEW YORK CITY IS JUST ON THE OTHER SIDE OF THAT SEWER GRATE.
KSSSSH
SAND?!
MARC?!
MARLENE! KEEP HER FACE CLEAR OF THE SAND!
I'VE GOT YOU, MARLENE. HOLD ON...

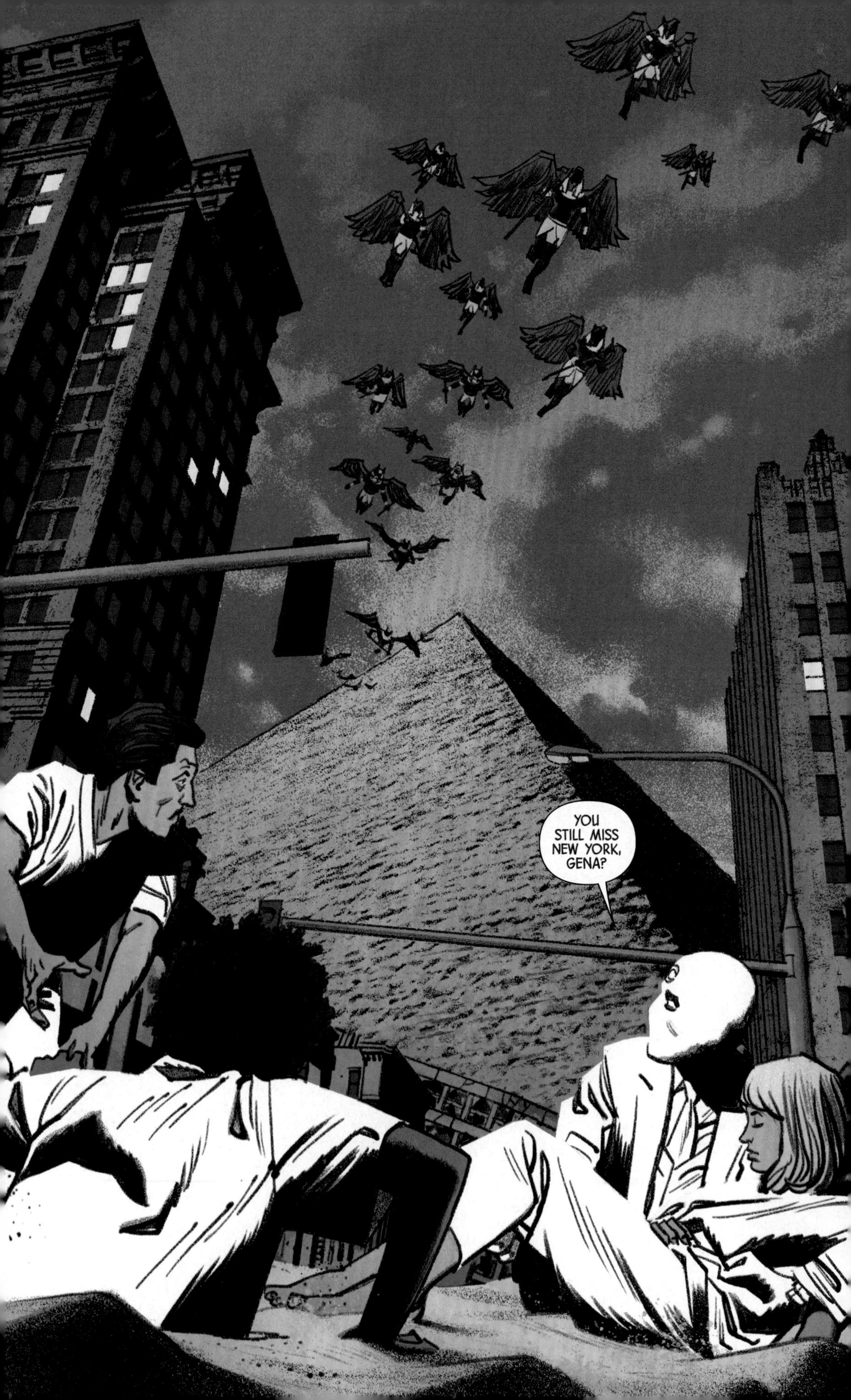
YOU STILL MISS NEW YORK, GENA?

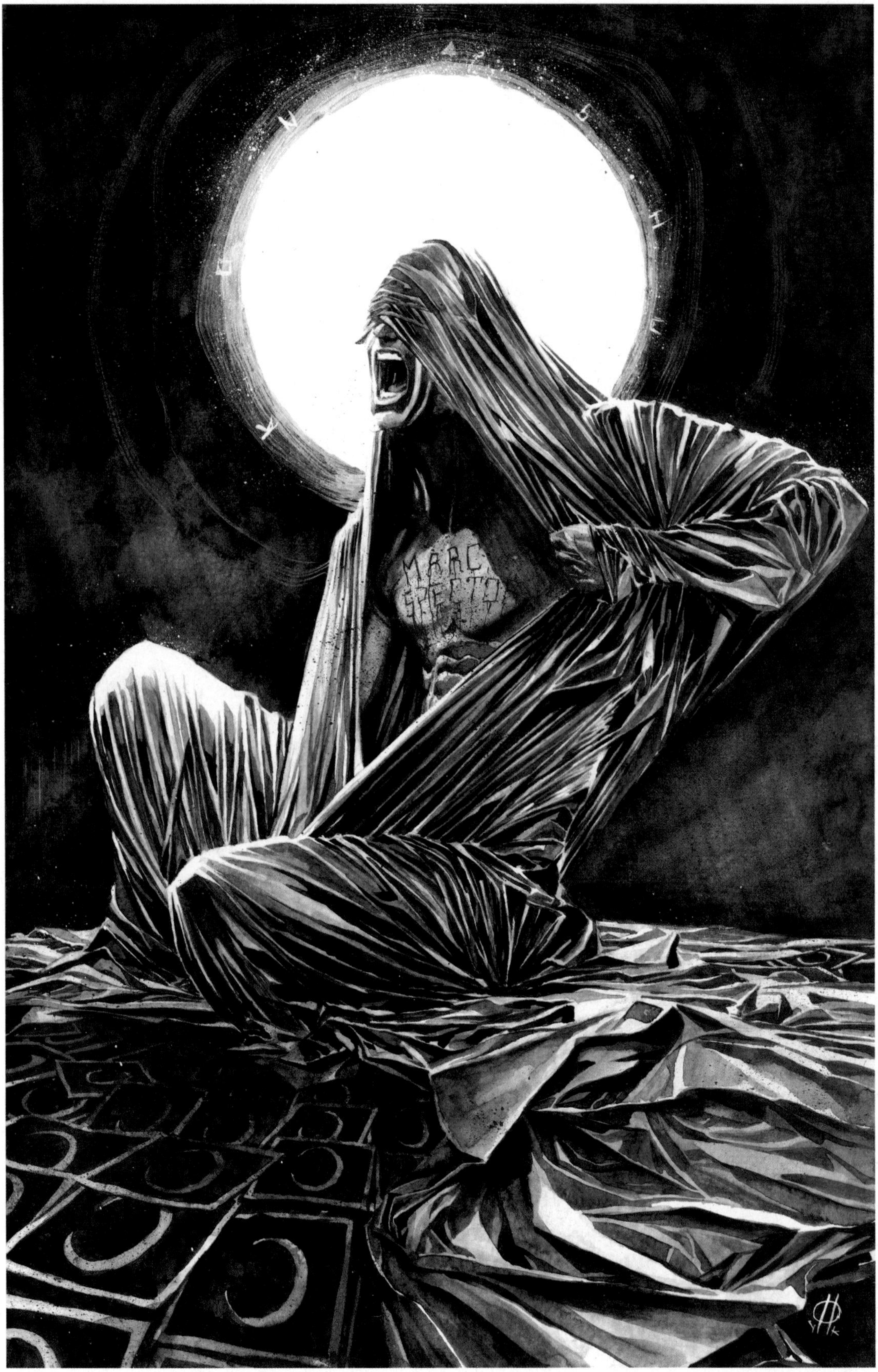
MARC

#1 VARIANT BY MARCO RUDY

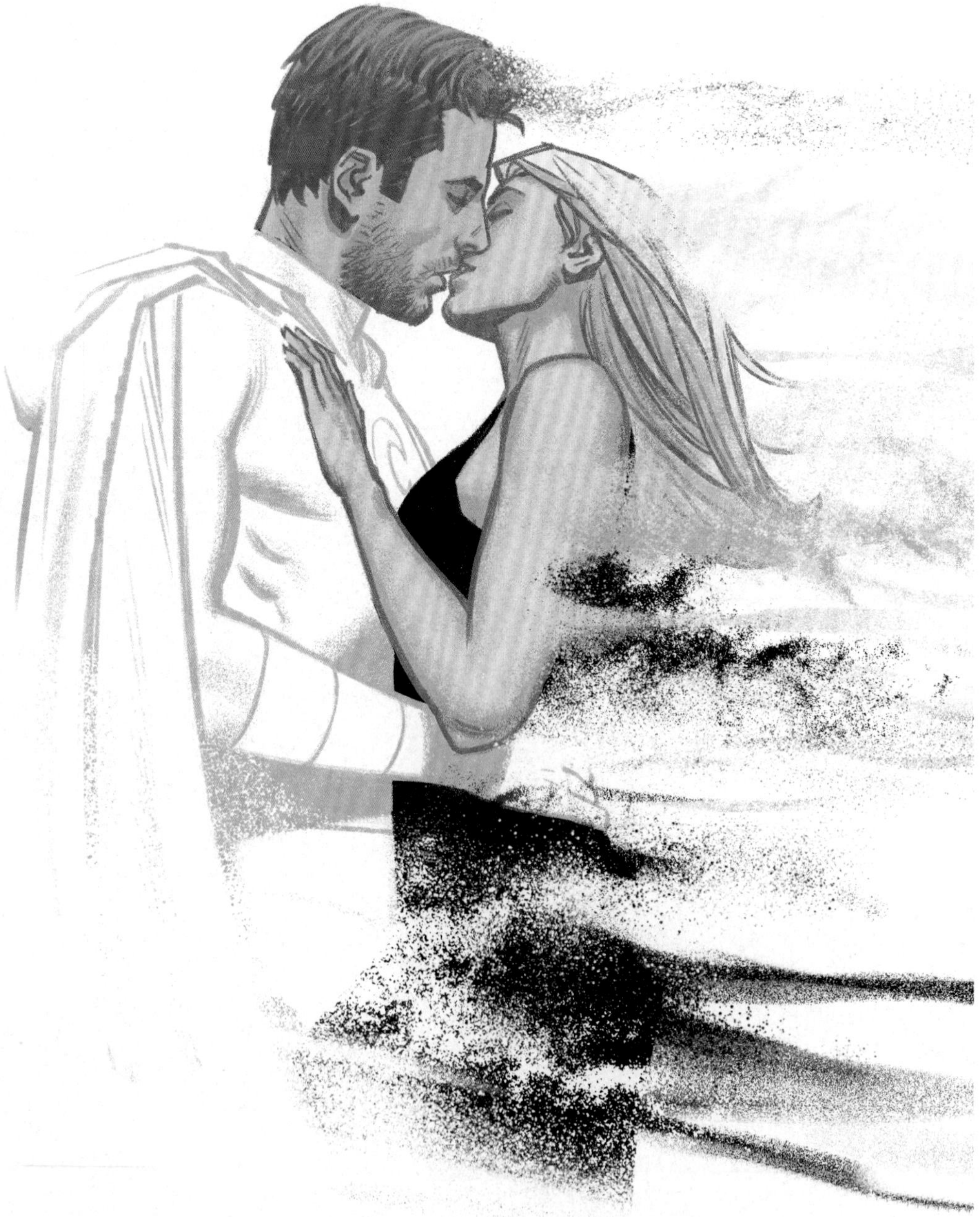

WELCOME TO NEW EGYPT
PART FOUR

4

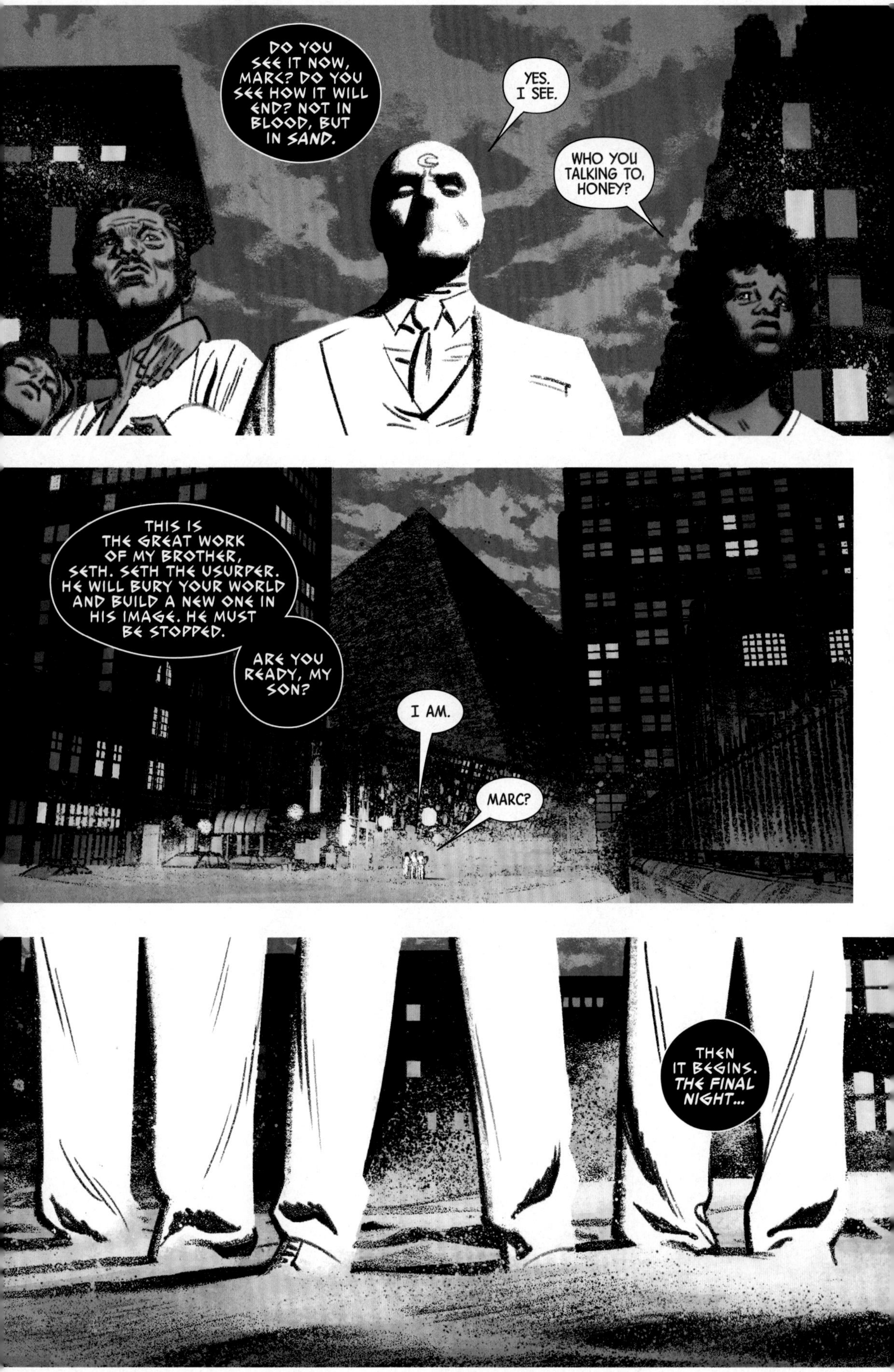
DO YOU SEE IT NOW, MARC? DO YOU SEE HOW IT WILL END? NOT IN BLOOD, BUT IN *SAND*.
YES. I SEE.
WHO YOU TALKING TO, HONEY?
THIS IS THE GREAT WORK OF MY BROTHER, SETH. SETH THE USURPER. HE WILL BURY YOUR WORLD AND BUILD A NEW ONE IN HIS IMAGE. HE MUST BE STOPPED.
ARE YOU READY, MY SON?
I AM.
MARC?
THEN IT BEGINS. *THE FINAL NIGHT*...

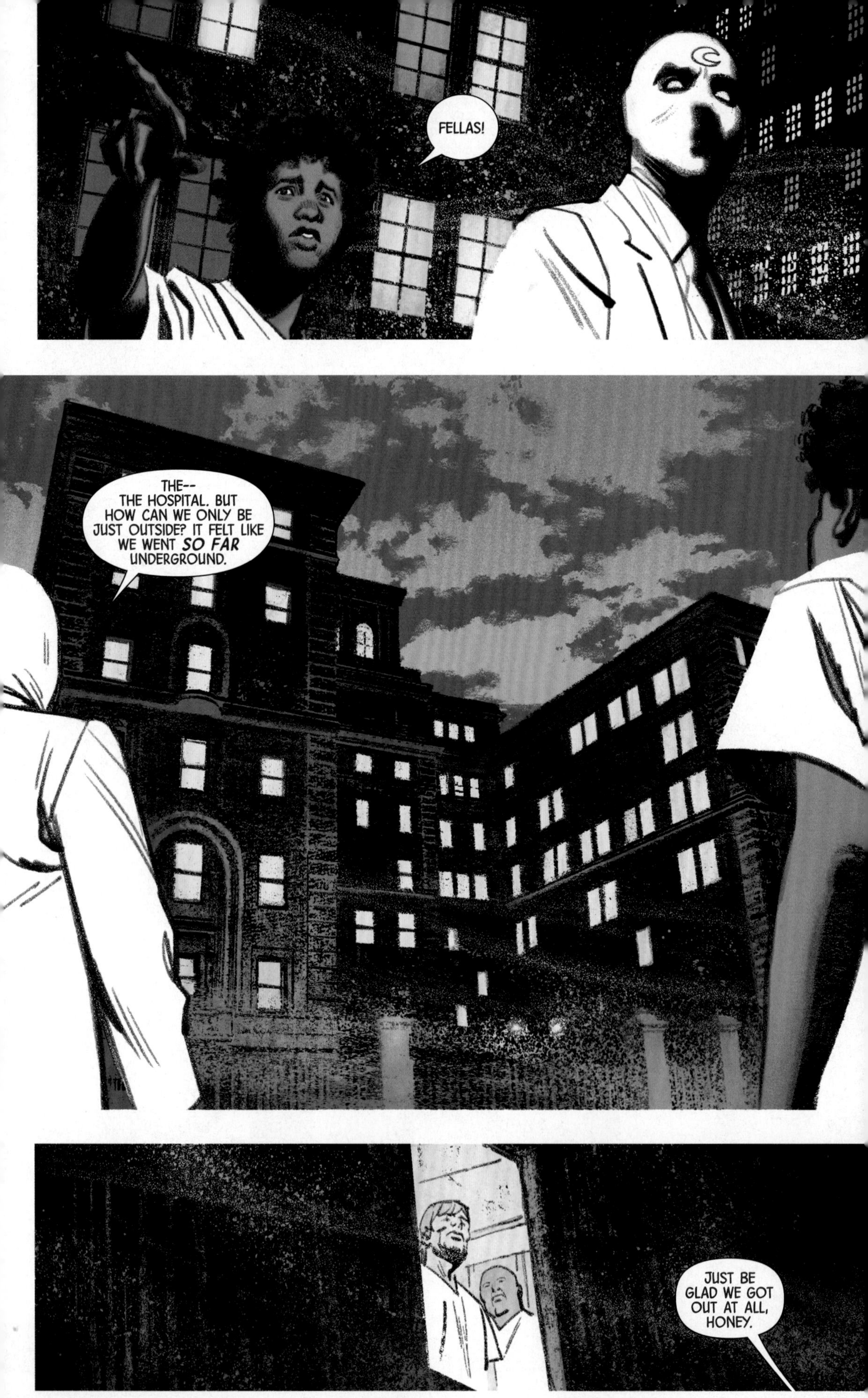
FELLAS!
THE-- THE HOSPITAL. BUT HOW CAN WE ONLY BE JUST OUTSIDE? IT FELT LIKE WE WENT SO FAR UNDERGROUND.
JUST BE GLAD WE GOT OUT AT ALL, HONEY.

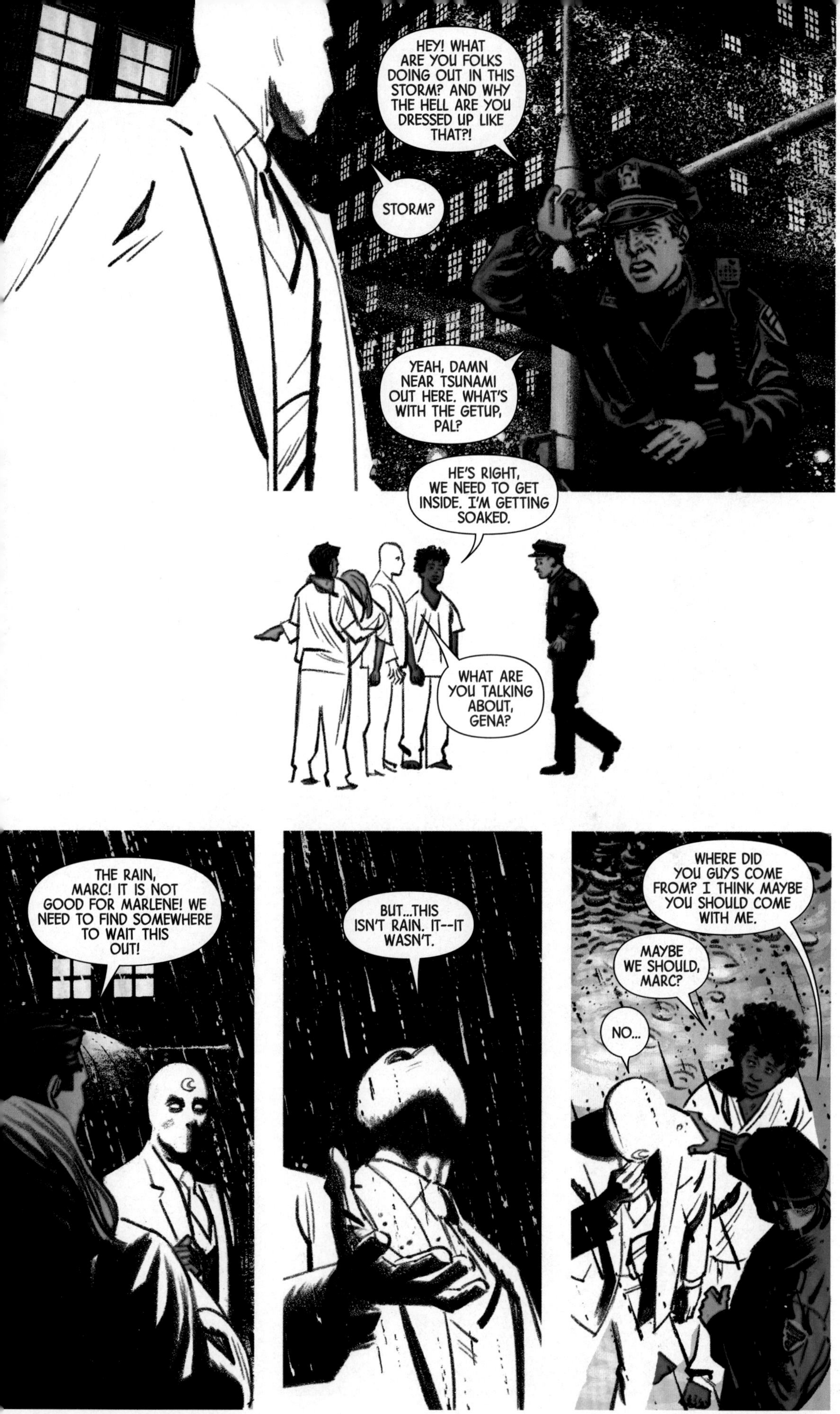
HEY! WHAT ARE YOU FOLKS DOING OUT IN THIS STORM? AND WHY THE HELL ARE YOU DRESSED UP LIKE THAT?!
STORM?
YEAH, DAMN NEAR TSUNAMI OUT HERE. WHAT'S WITH THE GETUP, PAL?
HE'S RIGHT, WE NEED TO GET INSIDE. I'M GETTING SOAKED.
WHAT ARE YOU TALKING ABOUT, GENA?
THE RAIN, MARC! IT IS NOT GOOD FOR MARLENE! WE NEED TO FIND SOMEWHERE TO WAIT THIS OUT!
BUT...THIS ISN'T RAIN. IT--IT WASN'T.
WHERE DID YOU GUYS COME FROM? I THINK MAYBE YOU SHOULD COME WITH ME.
MAYBE WE SHOULD, MARC?
NO...

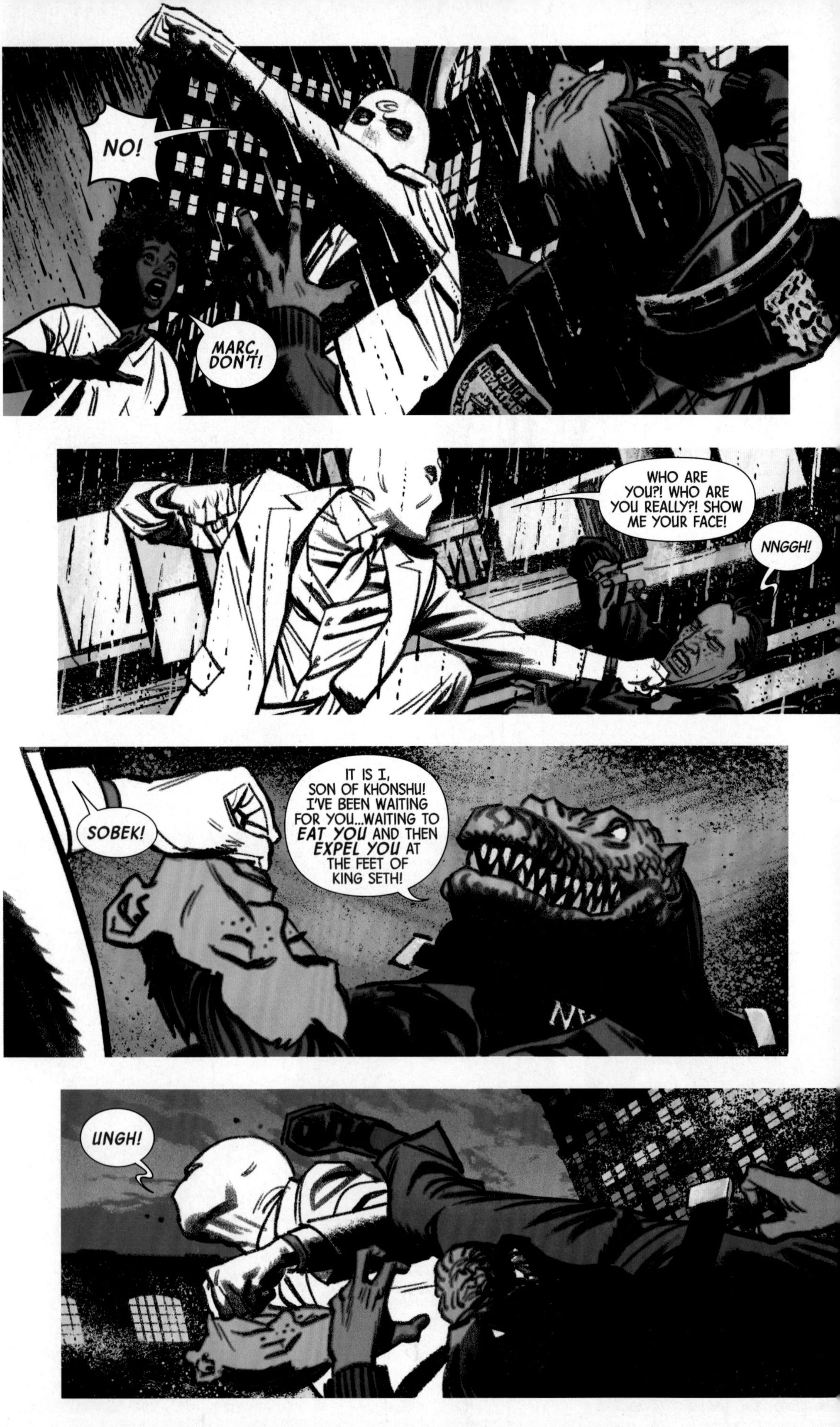
NO!
MARC, DON'T!
WHO ARE YOU?! WHO ARE YOU REALLY?! SHOW ME YOUR FACE!
NNGGH!
SOBEK!
IT IS I, SON OF KHONSHU! I'VE BEEN WAITING FOR YOU...WAITING TO EAT YOU AND THEN EXPEL YOU AT THE FEET OF KING SETH!
UNGH!

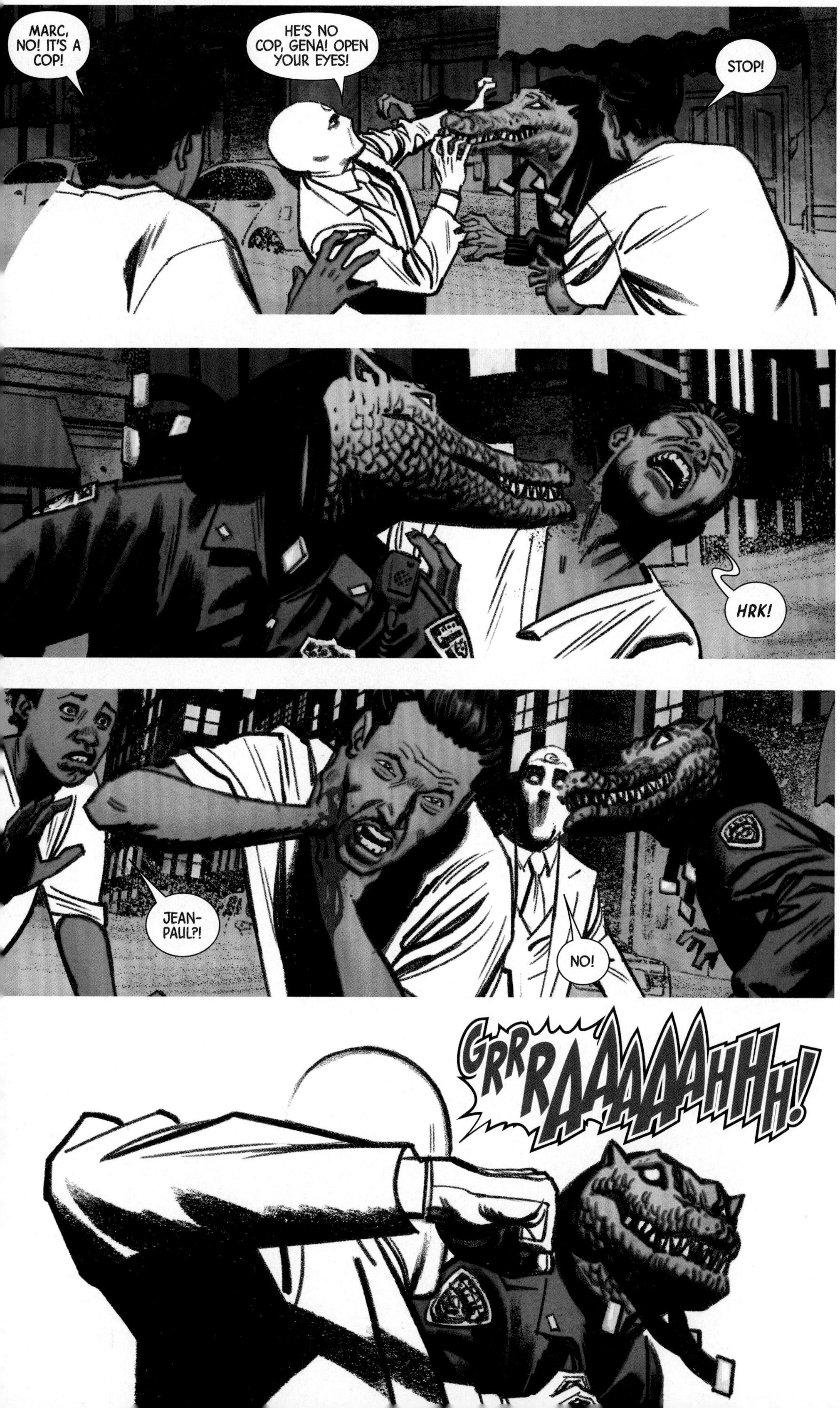
MARC, NO! IT'S A COP!
HE'S NO COP, GENA! OPEN YOUR EYES!
STOP!
HRK!
JEAN-PAUL?!
NO!
GRRRAAAAAHHH!

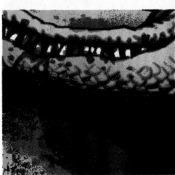

OH, GOD!

FRENCHIE? JEAN-PAUL?

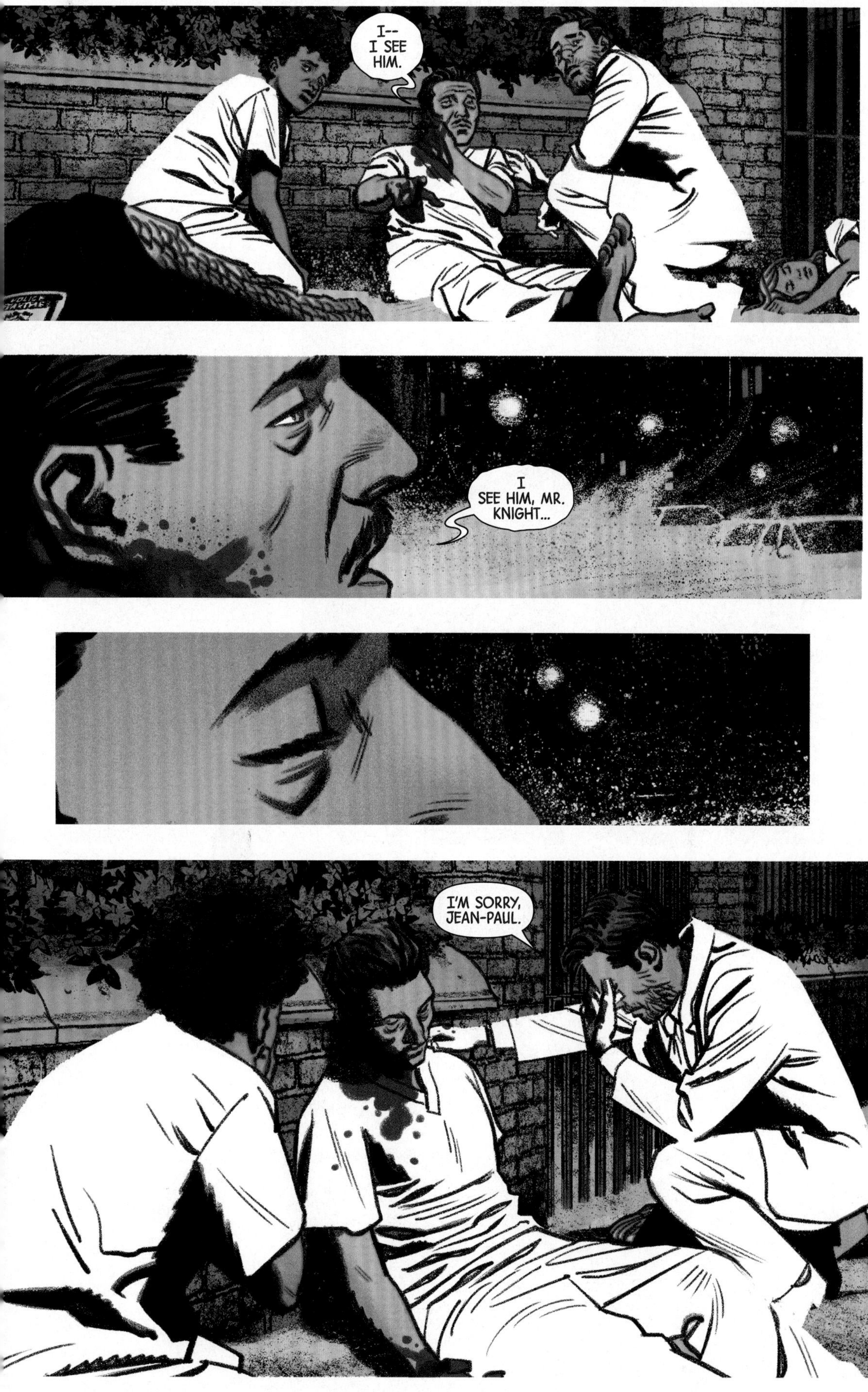
I-- I SEE HIM.
I SEE HIM, MR. KNIGHT...
I'M SORRY, JEAN-PAUL.

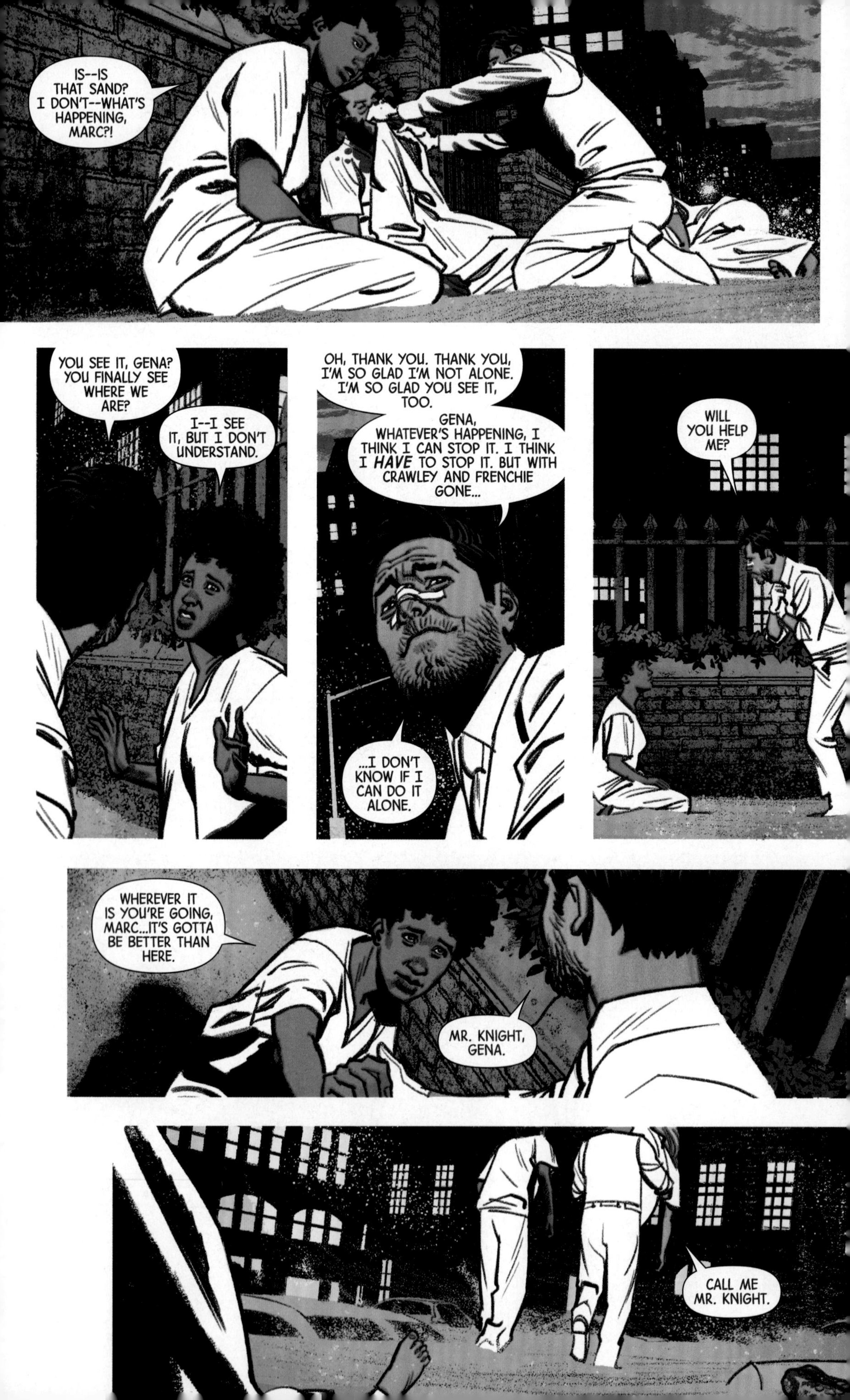
IS--IS THAT SAND? I DON'T--WHAT'S HAPPENING, MARC?!
YOU SEE IT, GENA? YOU FINALLY SEE WHERE WE ARE?
I--I SEE IT, BUT I DON'T UNDERSTAND.
OH, THANK YOU. THANK YOU, I'M SO GLAD I'M NOT ALONE. I'M SO GLAD YOU SEE IT, TOO.
GENA, WHATEVER'S HAPPENING, I THINK I CAN STOP IT. I THINK I HAVE TO STOP IT. BUT WITH CRAWLEY AND FRENCHIE GONE...
...I DON'T KNOW IF I CAN DO IT ALONE.
WILL YOU HELP ME?
WHEREVER IT IS YOU'RE GOING, MARC...IT'S GOTTA BE BETTER THAN HERE.
MR. KNIGHT, GENA.
CALL ME MR. KNIGHT.

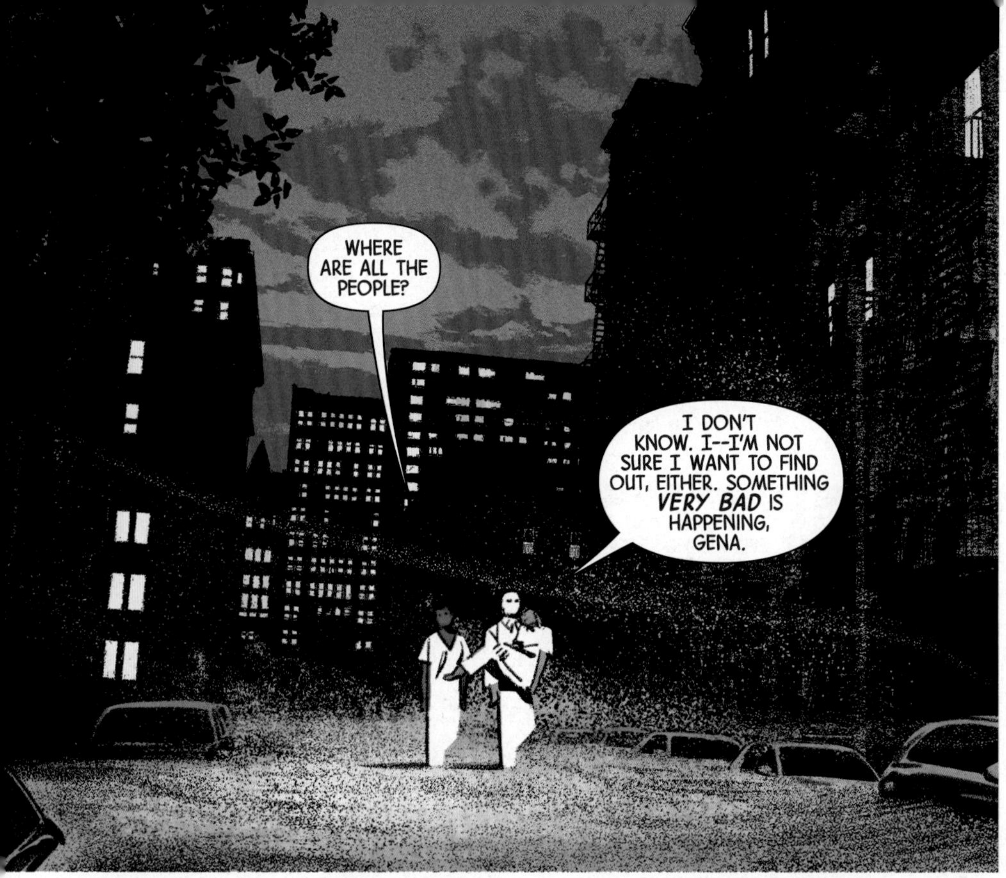
WHERE ARE ALL THE PEOPLE?
I DON'T KNOW. I--I'M NOT SURE I WANT TO FIND OUT, EITHER. SOMETHING *VERY BAD* IS HAPPENING, GENA.

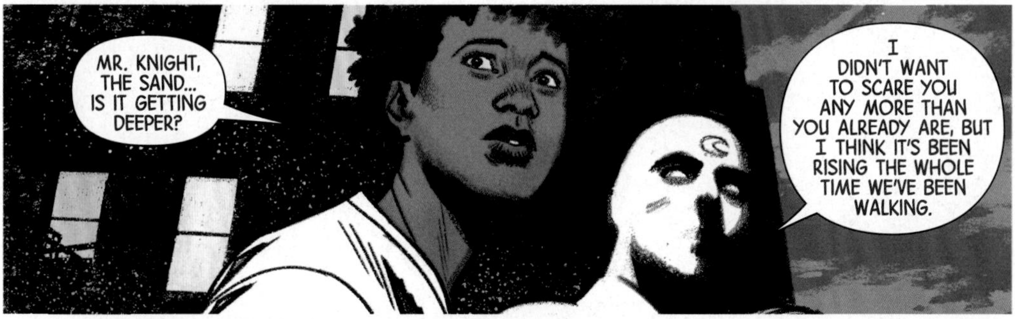
MR. KNIGHT, THE SAND... IS IT GETTING DEEPER?
I DIDN'T WANT TO SCARE YOU ANY MORE THAN YOU ALREADY ARE, BUT I THINK IT'S BEEN RISING THE WHOLE TIME WE'VE BEEN WALKING.

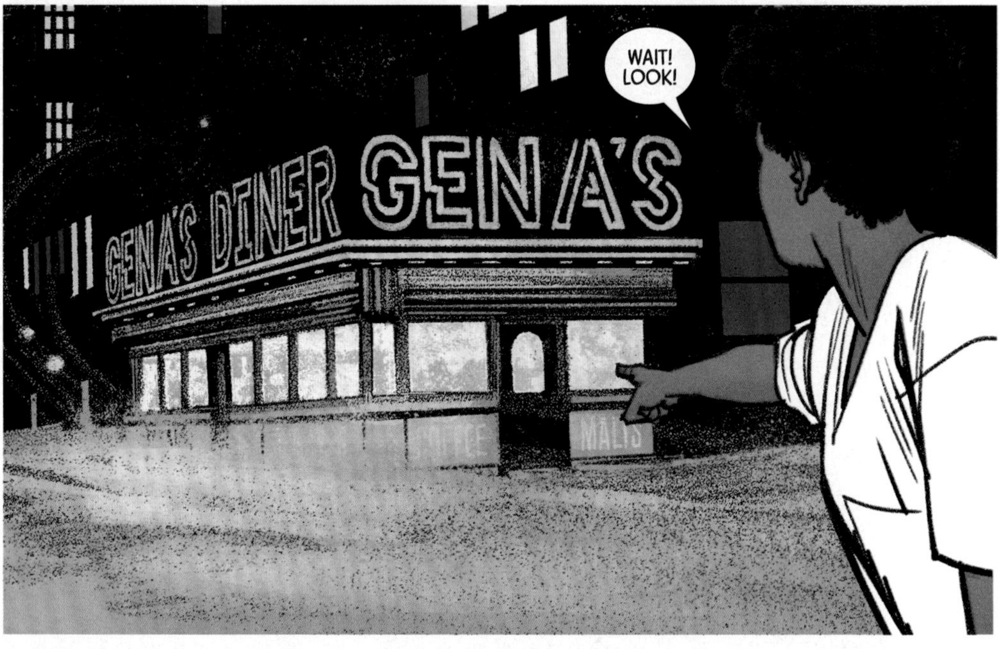
WAIT! LOOK!
GENA'S DINER
GENA'S

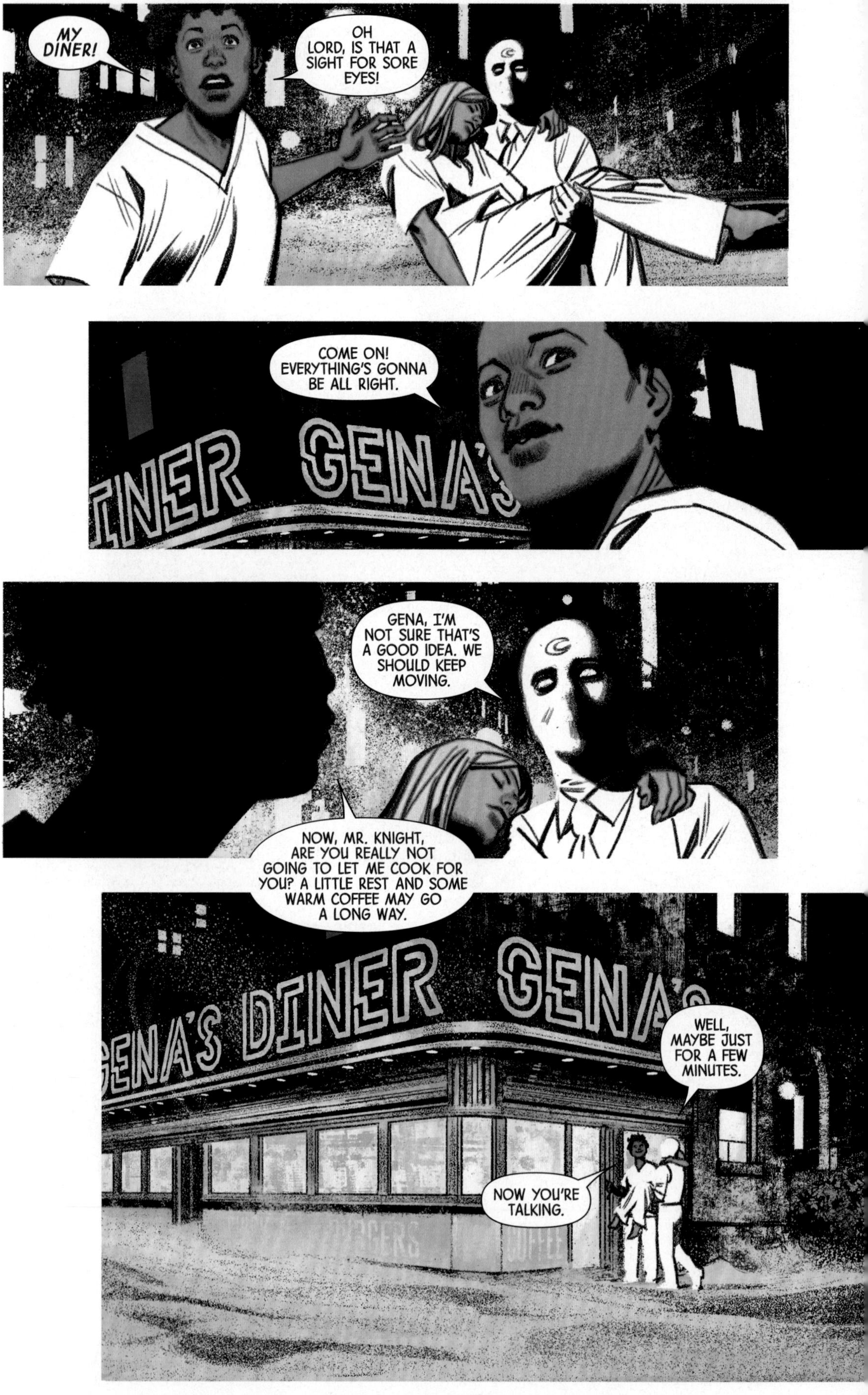
MY DINER!
OH LORD, IS THAT A SIGHT FOR SORE EYES!
COME ON! EVERYTHING'S GONNA BE ALL RIGHT.
GENA'S DINER
GENA, I'M NOT SURE THAT'S A GOOD IDEA. WE SHOULD KEEP MOVING.
NOW, MR. KNIGHT, ARE YOU REALLY NOT GOING TO LET ME COOK FOR YOU? A LITTLE REST AND SOME WARM COFFEE MAY GO A LONG WAY.
GENA'S DINER GENA'S
WELL, MAYBE JUST FOR A FEW MINUTES.
NOW YOU'RE TALKING.

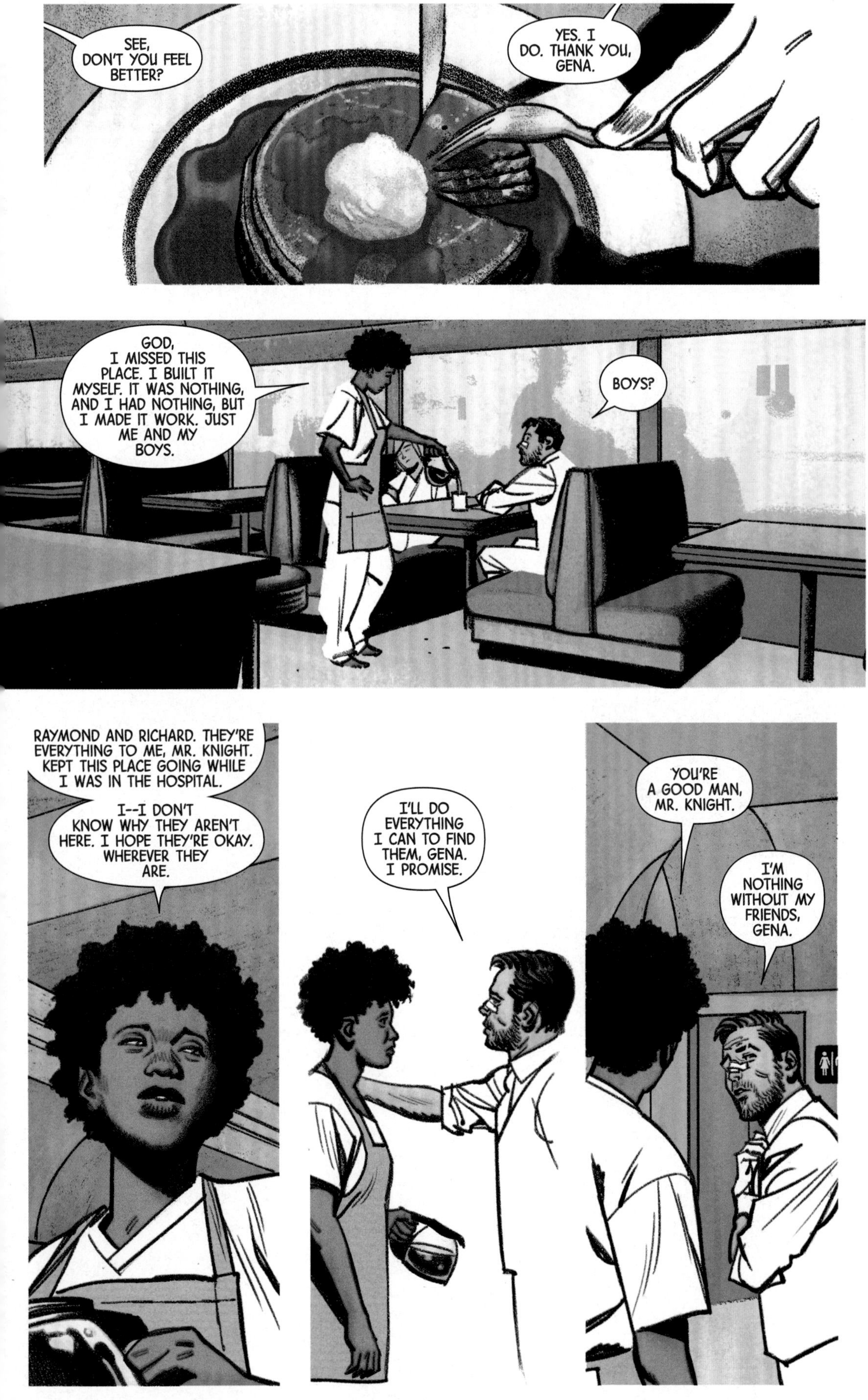
SEE, DON'T YOU FEEL BETTER?
YES. I DO. THANK YOU, GENA.
GOD, I MISSED THIS PLACE. I BUILT IT MYSELF. IT WAS NOTHING, AND I HAD NOTHING, BUT I MADE IT WORK. JUST ME AND MY BOYS.
BOYS?
RAYMOND AND RICHARD. THEY'RE EVERYTHING TO ME, MR. KNIGHT. KEPT THIS PLACE GOING WHILE I WAS IN THE HOSPITAL.
I--I DON'T KNOW WHY THEY AREN'T HERE. I HOPE THEY'RE OKAY. WHEREVER THEY ARE.
I'LL DO EVERYTHING I CAN TO FIND THEM, GENA. I PROMISE.
YOU'RE A GOOD MAN, MR. KNIGHT.
I'M NOTHING WITHOUT MY FRIENDS, GENA.

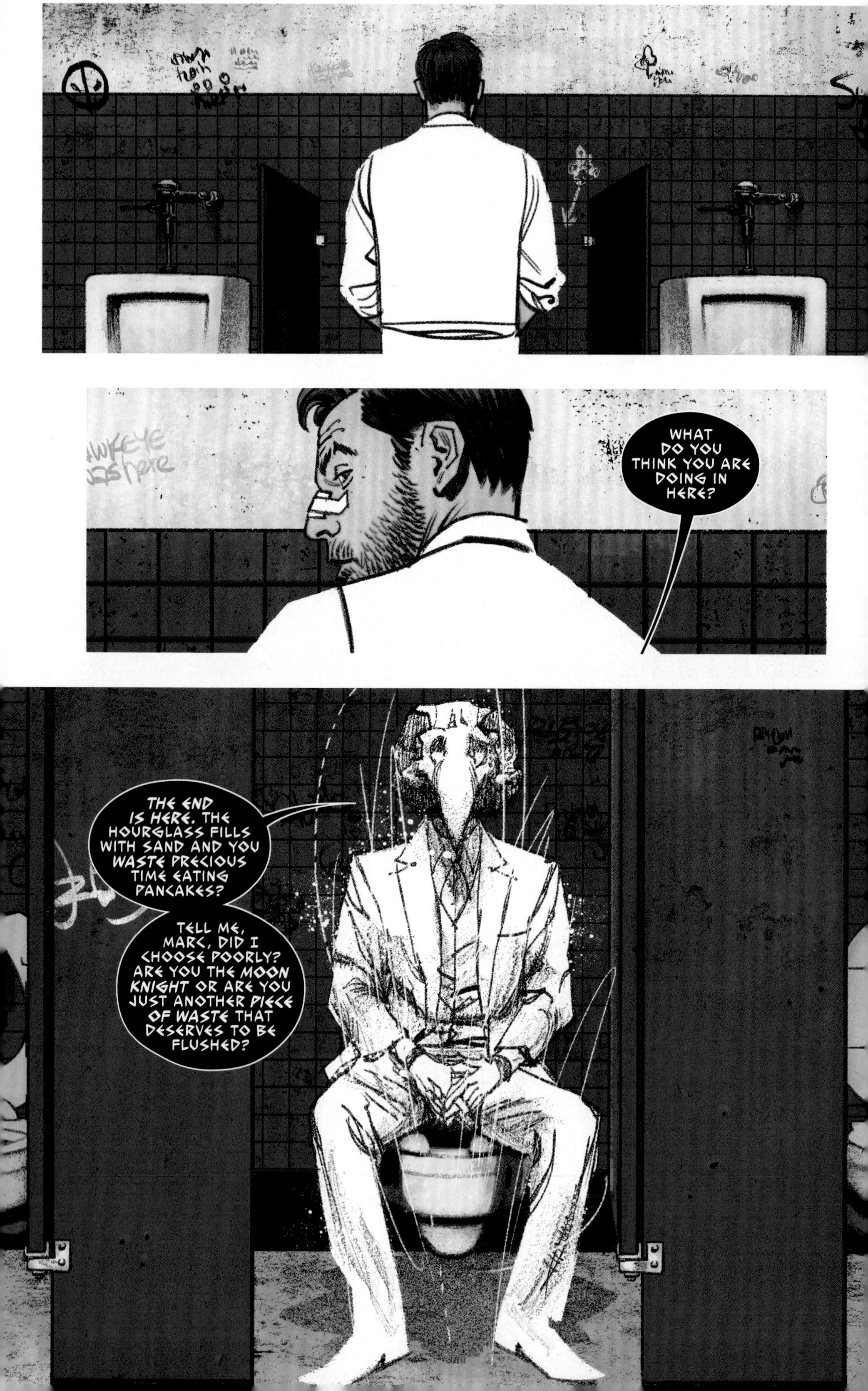
WHAT DO YOU THINK YOU ARE DOING IN HERE?
THE END IS HERE. THE HOURGLASS FILLS WITH SAND AND YOU WASTE PRECIOUS TIME EATING PANCAKES?
TELL ME, MARC, DID I CHOOSE POORLY? ARE YOU THE MOON KNIGHT OR ARE YOU JUST ANOTHER PIECE OF WASTE THAT DESERVES TO BE FLUSHED?

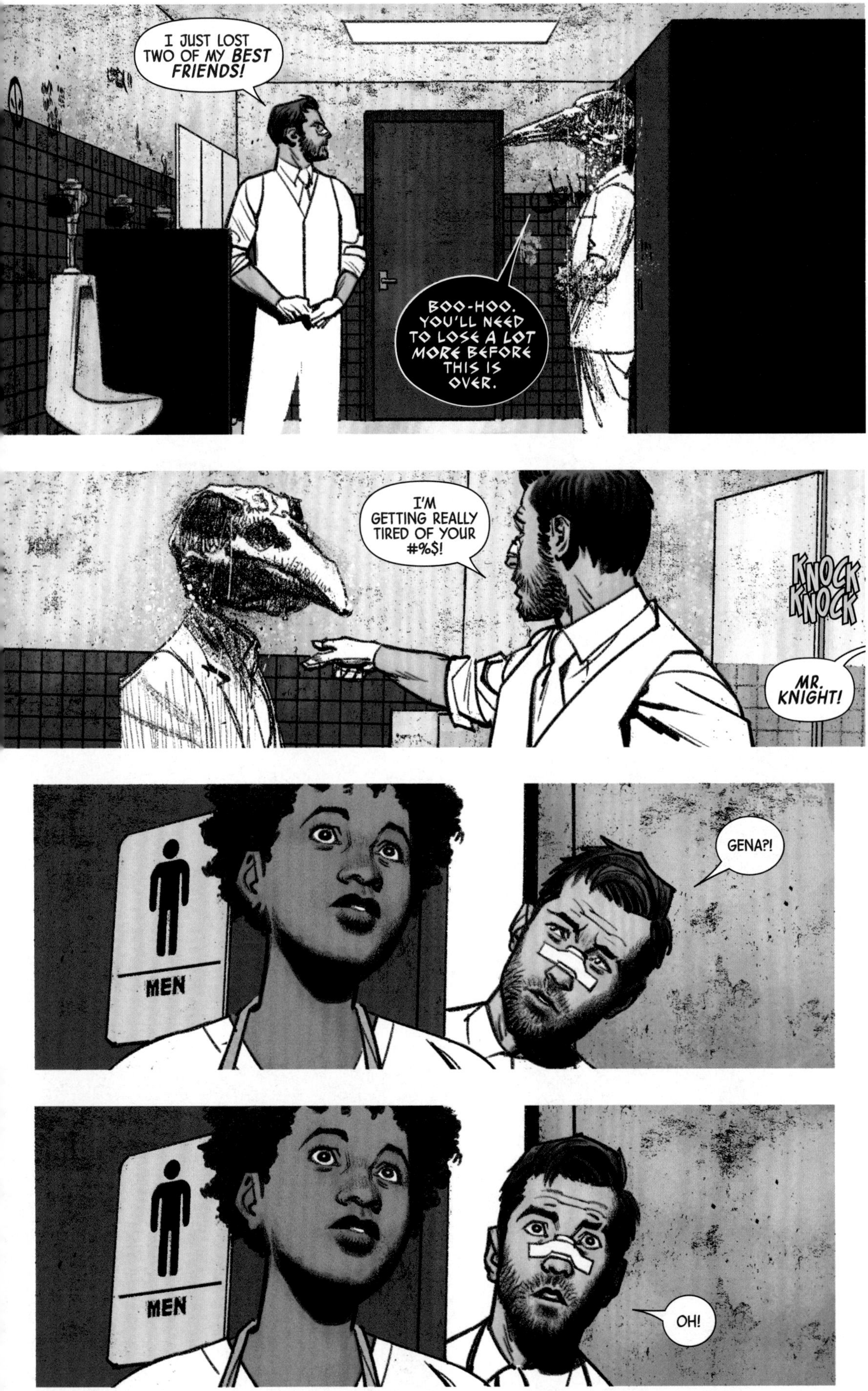
I JUST LOST TWO OF MY BEST FRIENDS!
BOO-HOO. YOU'LL NEED TO LOSE A LOT MORE BEFORE THIS IS OVER.
I'M GETTING REALLY TIRED OF YOUR #%$!
KNOCK KNOCK
MR. KNIGHT!
MEN
GENA?!
MEN
OH!

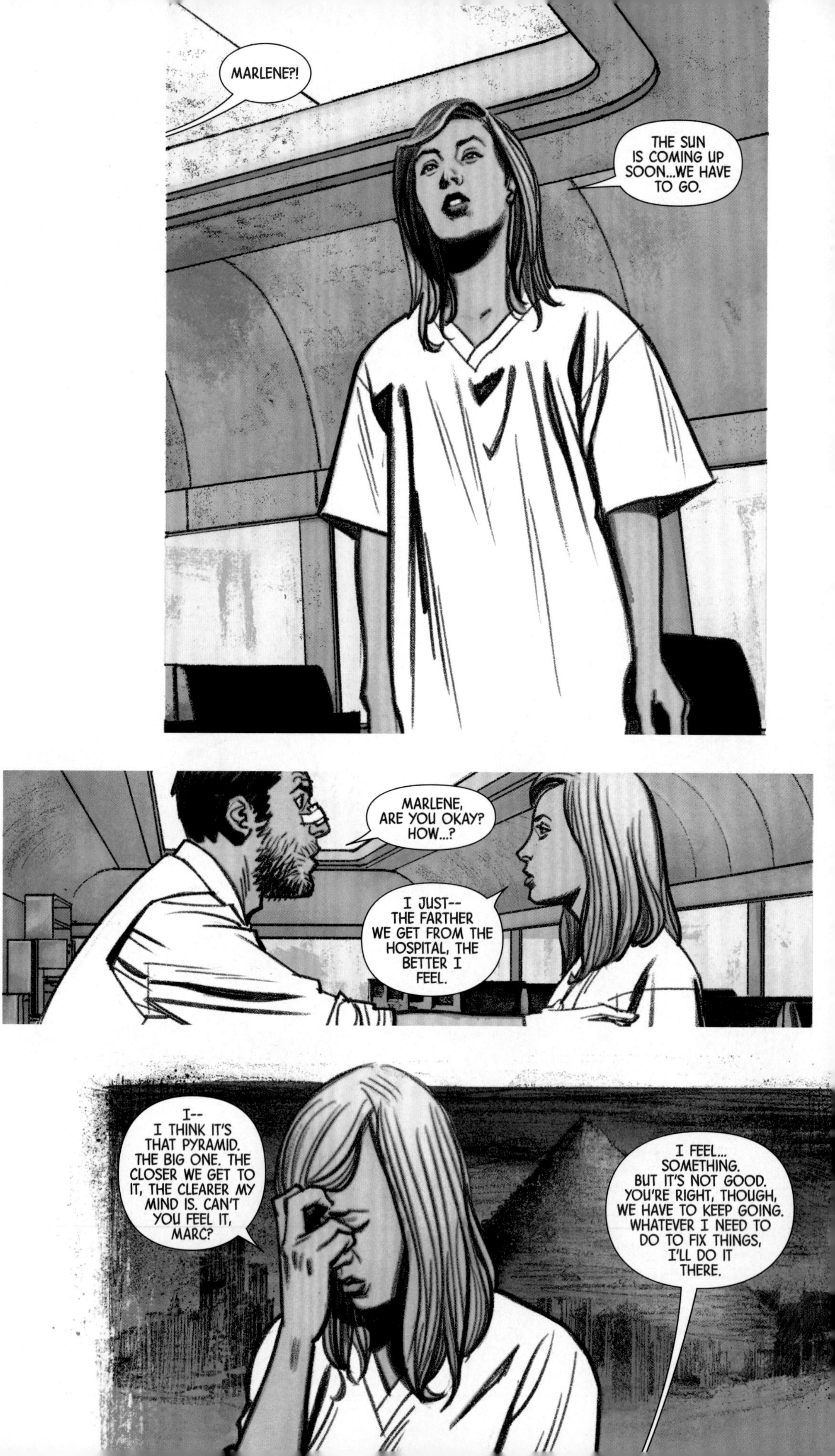
MARLENE?!
THE SUN IS COMING UP SOON...WE HAVE TO GO.
MARLENE, ARE YOU OKAY? HOW...?
I JUST-- THE FARTHER WE GET FROM THE HOSPITAL, THE BETTER I FEEL.
I-- I THINK IT'S THAT PYRAMID. THE BIG ONE. THE CLOSER WE GET TO IT, THE CLEARER MY MIND IS. CAN'T YOU FEEL IT, MARC?
I FEEL... SOMETHING. BUT IT'S NOT GOOD. YOU'RE RIGHT, THOUGH, WE HAVE TO KEEP GOING. WHATEVER I NEED TO DO TO FIX THINGS, I'LL DO IT THERE.

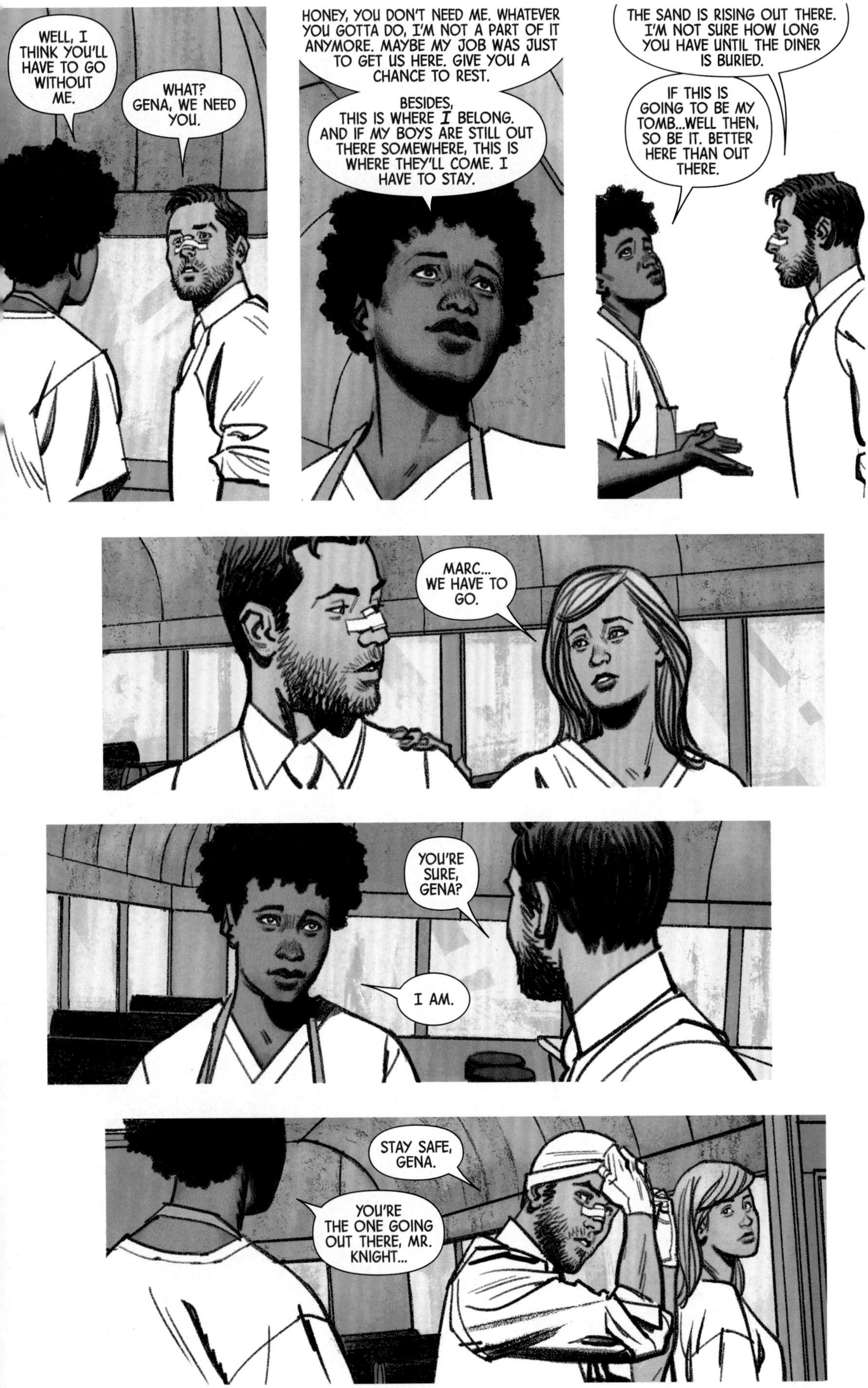
WELL, I THINK YOU'LL HAVE TO GO WITHOUT ME.
WHAT? GENA, WE NEED YOU.
HONEY, YOU DON'T NEED ME. WHATEVER YOU GOTTA DO, I'M NOT A PART OF IT ANYMORE. MAYBE MY JOB WAS JUST TO GET US HERE. GIVE YOU A CHANCE TO REST.
BESIDES, THIS IS WHERE *I* BELONG. AND IF MY BOYS ARE STILL OUT THERE SOMEWHERE, THIS IS WHERE THEY'LL COME. I HAVE TO STAY.
THE SAND IS RISING OUT THERE. I'M NOT SURE HOW LONG YOU HAVE UNTIL THE DINER IS BURIED.
IF THIS IS GOING TO BE MY TOMB...WELL THEN, SO BE IT. BETTER HERE THAN OUT THERE.
MARC... WE HAVE TO GO.
YOU'RE SURE, GENA?
I AM.
STAY SAFE, GENA.
YOU'RE THE ONE GOING OUT THERE, MR. KNIGHT...

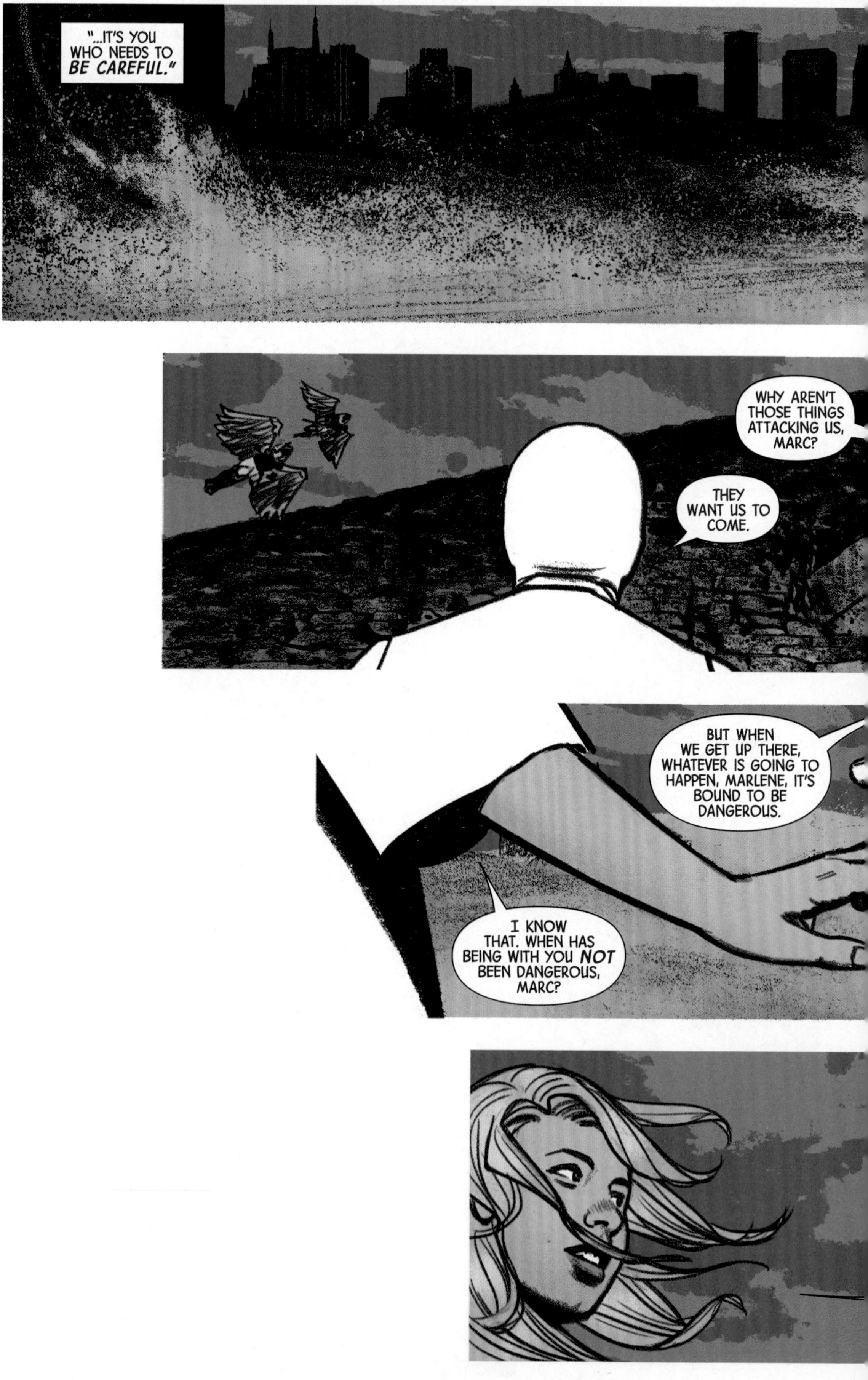
"...IT'S YOU WHO NEEDS TO BE CAREFUL."
WHY AREN'T THOSE THINGS ATTACKING US, MARC?
THEY WANT US TO COME.
BUT WHEN WE GET UP THERE, WHATEVER IS GOING TO HAPPEN, MARLENE, IT'S BOUND TO BE DANGEROUS.
I KNOW THAT. WHEN HAS BEING WITH YOU NOT BEEN DANGEROUS, MARC?

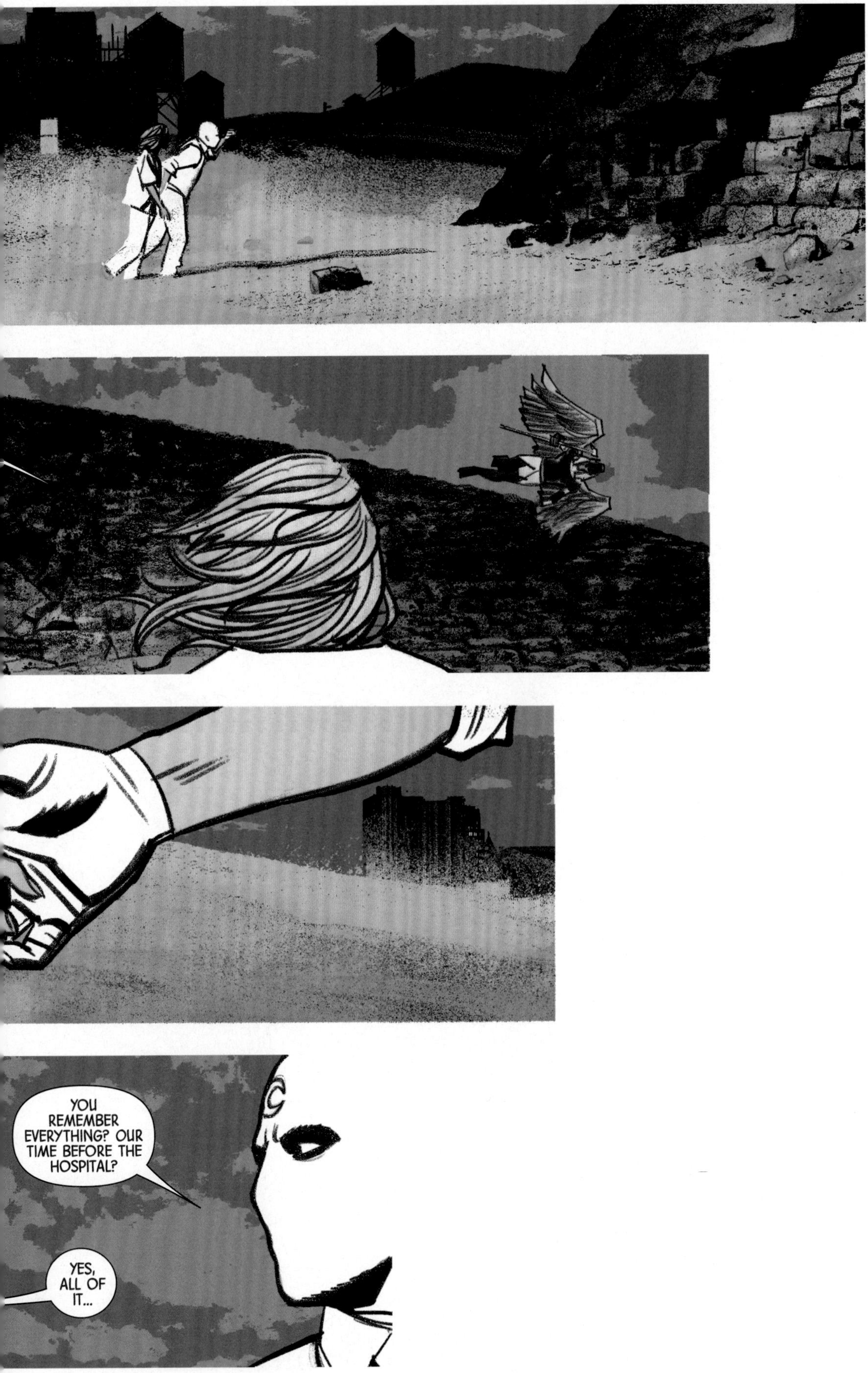
YOU REMEMBER EVERYTHING? OUR TIME BEFORE THE HOSPITAL?
YES, ALL OF IT...

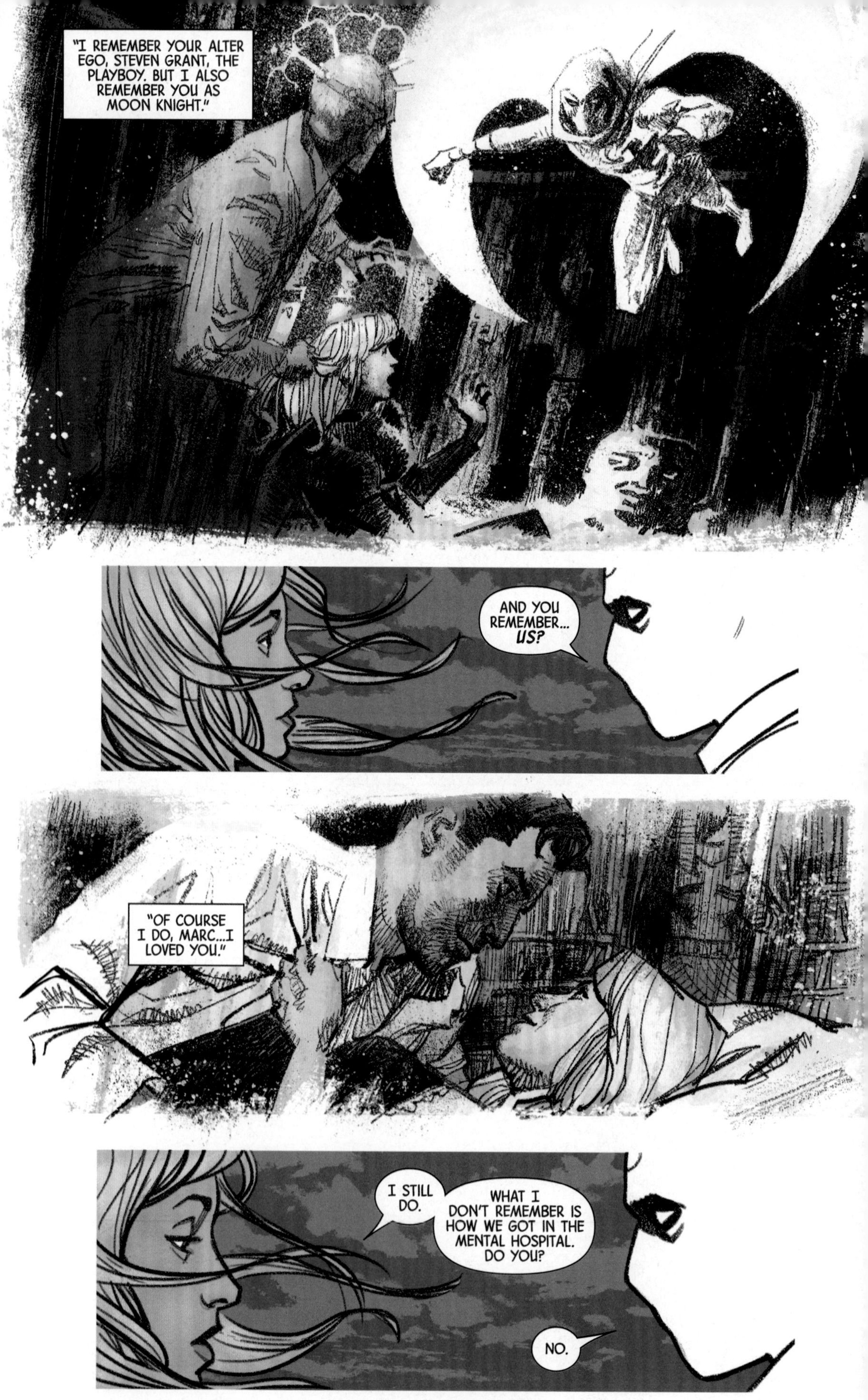
"I REMEMBER YOUR ALTER EGO, STEVEN GRANT, THE PLAYBOY. BUT I ALSO REMEMBER YOU AS MOON KNIGHT."
AND YOU REMEMBER... US?
"OF COURSE I DO, MARC...I LOVED YOU."
I STILL DO.
WHAT I DON'T REMEMBER IS HOW WE GOT IN THE MENTAL HOSPITAL. DO YOU?
NO.

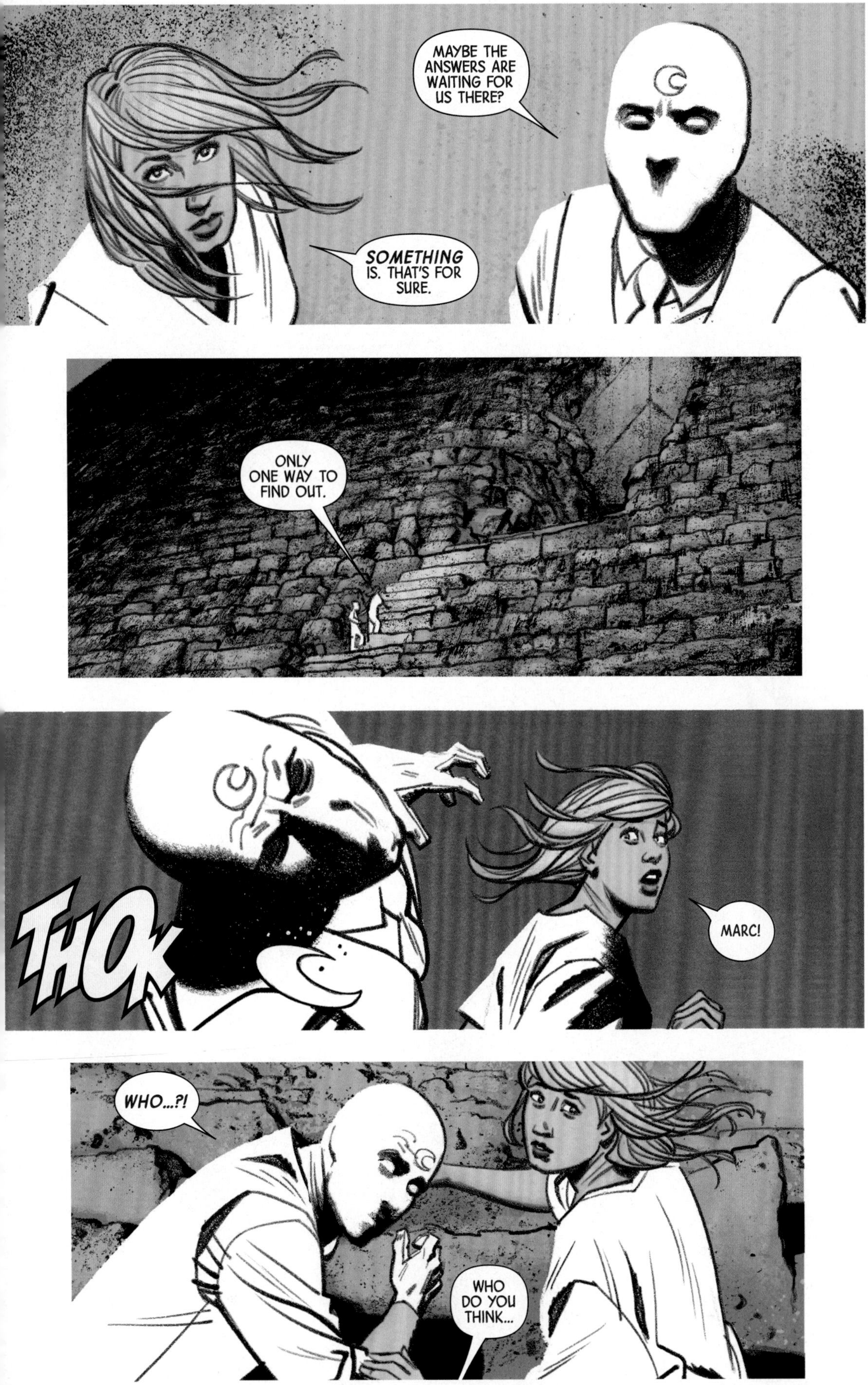
MAYBE THE ANSWERS ARE WAITING FOR US THERE?
SOMETHING IS. THAT'S FOR SURE.
ONLY ONE WAY TO FIND OUT.
THOK
MARC!
WHO...?!
WHO DO YOU THINK...

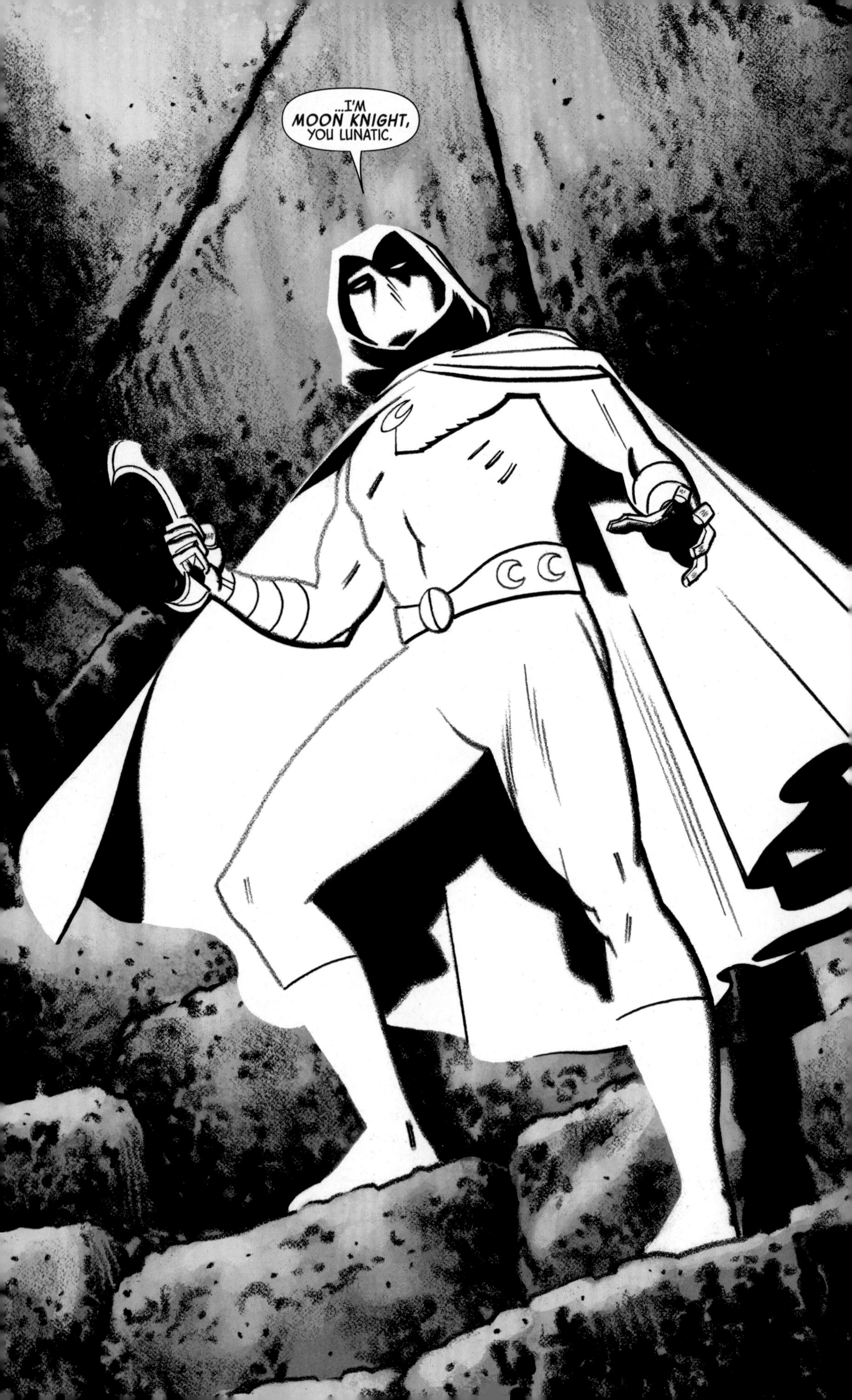
...I'M MOON KNIGHT, YOU LUNATIC.

Moon Knight 001
variant edition
rated T+
$4.99 US
direct edition
MARVEL.com

series 1

MARVEL

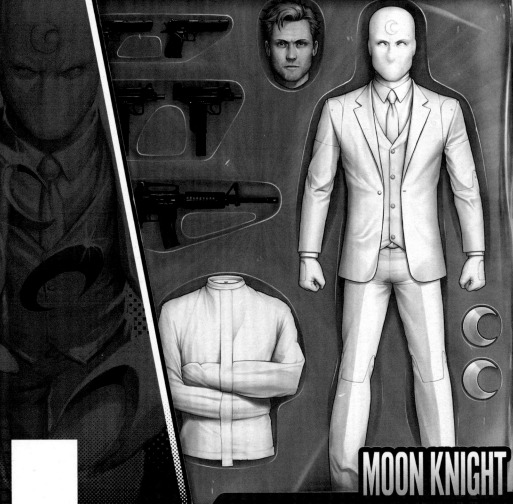

MOON KNIGHT
MOON KNIGHT
fist of khonshu

#1 ACTION FIGURE VARIANT BY JOHN TYLER CHRISTOPHER

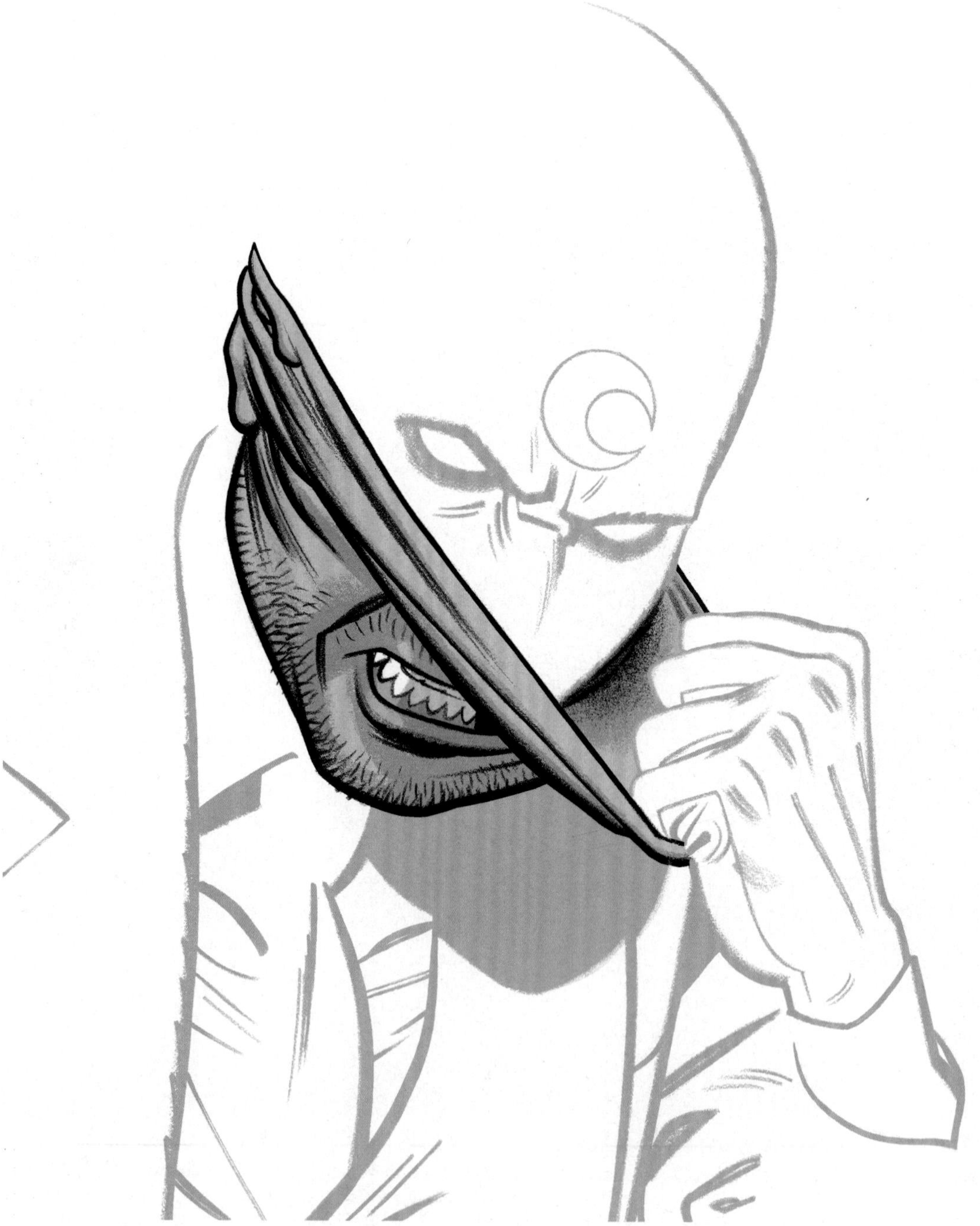

WELCOME TO NEW EGYPT
PART FIVE

5

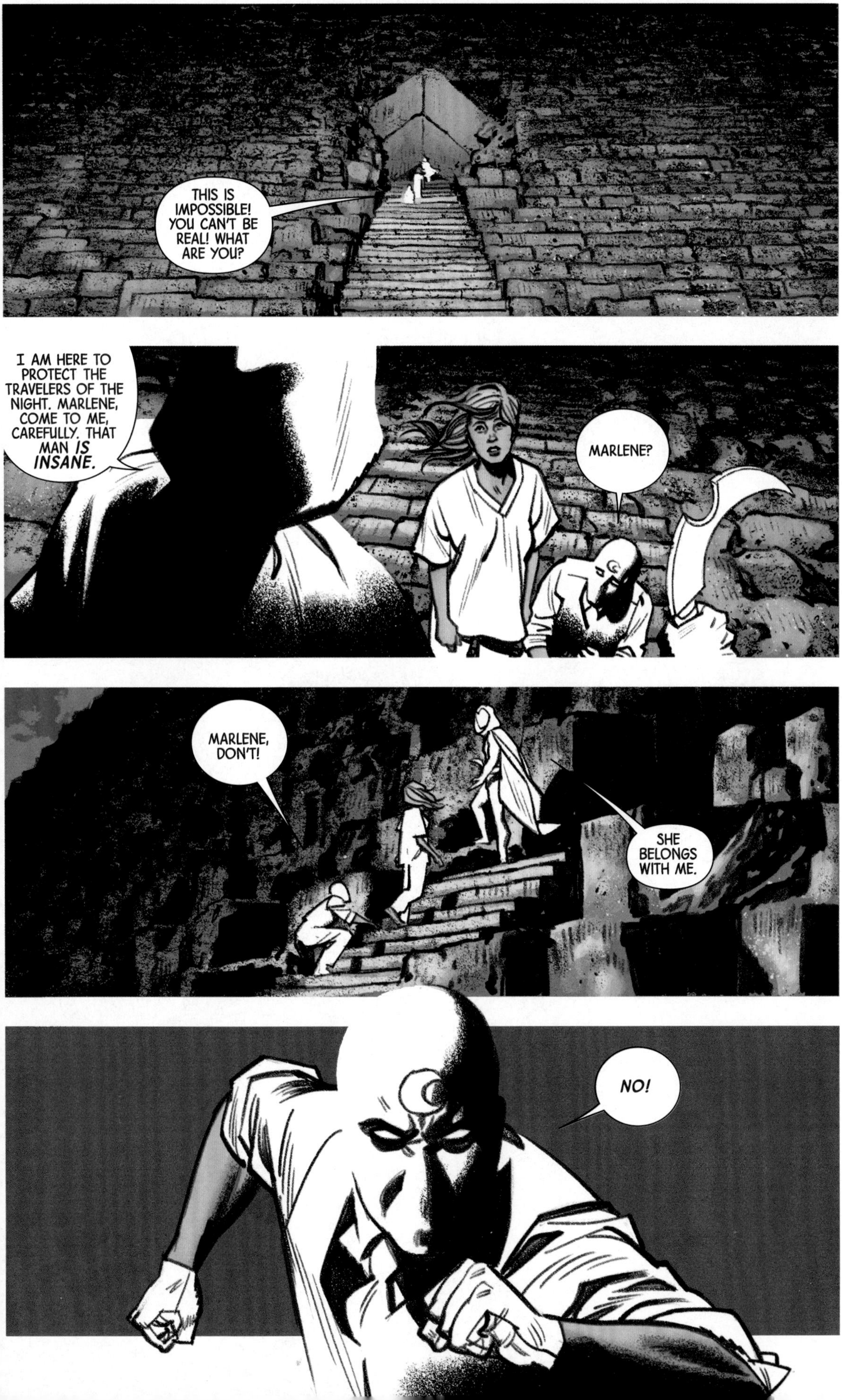
THIS IS IMPOSSIBLE! YOU CAN'T BE REAL! WHAT ARE YOU?
I AM HERE TO PROTECT THE TRAVELERS OF THE NIGHT. MARLENE, COME TO ME, CAREFULLY. THAT MAN *IS INSANE.*
MARLENE?
MARLENE, DON'T!
SHE BELONGS WITH ME.
NO!

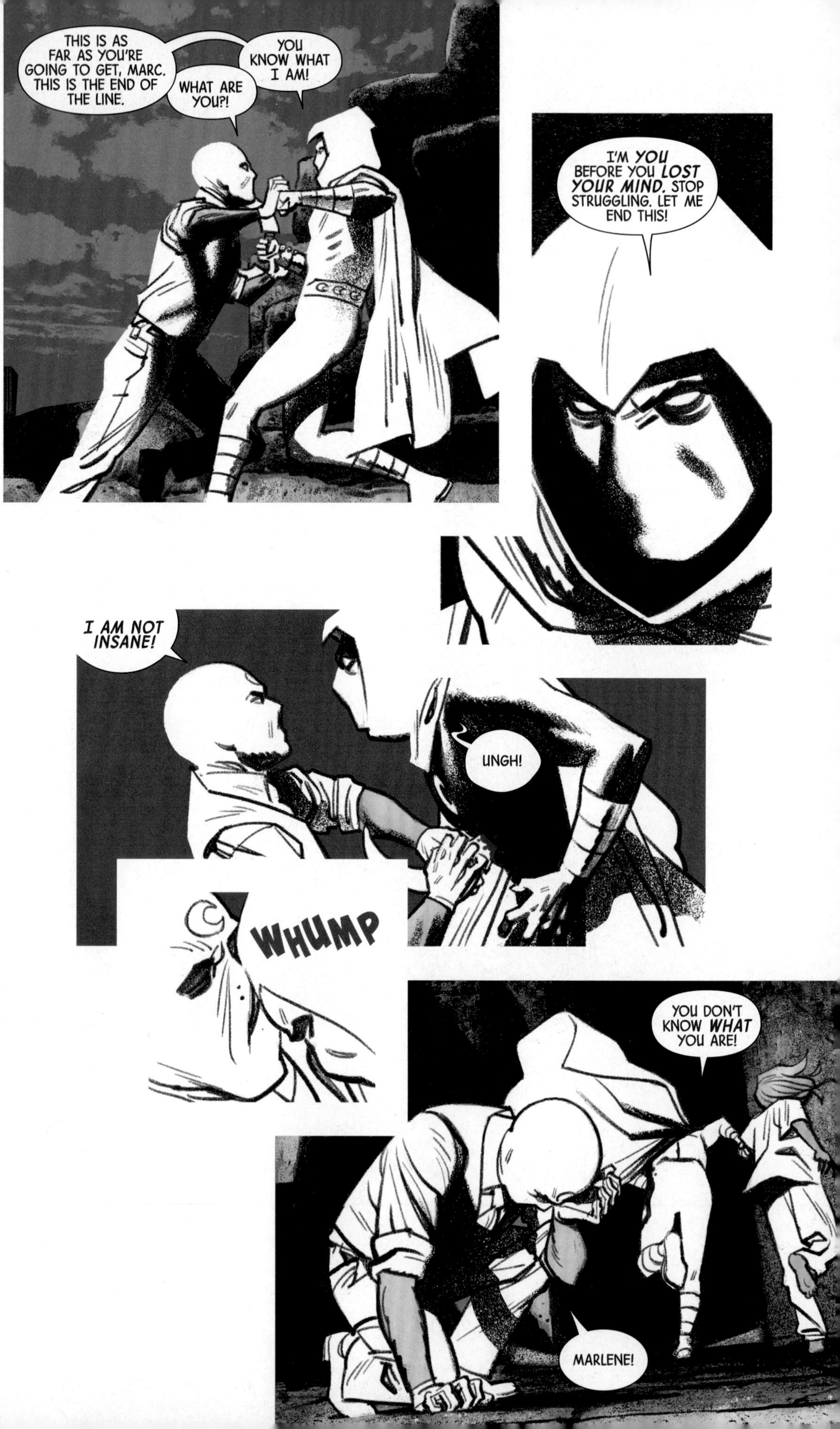
THIS IS AS FAR AS YOU'RE GOING TO GET, MARC. THIS IS THE END OF THE LINE.
WHAT ARE YOU?!
YOU KNOW WHAT I AM!
I'M YOU BEFORE YOU LOST YOUR MIND. STOP STRUGGLING. LET ME END THIS!
I AM NOT INSANE!
UNGH!
WHUMP
YOU DON'T KNOW WHAT YOU ARE!
MARLENE!

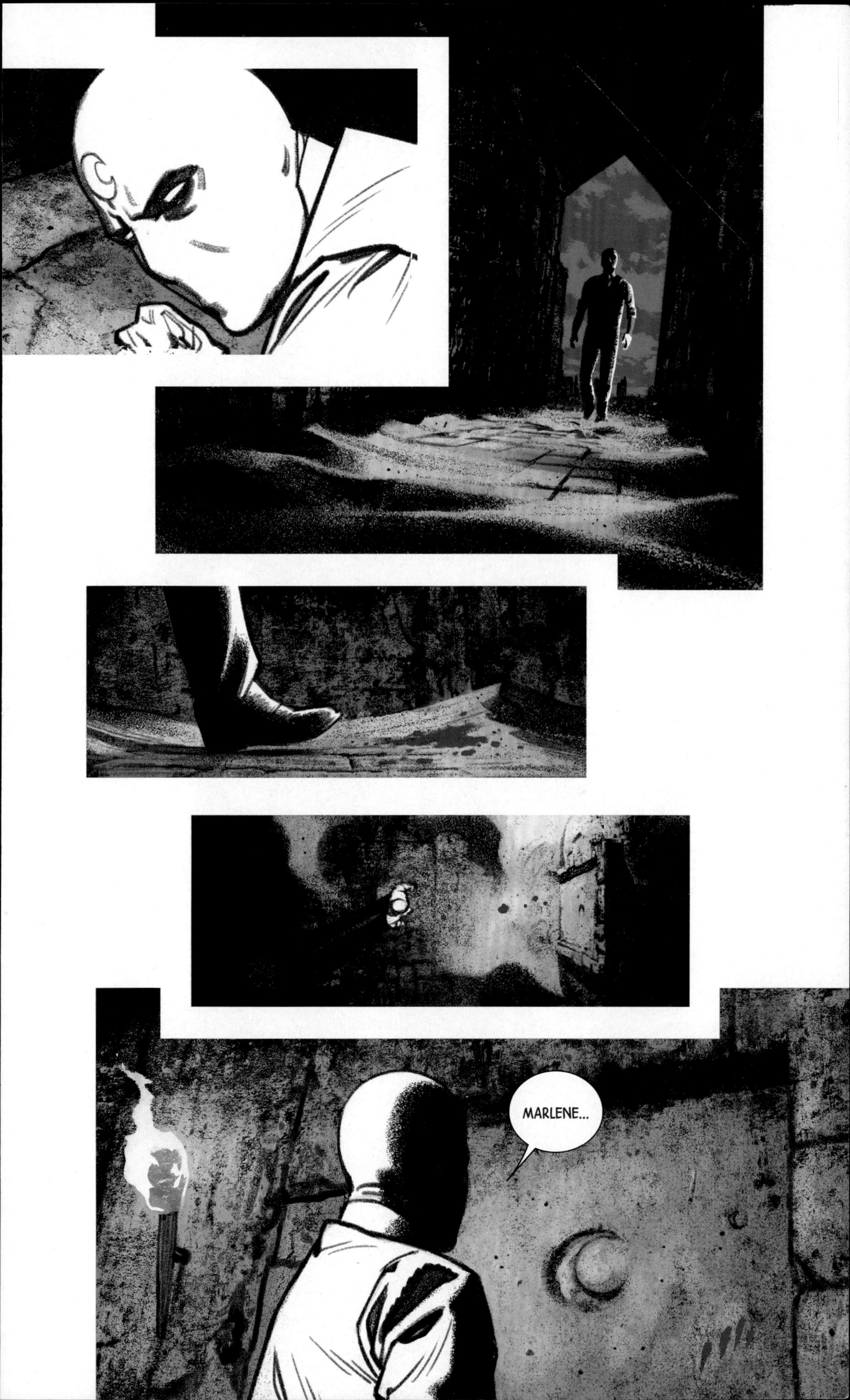
MARLENE...

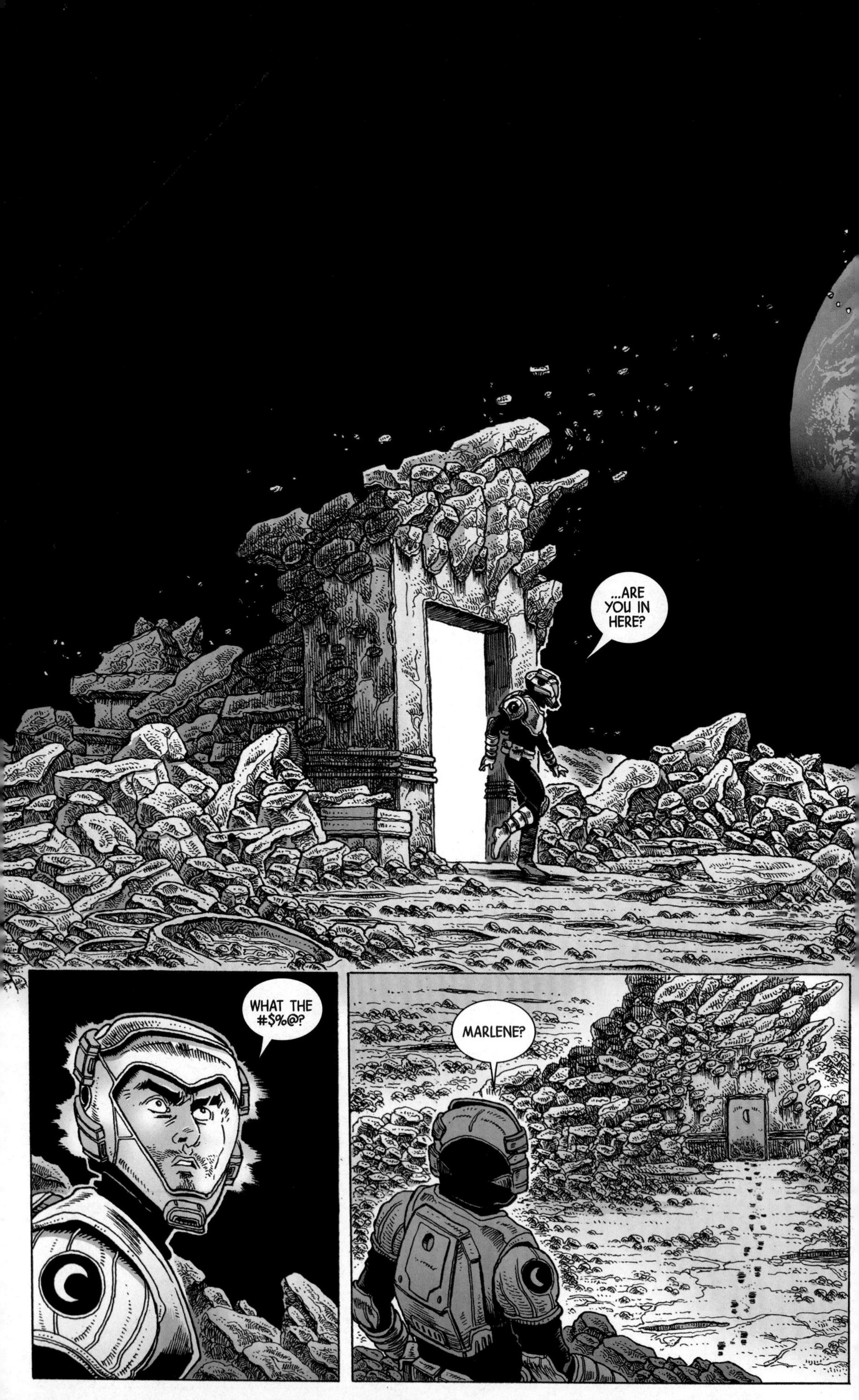
...ARE YOU IN HERE?
WHAT THE #$%@?
MARLENE?

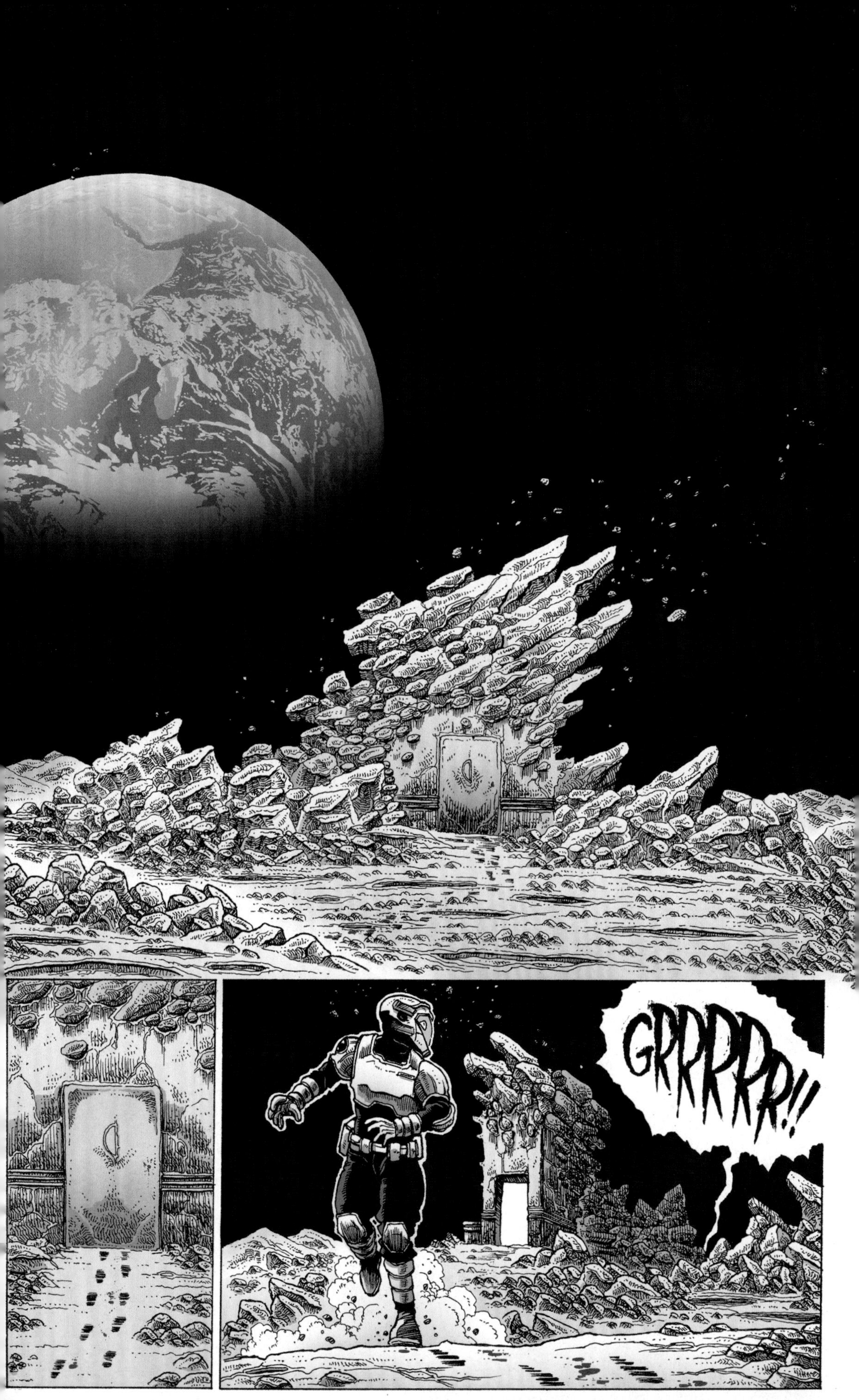
GRRRRRR!!

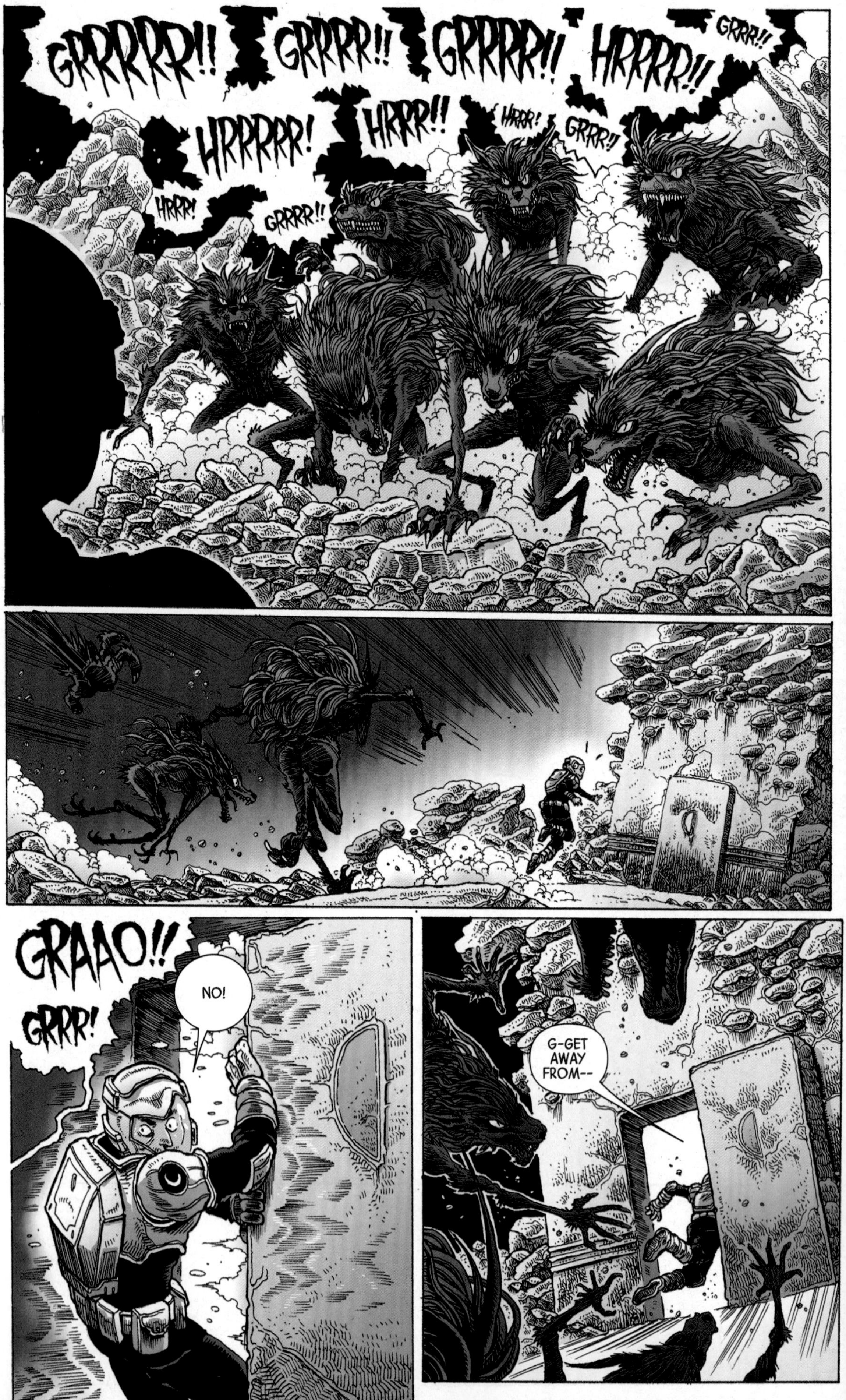
GRRRRR!!
GRRRR!!
GRRRR!!
HRRRR!!
GRRR!!
HRRRRR!
HRRR!!
HRRR!
GRRR!!
HRRR!
GRRRR!!
GRAAO!!
GRRR!
NO!
G-GET AWAY FROM--

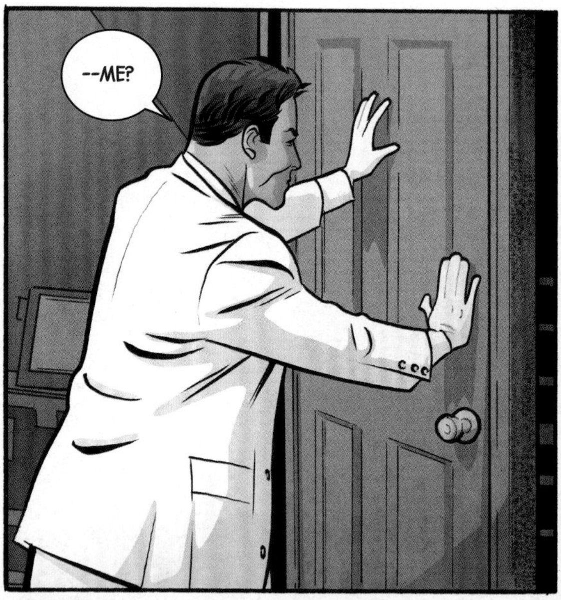
--ME?

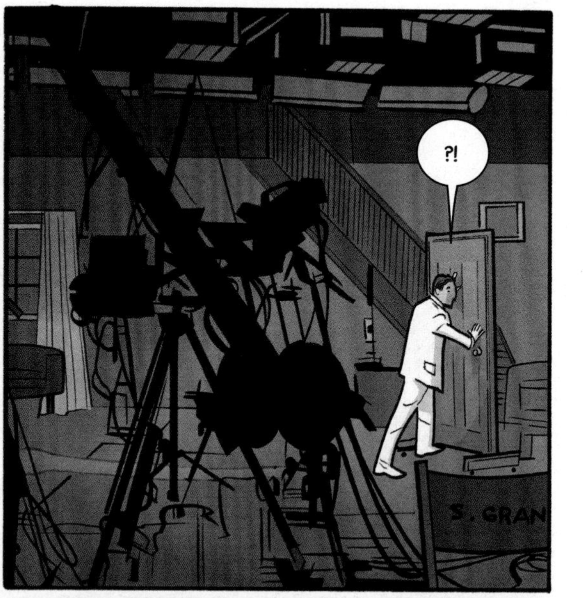
?!
S. GRAN

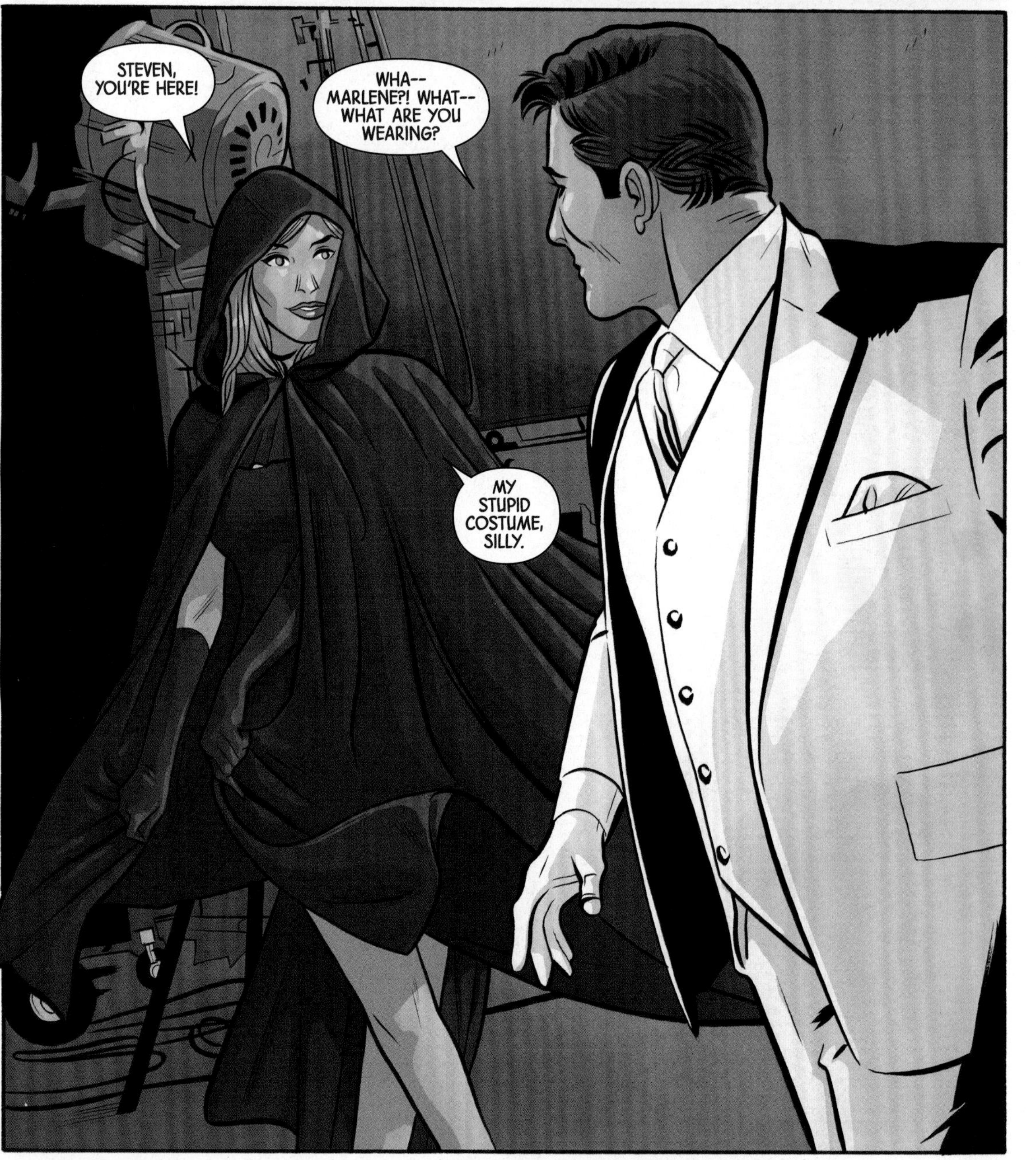
STEVEN, YOU'RE HERE!
WHA-- MARLENE?! WHAT-- WHAT ARE YOU WEARING?
MY STUPID COSTUME, SILLY.

I--I DON'T UNDERSTAND.

YOU WILL. THERE IS ONE THING I NEED TO TELL YOU, THOUGH.

WHAT?

YOU SHOULD GET GOING. *THEY* WILL BE HERE ANY SECOND.

WHO?

WELL, WELL, BILLY. LOOK WHO WE FOUND!

OUR LUCKY DAY, BOBBY!

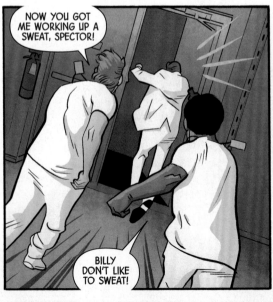

NOW YOU GOT ME WORKING UP A SWEAT, SPECTOR!

BILLY DON'T LIKE TO SWEAT!

GONNA HAVE TO TEACH YOU A LESSON!

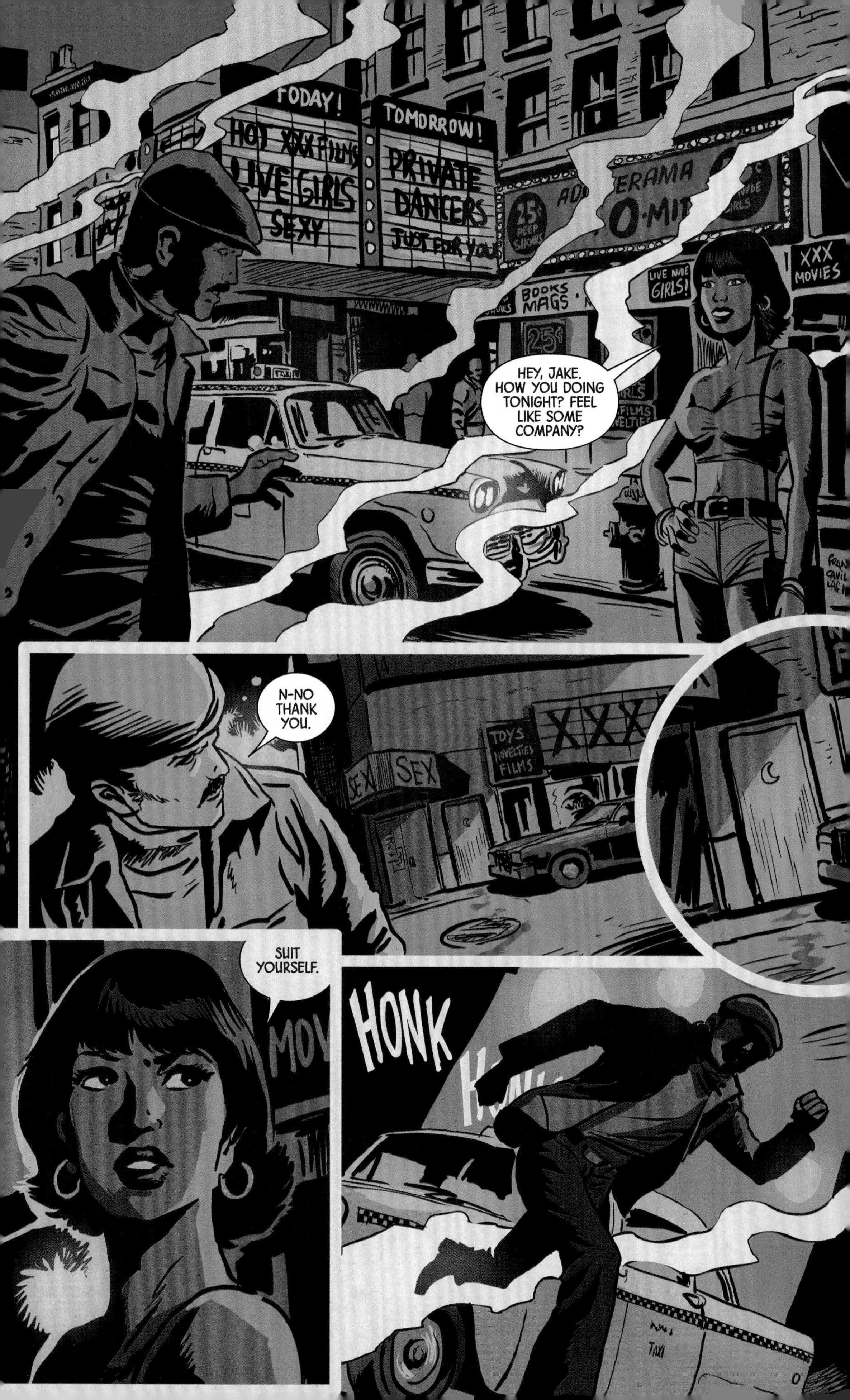
TODAY!
HOT XXX FILMS
LIVE GIRLS
SEXY
TOMORROW!
PRIVATE DANCERS
JUST FOR YOU
25¢ PEEP SHOWS
BOOKS MAGS
LIVE NUDE GIRLS!
XXX MOVIES
HEY, JAKE. HOW YOU DOING TONIGHT? FEEL LIKE SOME COMPANY?
N-NO THANK YOU.
TOYS NOVELTIES FILMS
SEX SEX
XXX
SUIT YOURSELF.
HONK

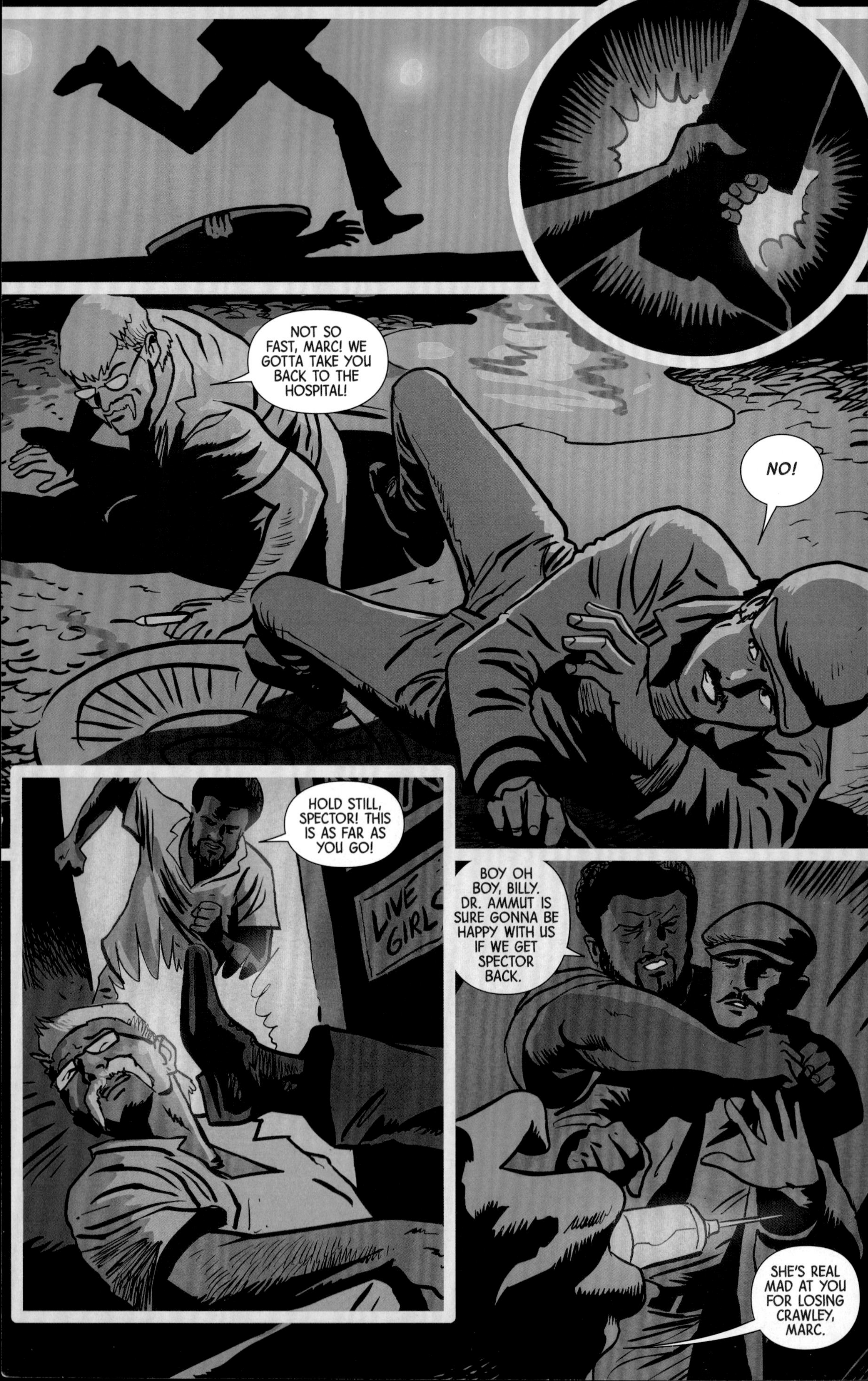
NOT SO FAST, MARC! WE GOTTA TAKE YOU BACK TO THE HOSPITAL!
NO!
HOLD STILL, SPECTOR! THIS IS AS FAR AS YOU GO!
LIVE GIRLS
BOY OH BOY, BILLY. DR. AMMUT IS SURE GONNA BE HAPPY WITH US IF WE GET SPECTOR BACK.
SHE'S REAL MAD AT YOU FOR LOSING CRAWLEY, MARC.

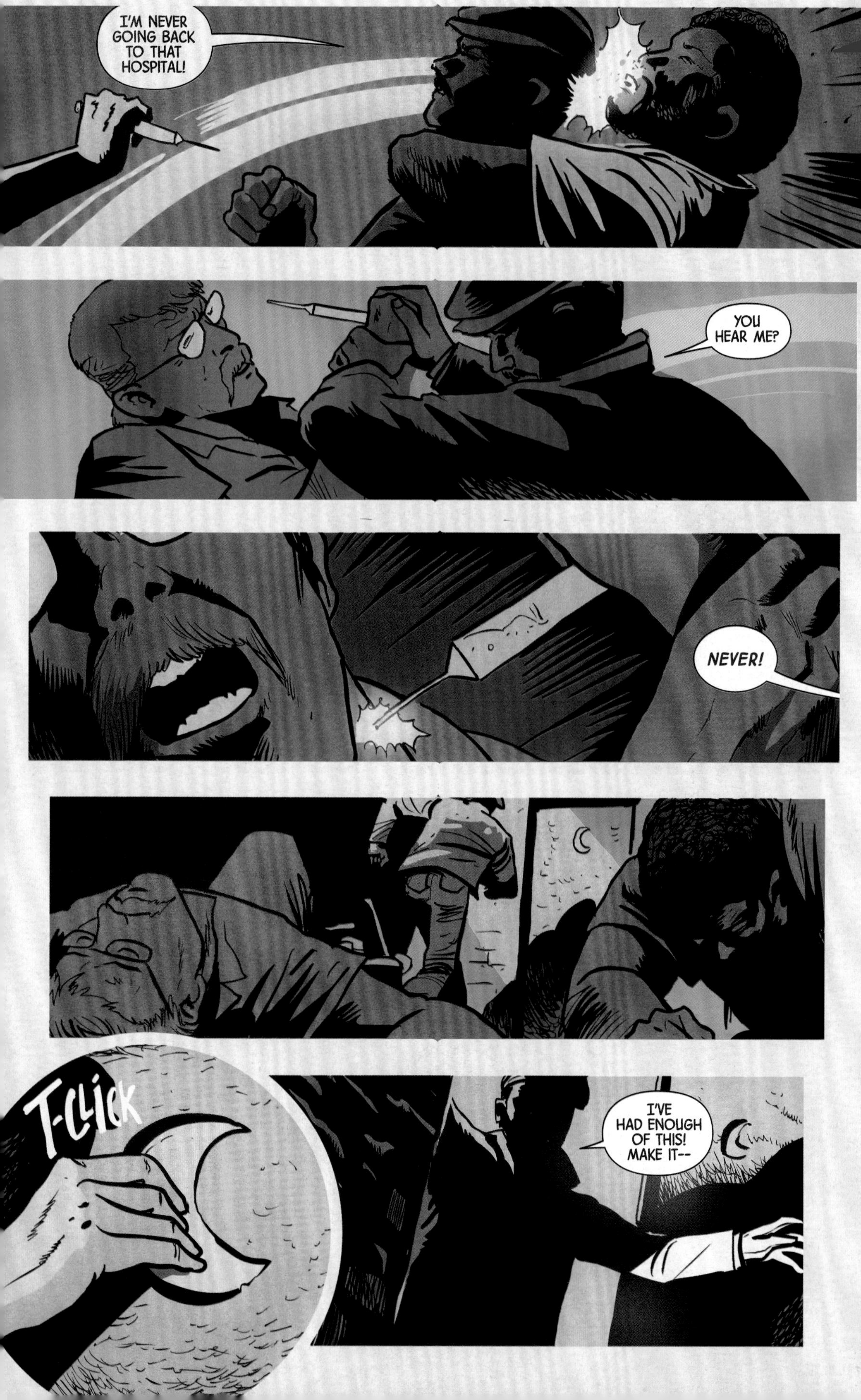
I'M NEVER GOING BACK TO THAT HOSPITAL!
YOU HEAR ME?
NEVER!
T-CLICK
I'VE HAD ENOUGH OF THIS! MAKE IT--

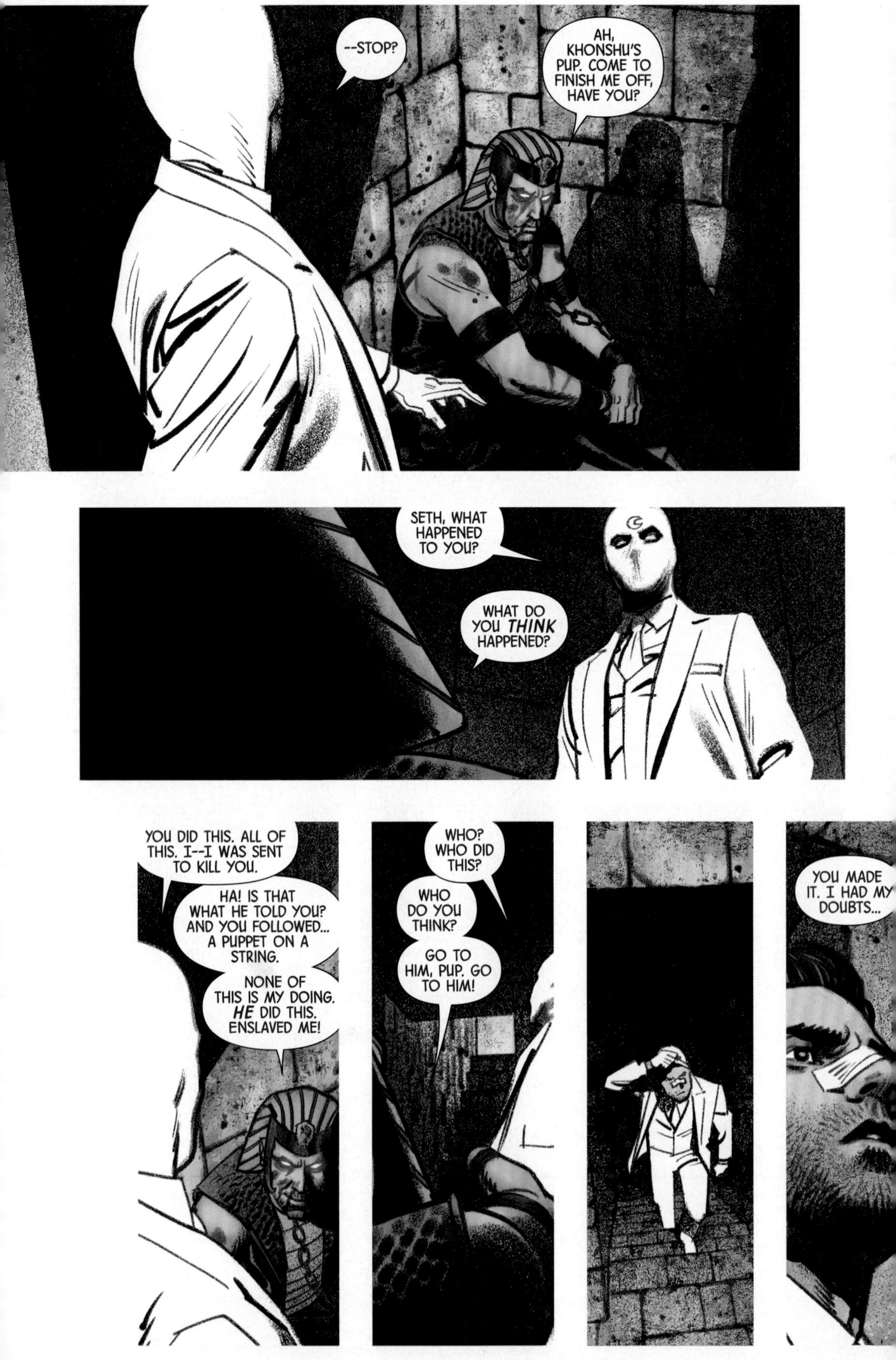

--STOP?
AH, KHONSHU'S PUP. COME TO FINISH ME OFF, HAVE YOU?
SETH, WHAT HAPPENED TO YOU?
WHAT DO YOU THINK HAPPENED?
YOU DID THIS. ALL OF THIS. I--I WAS SENT TO KILL YOU.
HA! IS THAT WHAT HE TOLD YOU? AND YOU FOLLOWED... A PUPPET ON A STRING.
NONE OF THIS IS MY DOING. HE DID THIS. ENSLAVED ME!
WHO? WHO DID THIS?
WHO DO YOU THINK?
GO TO HIM, PUP. GO TO HIM!
YOU MADE IT. I HAD MY DOUBTS...

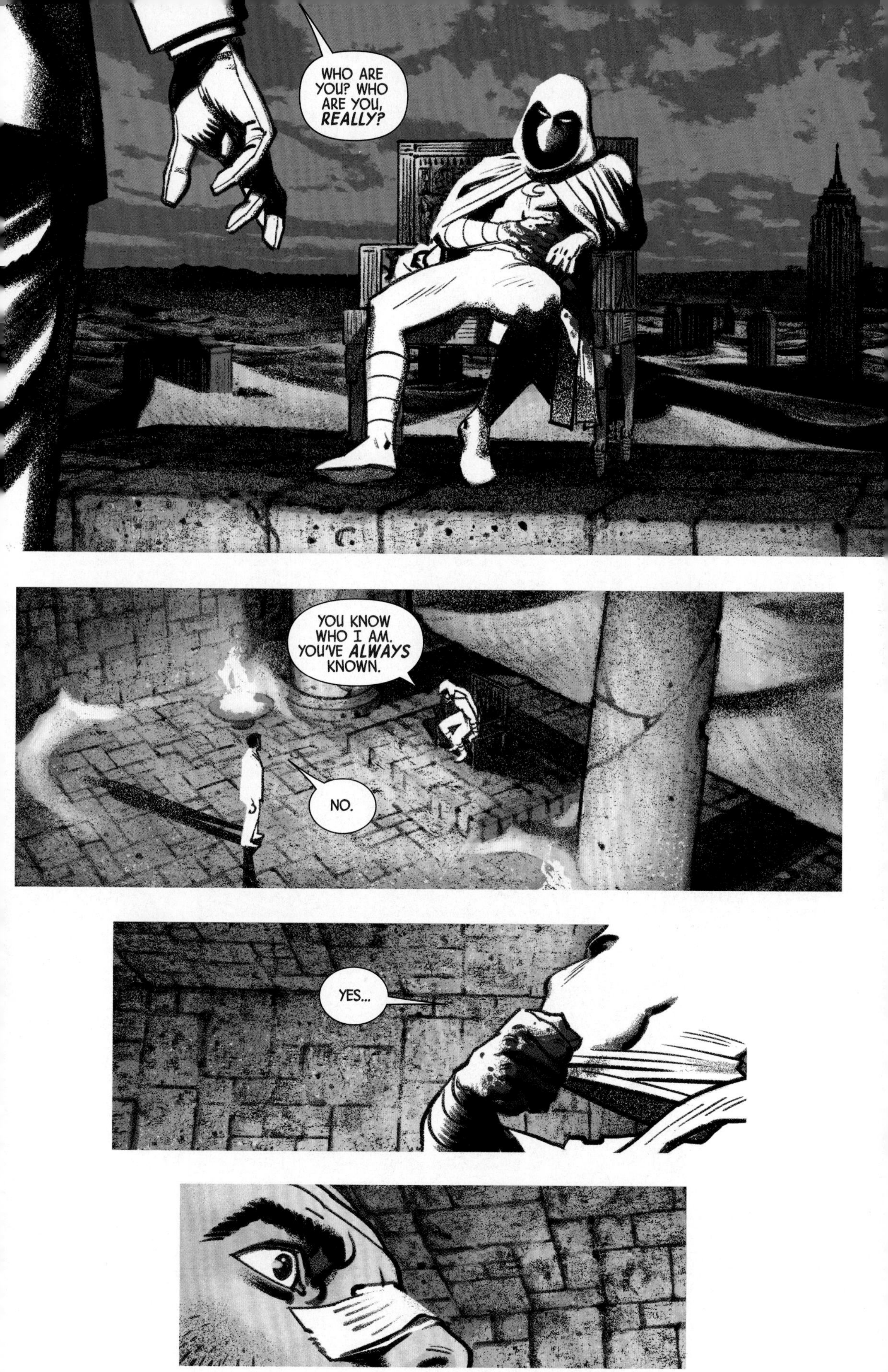
WHO ARE YOU? WHO ARE YOU, *REALLY?*
YOU KNOW WHO I AM. YOU'VE *ALWAYS* KNOWN.
NO.
YES...

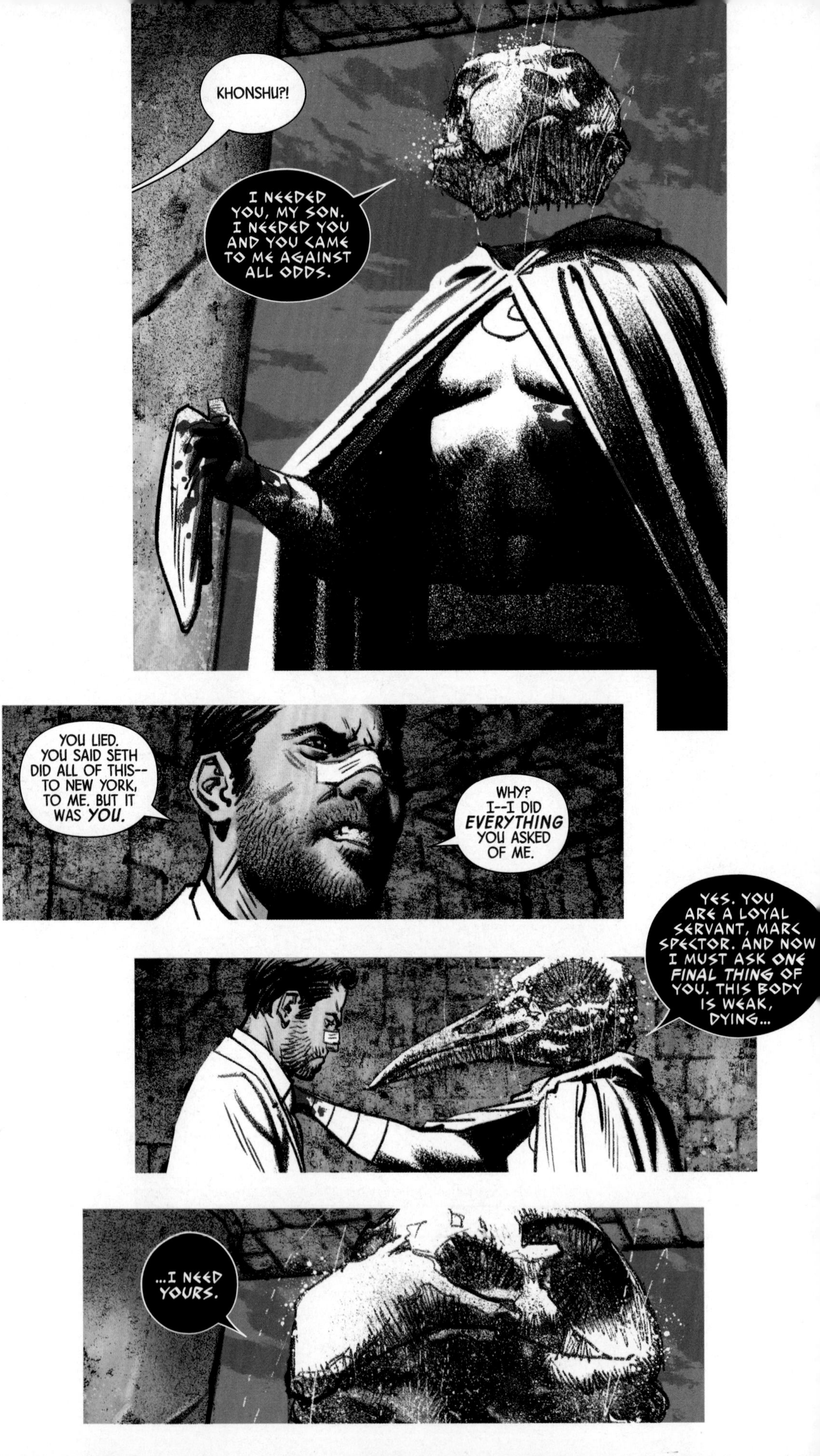
KHONSHU?!
I NEEDED YOU, MY SON. I NEEDED YOU AND YOU CAME TO ME AGAINST ALL ODDS.
YOU LIED. YOU SAID SETH DID ALL OF THIS-- TO NEW YORK, TO ME. BUT IT WAS YOU.
WHY? I--I DID EVERYTHING YOU ASKED OF ME.
YES. YOU ARE A LOYAL SERVANT, MARC SPECTOR. AND NOW I MUST ASK ONE FINAL THING OF YOU. THIS BODY IS WEAK, DYING...
...I NEED YOURS.

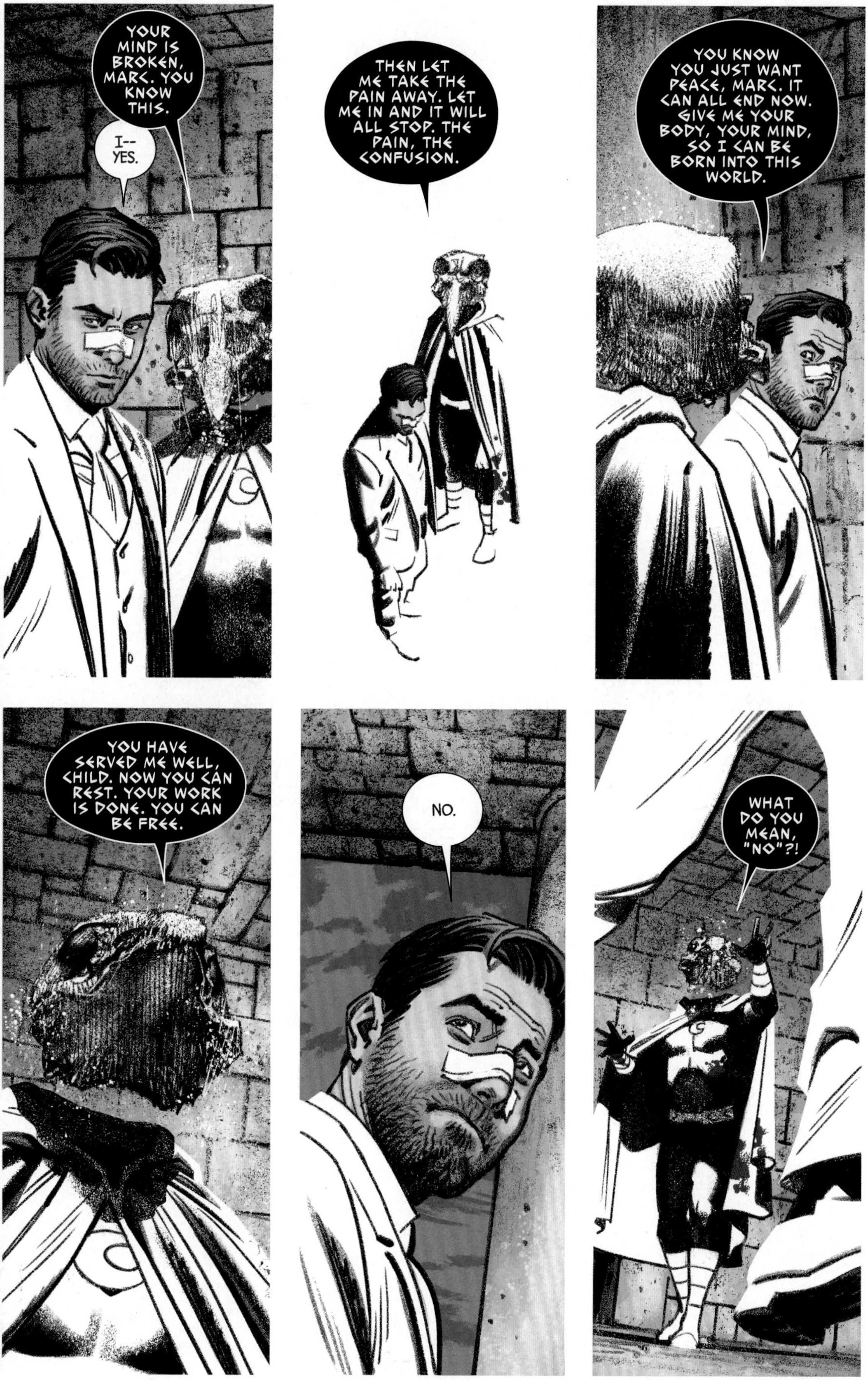
YOUR MIND IS BROKEN, MARC. YOU KNOW THIS.
I-- YES.
THEN LET ME TAKE THE PAIN AWAY. LET ME IN AND IT WILL ALL STOP. THE PAIN, THE CONFUSION.
YOU KNOW YOU JUST WANT PEACE, MARC. IT CAN ALL END NOW. GIVE ME YOUR BODY, YOUR MIND, SO I CAN BE BORN INTO THIS WORLD.
YOU HAVE SERVED ME WELL, CHILD. NOW YOU CAN REST. YOUR WORK IS DONE. YOU CAN BE FREE.
NO.
WHAT DO YOU MEAN, "NO"?!

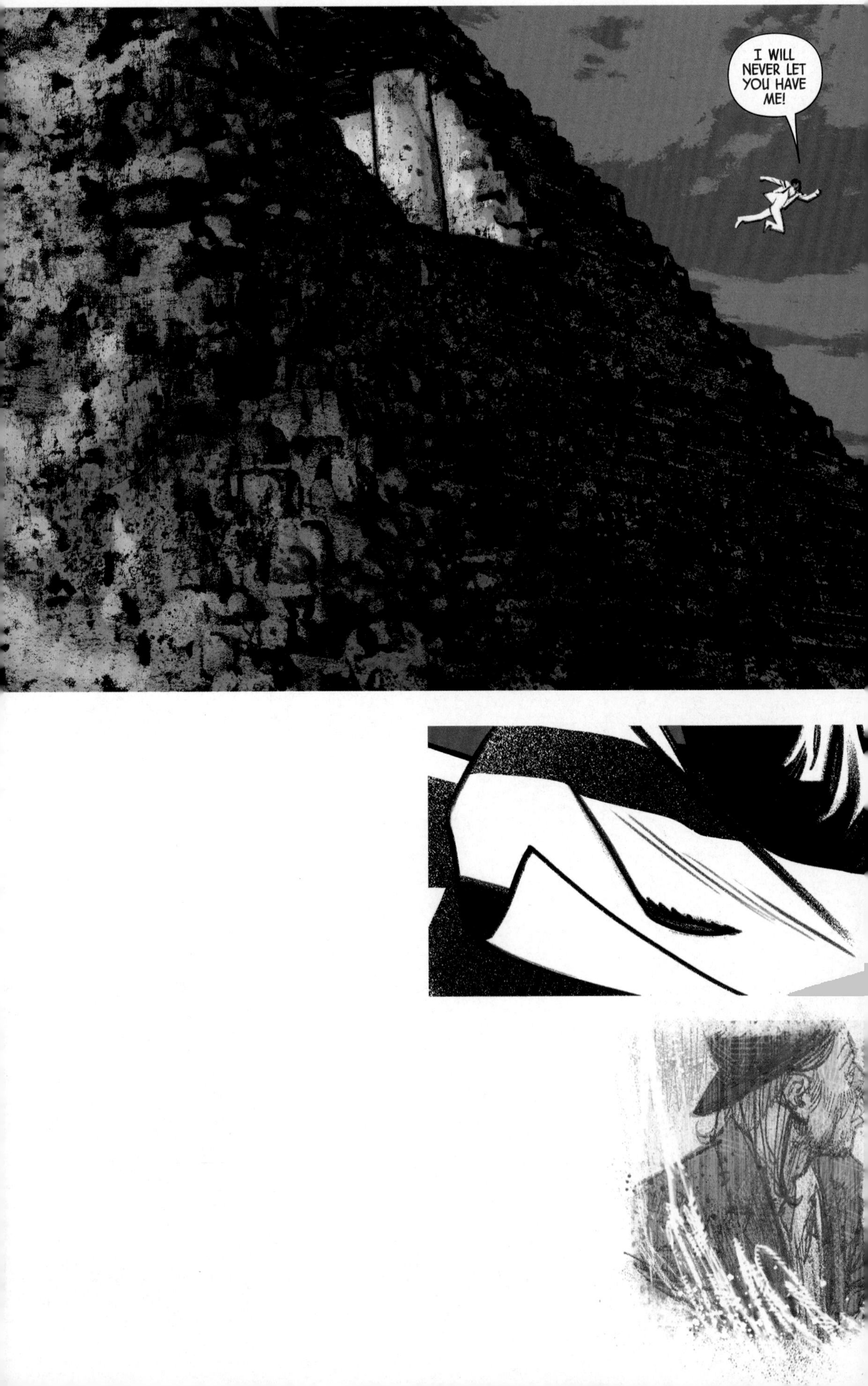
I WILL NEVER LET YOU HAVE ME!

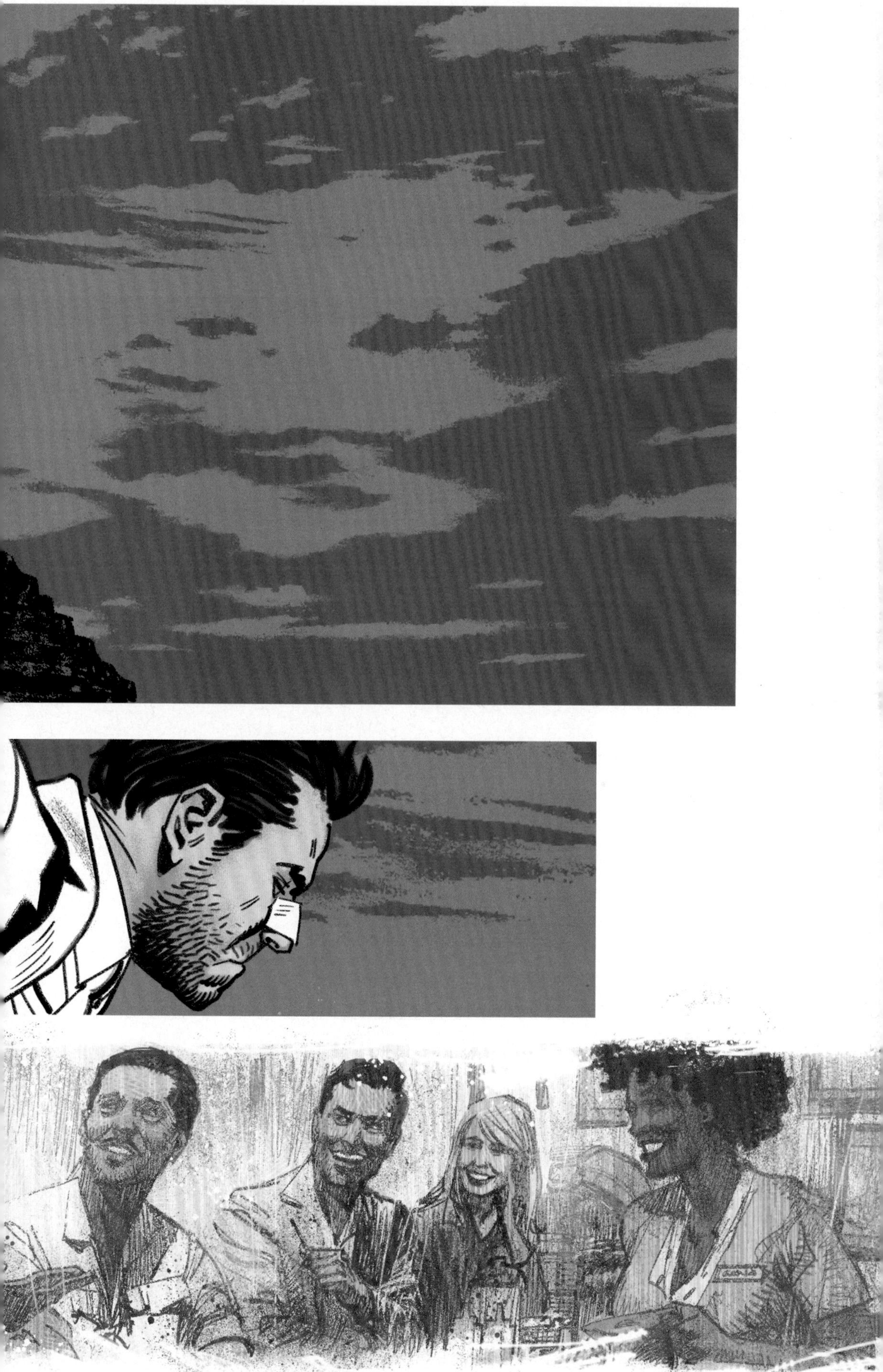

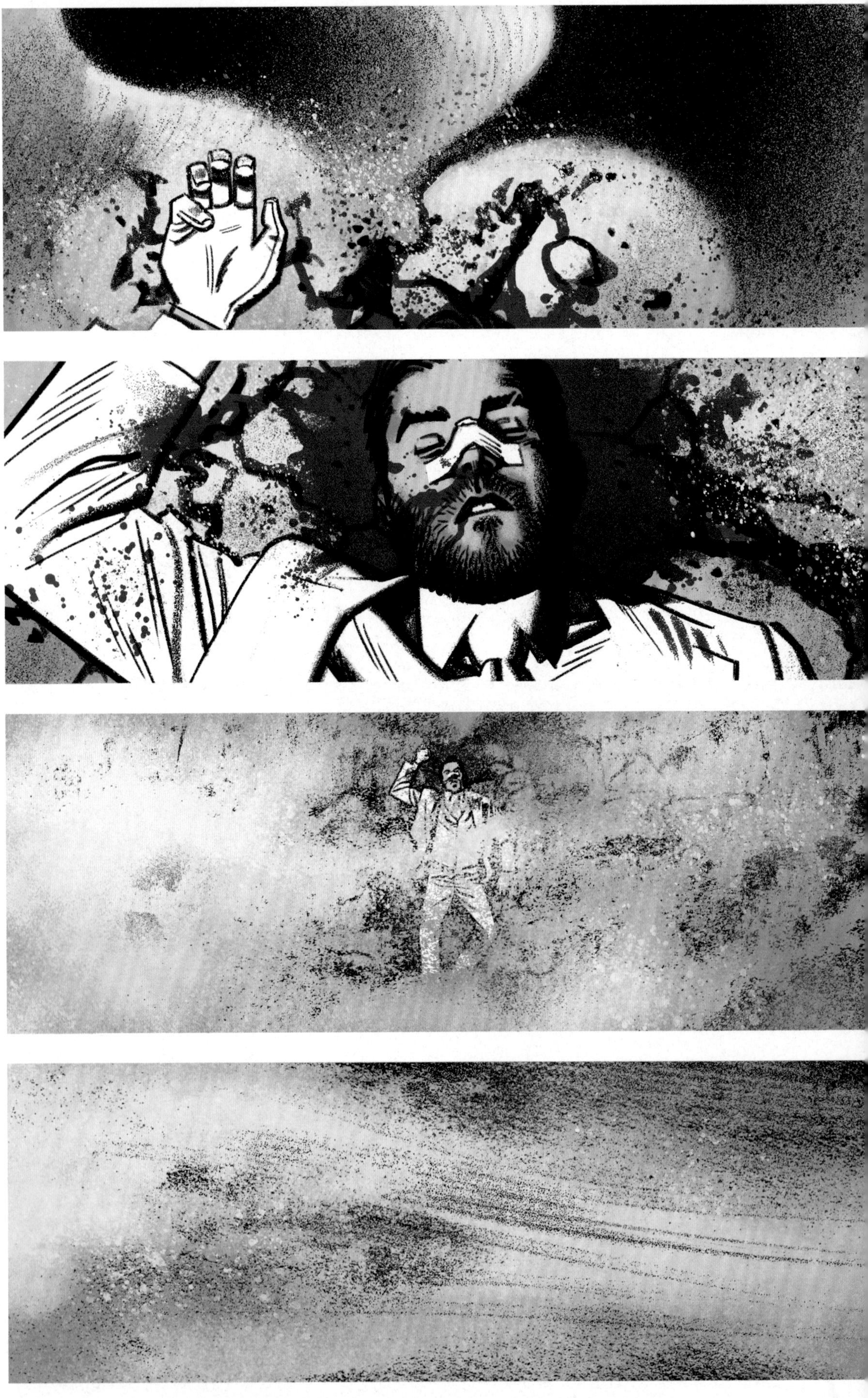

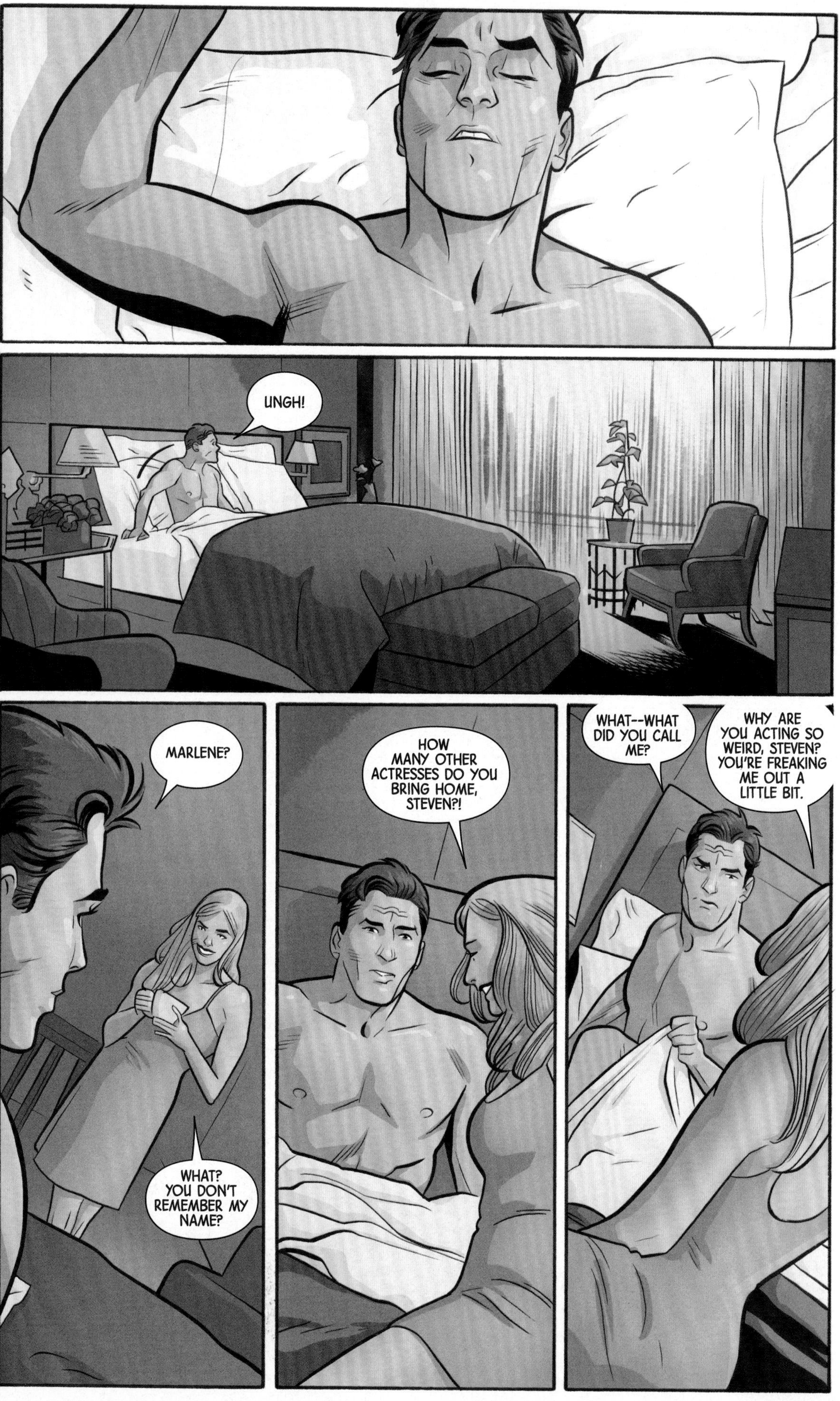
UNGH!
MARLENE?
WHAT? YOU DON'T REMEMBER MY NAME?
HOW MANY OTHER ACTRESSES DO YOU BRING HOME, STEVEN?!
WHAT--WHAT DID YOU CALL ME?
WHY ARE YOU ACTING SO WEIRD, STEVEN? YOU'RE FREAKING ME OUT A LITTLE BIT.

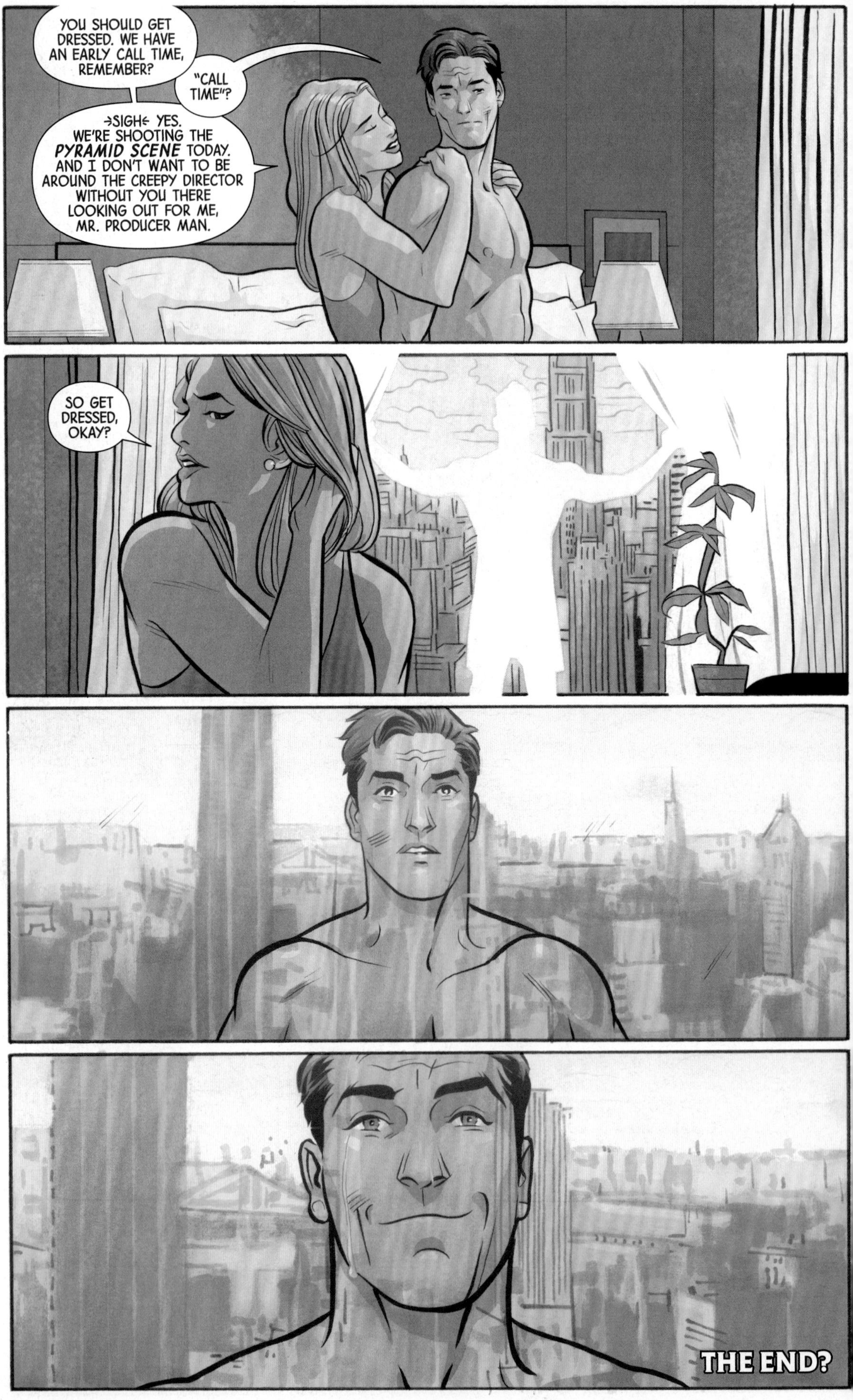
YOU SHOULD GET DRESSED. WE HAVE AN EARLY CALL TIME, REMEMBER?
"CALL TIME"?
⇾SIGH⇽ YES. WE'RE SHOOTING THE PYRAMID SCENE TODAY. AND I DON'T WANT TO BE AROUND THE CREEPY DIRECTOR WITHOUT YOU THERE LOOKING OUT FOR ME, MR. PRODUCER MAN.
SO GET DRESSED, OKAY?
THE END?

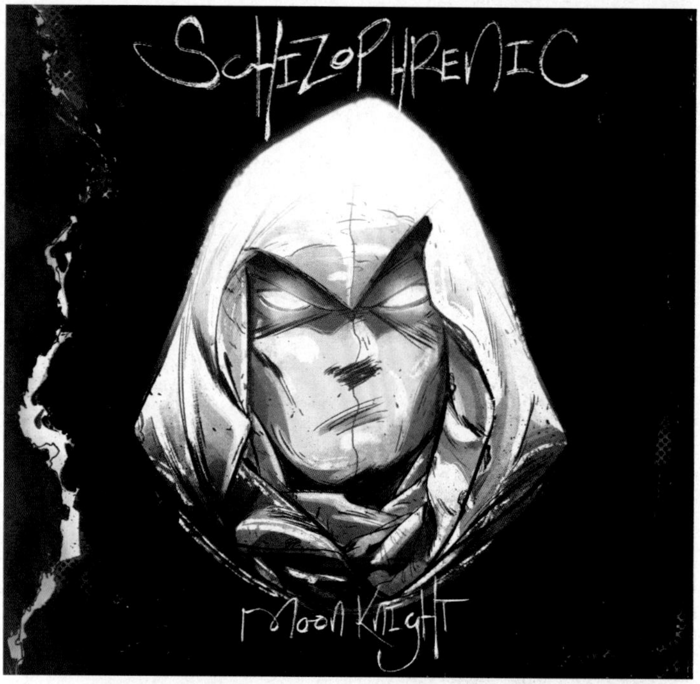
SCHIZOPHRENIC
Moon Knight

#1 HIP-HIP VARIANT BY RICARDO LÓPEZ ORTIZ

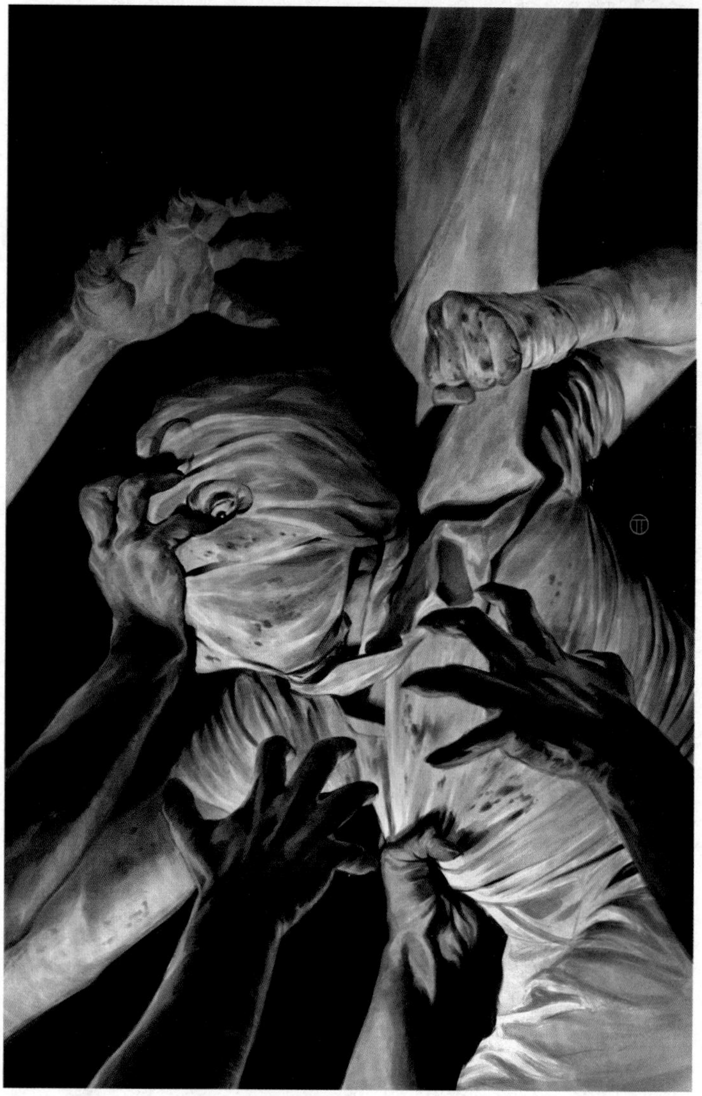

#2 VARIANT BY JULIAN TOTINO TEDESCO

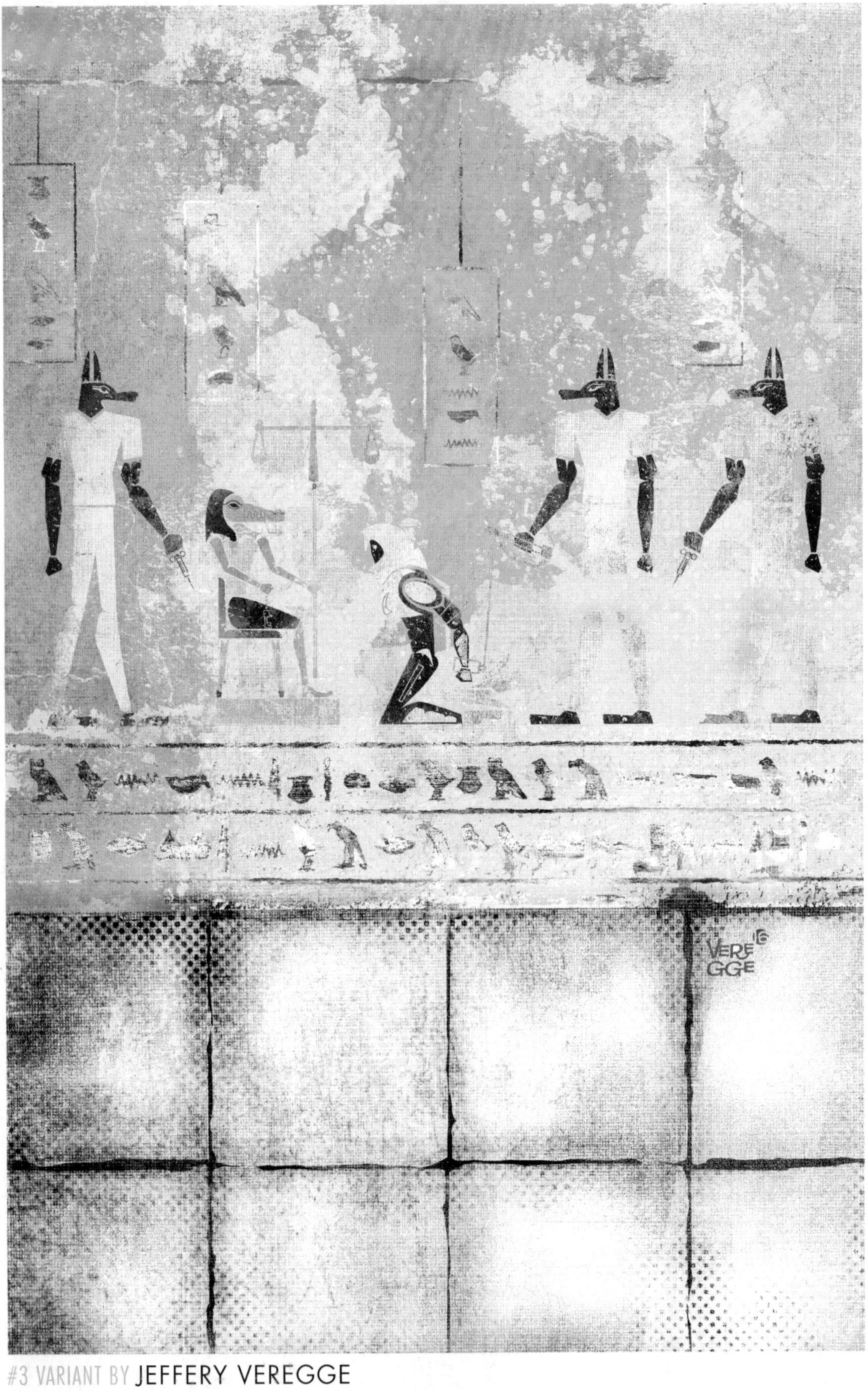
VEREGGE

#3 VARIANT BY JEFFERY VEREGGE